The Childrens' St

(Volume 1)

From the Beginning of the War to the Landing of the British Army in France

Edward Parrott

Alpha Editions

This edition published in 2024

ISBN : 9789367245958

Design and Setting By
Alpha Editions
www.alphaedis.com
Email - info@alphaedis.com

As per information held with us this book is in Public Domain.
This book is a reproduction of an important historical work. Alpha Editions uses the best technology to reproduce historical work in the same manner it was first published to preserve its original nature. Any marks or number seen are left intentionally to preserve its true form.

Contents

CHAPTER I.	- 1 -
CHAPTER II.	- 14 -
CHAPTER III.	- 29 -
CHAPTER IV.	- 40 -
THE MARSEILLAISE HYMN.	- 45 -
CHAPTER V.	- 54 -
CHAPTER VI.	- 61 -
CHAPTER VII.	- 66 -
CHAPTER VIII.	- 71 -
CHAPTER IX.	- 75 -
CHAPTER X.	- 78 -
CHAPTER XI.	- 89 -
CHAPTER XII.	- 95 -
CHAPTER XIII.	- 102 -
CHAPTER XIV.	- 116 -
CHAPTER XV.	- 123 -
CHAPTER XVI.	- 127 -
CHAPTER XVII.	- 139 -
CHAPTER XVIII.	- 147 -
CHAPTER XIX.	- 153 -
CHAPTER XX.	- 168 -
CHAPTER XXI.	- 178 -
CHAPTER XXII.	- 182 -
CHAPTER XXIII.	- 198 -
CHAPTER XXIV.	- 204 -
CHAPTER XXV.	- 209 -

CHAPTER XXVI. ....- 223 -
CHAPTER XXVII. ....- 236 -
CHAPTER XXVIII..- 241 -
CHAPTER XXIX. ....- 249 -
CHAPTER XXX..- 253 -
FOOTNOTES: ....- 262 -

CHAPTER I.

A BOLT FROM THE BLUE.

One Sunday afternoon, in the month of December 1908, the beautiful city of Messina[1] was all life and light and gaiety. The sky was blue and cloudless, and out in the Strait the little, crested waves leaped and sparkled in the sunshine. The squares and gardens were thronged with townsfolk in holiday attire; laughing groups of young men and maidens went to and fro or paused to listen to the band; fathers of families were romping with their children on the grass; mothers were quietly knitting hard by: all was merry as a marriage bell. Happy, careless ease reigned everywhere, and when night fell, the big, round moon shone upon a silent town in which thousands of people were wrapped in peaceful slumber.

But ere the dawn had begun to brighten the eastern sky an awful doom fell upon that city. The thunder roared, the lightning flashed, the earth heaved and cracked, houses and churches and public buildings came crashing to the ground, fires broke out, and a huge, angry wave from the sea swept over the land. The morning sun shone upon a terrible scene of destruction. The fair city was no more; thousands of the happy folks of yesterday had been hurried into eternity, and those who were spared found themselves homeless and ruined.

With almost the same startling suddenness the Great War broke upon Europe. The thunderbolt fell upon us from a sky of blue; the peace of the world was broken on a smiling day. Five of the Great Powers[2] of Europe blew their war trumpets, and millions of armed men stood ready to carry death and destruction into countless homes in many lands. The Great War had begun.

In the Summer Holidays.

A scene on the Thames at Henley Regatta, held every year in the month of July.
(*From a photograph by the Sport and General Press Agency.*)

Do you remember the 24th of July 1914? I think you do, for it was just about the beginning of that time which most boys and girls consider the very happiest of all the year. Your school had just broken up, the books were all put away, and you fondly hoped that you would see no more of them for a month or six weeks. You were all agog for the holidays. Your mind was full of that jolly seaside place to which you were going to-morrow or the next day. You were dreaming of boats and bathing, of games on the sands, of bicycle spins in the country lanes, and picnics in the woods. And in the midst of all these happy dreams, perhaps you heard your father say, as he turned his newspaper at breakfast time,—

"*Yesterday Austria sent a very harsh Note* [1] *to Servia. Looks like more war in the East.*"

I daresay you paid no attention to this remark. To you it meant nothing at all. You would have been far more interested if your father had told you how Middlesex was getting on with Kent, and whether Woolley or Hearne or P. F. Warner had made another century or not. But your father's remark was really far more important than all the cricket matches that were ever played, or that ever will be played. It was the first appearance of the bolt from the blue. Few, even the wisest of us, realized that it was the beginning of the greatest war that the world has ever known; a war of such vastness and terror that men would speak of it as *Armageddon*[4]—that is, a war similar to that which is described in the Book of Revelation, when "the kings of the earth and of the whole world gather them to the battle of God Almighty."

War.

(*From the picture by Sir Edwin Landseer, R.A., in the National Gallery of British Art.*)

As your father's remark was so important, let us try to understand its meaning. He mentioned two countries, Austria and Servia, and you would easily guess that there was some quarrel between them. It is not easy to explain to you exactly what the quarrel was about, and perhaps you will find the explanation a little dull; but if you are really to understand how the war arose, you must not mind a little dulness. We shall come to the exciting events by-and-by.

Look at the map on the next page. It shows you the two countries which had fallen out—Austria and Servia. You see at a glance that the Austrian Empire, which consists of Austria and Hungary, is by far the larger country; in fact, Austria-Hungary is seven times as large as Servia, and has eleven times as many people. There is no country on earth which contains so many different races as Austria-Hungary. Within its bounds we find Germans, Italians, Magyars,[5] Jews, Armenians,[6] and Gypsies, as well as eight distinct Slav races.

You will come across the word *Slav* many times in these pages, so I must explain it to you at once. By the word Slav we mean a member of that branch of mankind known as the Slavonic race. The Slavs inhabit most of the east of Europe and a large part of Asia, and they are really more Asiatic than European. Most of the Russians and the Christian peoples of the Balkan Peninsula are Slavs, and so, too, are the Poles, who live partly in Austria, partly in Germany, and partly in Russia. In Austria, and especially in Hungary, there are many Slav races, but the ruling peoples in these countries are Germans in Austria and Magyars in Hungary.

The Servians are Slavs. They are a tall, handsome race, and are very warlike in character. During the recent war in the Balkans they fought very bravely and successfully against the Turks. At the end of the war the Powers of Europe gave them more than 15,000 square miles of fresh territory. The Servians have always been ambitious, and they wish their country to become great and powerful.

Now look at your map again, and find the river Save, which joins the Danube at Belgrade,[7] the capital of Servia. South of the Save you see a country marked Bosnia,[8] and, still farther south, another country marked Herzegovina.[9] You are sure to notice that these two countries stand between Servia and the Adriatic Sea, and that they belong to Austria. Both Bosnia and Herzegovina are inhabited by Slavs, who hate being under Austria, and are eager to join their kinsmen the Servians. You cannot blame them for this, because they naturally would like to form one kingdom with men of their own race, religion, and modes of life. Besides, they feel that they have been very badly treated. Let me explain.

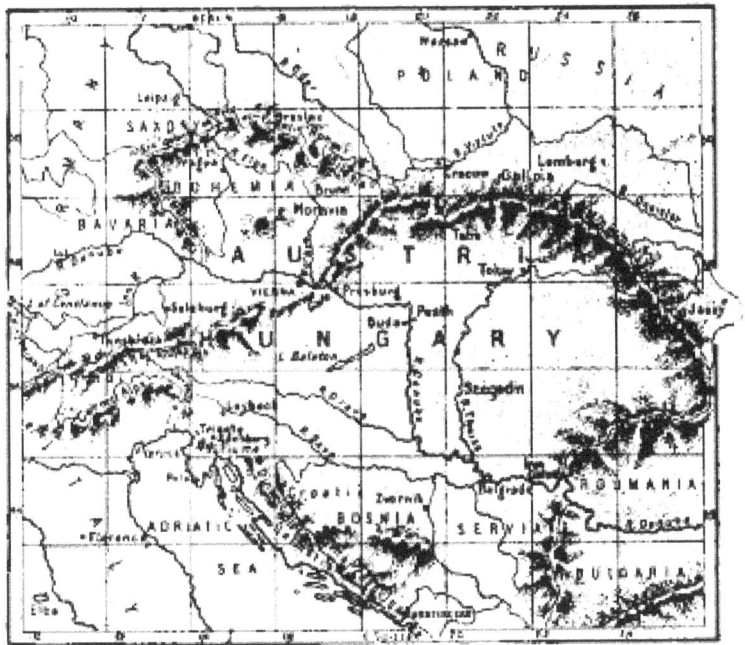

In the year 1877, when Turkey was master of the Balkan Peninsula, Russia made up her mind to fight the Turks. The Austrians were afraid that the Russians would beat the Turks, and take from them the city of Constantinople. The Russians, as you know, have a very poor sea coast. Away fronting the Arctic Ocean they have a strip of coast, but it is of very little use to them, as it is frozen up for a large part of the year. So, too, is their coast on the Baltic Sea. In the south they have a good deal of coast on the Black Sea; but in order to get from the Black Sea to the Mediterranean Sea, and so to the oceans of the world, they have to pass through two narrow straits, known as the Bosporus[10] and the Dardanelles.[11] The Turks hold these straits, and they can shut them against ships at any time. So you see that the Russians can only carry on trade in the south by leave and licence of Turkey. If they could obtain possession of Constantinople all their difficulties would vanish. They would be masters of a port which would enable them to become a great sea power.

Servia is a land of peasant soldiers. Here you see some of them coming into Belgrade to join the colours. *Photo, Topical.*

Now, Austria is even worse off than Russia in the matter of sea coast. She has about a thousand miles of seaboard on the Adriatic Sea, and there are many excellent harbours and deep and sheltered bays on it; but, unfortunately, a long range of steep limestone mountains cuts them off from the interior, and makes communication very difficult. There is a mountain railway joining the port of Trieste[12] with the interior, but it is easier to send bulky produce down the Danube to the Black Sea than across the mountains. Austria has always longed for better access to the sea, and lately she has coveted the port of Salonica,[13] which you will find on the Ægean[14] Sea.

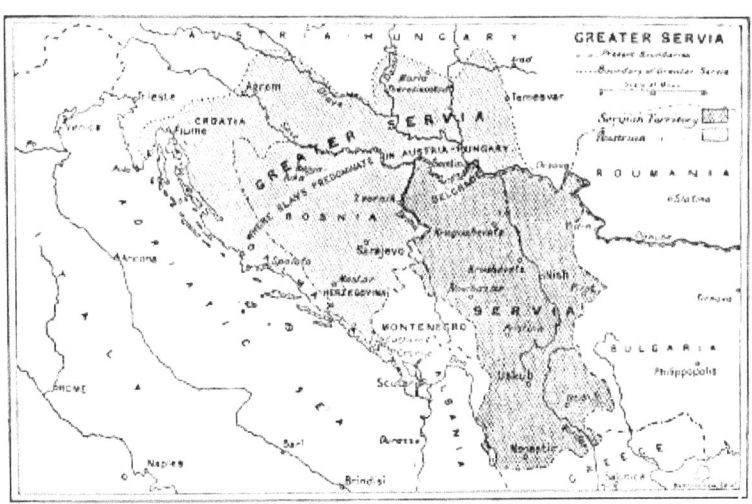

This map shows what Servia would become if Bosnia and Herzegovina were to be united with her.

When, therefore, Russia was about to fight Turkey, the Austrians feared that all the Balkans would come under Russian sway, and that their hopes of gaining power in the peninsula would be vain. So they prepared to fight Russia, but were bought off. Russia secretly promised Austria that if she would stand out of the fight she should receive as her reward the provinces of Bosnia and Herzegovina. Austria stood out, and when the war was over the Great Powers said that she might rule these two provinces, though they were not to become her actual property. You can easily imagine the anger of the people of Bosnia and Herzegovina when they found themselves handed over to Austria, just as though they were a flock of sheep to be bought and sold. Ever since 1878 the Austrians have ruled them; but they have always been discontented, and when, in 1908, they were told that they now belonged wholly and entirely to Austria, their anger knew no bounds. During the recent Balkan War they saw the peasant soldiers of Servia conquering on the battlefield, and they hoped that when the war was over they might be allowed to join Servia, and with her form one strong state. Servia would have welcomed them with open arms, but, as you know, they were doomed to disappointment. Both Servia and Russia were much annoyed when Austria annexed the two provinces. The anger of Russia and Servia nearly brought about another war.

Such was the state of things at the beginning of June in the year 1914.

Franz Josef, Emperor of Austria. *Photo by C. Pietzner.*

Here is a portrait of the Emperor of Austria and King of Hungary, Franz Josef. He is an old man, eighty-five years of age—the oldest monarch in Europe. It is impossible not to be sorry for him; his life has been full of trouble, and he has had to rule over the most divided kingdom on earth. There has never been any love lost between Austrians and Hungarians, and the only bond that unites them is the aged king-emperor. Probably there never was so unfortunate a royal family as that of which Franz Josef is the head. His younger brother, Maximilian, after being invited to become Emperor of Mexico, was shot by the Mexicans in 1867; his heir, Rudolf, was found dead in a hunting-lodge in 1889; and his wife, the Empress, was stabbed to death in the streets of Geneva nine years later. Nor was this the last of his sorrows, as you will presently hear.

The heir to the Austrian throne in June 1914 was the Archduke Francis Ferdinand, the aged Emperor's nephew. He was a man of strong will and great ambition, and he eagerly desired to win power for Austria in the Balkans, and so secure for his country the port of Salonica. This port would enable Austria to develop her foreign trade, and become an important sea power.

Now, before Austria could send her army into the Balkans and carve out a road to Salonica, she must be sure that the Slavs of Bosnia and Herzegovina would not rise in rebellion and make her task doubly difficult. So, on the 23rd of June last, the Archduke Francis Ferdinand and his wife, the Duchess of Hohenberg, a lady who had Slav blood in her veins, left the Austrian capital to pay a state visit to Bosnia, for the purpose of reviewing the troops in that province and trying to secure the favour of the Bosnian people.

The Archduke Francis Ferdinand, the Archduchess, and their family.

If you and I proposed to visit Bosnia, our best route would be to take ship, say, from Venice, and cross the Adriatic Sea to the beautiful town of Ragusa,[15] with its castled walls, its dizzy cliffs, its quaint old buildings, its palaces, churches, and monasteries, all shut in between the blue sea and the steep gray hills that rise up suddenly in the rear. At Ragusa we should take the train through the wild, rugged country of Herzegovina, which has been called the Turkish Switzerland. Our train would run through rocky defiles, up steep passes, by the side of yawning chasms, until we reached Mostar,[16] the chief city of the country. The Austrian part of Mostar, we should find, consists of two white streets, a modern hotel, a public garden with a bandstand, and barracks for soldiers. All the rest of it is Turkish. You see the same narrow streets, the same kind of bazaars, the same mosques, the same solemn, white-turbaned Turks and veiled women that you see in Constantinople; but you also see swarthy, stalwart men of Herzegovina and

Albania,[17] every one of them carrying a sharp knife at his girdle and a gun in his hand.

We now leave Mostar for Sarajevo,[18] the capital of Bosnia, by a railway which is one of the wonders of the world. "In places whole cliffs have been blasted away to enable the metals to follow a narrow pathway with granite walls and a nasty precipice on either side. As the engine creeps carefully over the slender iron bridges towards the summit you may look down from your carriage window into a thousand feet of space, and feel thankful that cog-wheels are beneath you, for otherwise any hitch with the brakes might cause a frightful accident. At times the track twists and turns so much that an engine-driver may glance across a chasm, and without looking back see the rear van winding round a corner." Such is the railway by which we reach Sarajevo.

Let us suppose that we have arrived in Sarajevo on the morning of Sunday, June 28th of the year 1914. Upon the craggy heights above the town we see the citadel and fortifications, and here and there above the roofs of the houses the minarets and white domes of mosques; but we soon perceive that we are not in an Eastern but in a modern Western town. The Austrians have made wide streets, with fine shops, cafés, and beer-halls; they have erected handsome public buildings, theatres, and hotels; trams run along the streets, and taxis ply for hire; and on the outskirts of the town we find a racecourse and golf links. We must give the Austrians their due. They have done wonders in civilizing the country and in making it prosperous; but they have not won the hearts of the people, and that is the all-important business of rulers, after all.

To-day Sarajevo is in festive array. The yellow Austrian standard, with its black, double-headed eagle, flies above all the public buildings, and flutters from the upper windows of the shops along the Franz Josef Strasse; soldiers are marching through the streets; bugles are blowing, and bands are playing. On the pavements stand the townsfolk, and you notice that many of them are sullen and silent. They are waiting for the coming of their future king, but they show no signs of loyalty. When our beloved Prince of Wales visits one of our towns, we flock gladly to see him and greet him with the heartiest of cheers. Suppose, however, he was a man of another race, and that he was going some day to be our king against our will; how do you think we should receive him? Very much as the Bosnians are receiving their future king to-day.

View in the old part of Sarajevo, the capital of Bosnia.

Now the guns roar out from the citadel to announce the coming of the Archduke and his wife. The Archduke inspects the troops drawn up at the station, and then he and his wife enter a motor-car and drive towards the Town Hall, where the mayor is waiting to receive them. Suddenly, as they drive along one of the quays, you hear a loud report and see a cloud of smoke arise. What has happened? A young printer, twenty years of age, has hurled a bomb at the Archduke. He wards it off with his arm, but it has wounded an officer in the next car, and has inflicted injuries on several bystanders. Neither of the royal pair is hurt, though, as you may well imagine, they are much upset by this attempt on their lives.

The motor moves on, and arrives at the Town Hall, where the mayor, who knows nothing of what has happened, comes forward and begins to read an address of welcome. The Archduke, who is much annoyed at the treatment which he has received, cuts the mayor short angrily. "What," says he, "is the good of your speeches? I come to Sarajevo on a visit, and I get bombs thrown at me. It is outrageous!"

After a short stay at the Town Hall the Archduke and his wife re-enter their motor to return to the station. They have not gone far before a High School student hurls another bomb at them. It fails to explode, but the lad, who is armed with a pistol, fires three shots in quick succession. The first bullet strikes the Archduke in the throat. His wife, who loves him tenderly, throws herself in front of him, in order to shield him from further attack, and the second bullet enters her body. The third bullet completes the deadly work, and the dying pair are rapidly conveyed to the palace. The Archduke rouses himself. "Sophie," he says to his stricken wife, "live for our children." But she, too, is mortally wounded, and in a few minutes both are dead.

No possible excuse can be found for this foul deed. It was black murder—the worst of all possible crimes. The printer and the High School student were seized, and at first they denied that they knew each other. Bit by bit, however, it was discovered that not only were they working together, but that a great plot had been formed to kill the Archduke that day. Had they failed, there were others in the crowd ready and willing to take their places.

The date chosen for the Archduke's visit to Sarajevo was most unfortunate. On that day, in the year 1389, the Serbs[19] of Servia, which then included Bosnia, suffered the most terrible defeat in all their history. In the battle which was then fought, treachery was at work, and the best and bravest of their race perished on the battlefield. The Serbs have never forgotten the story of how their sires were slaughtered on the "Field of the Blackbirds." Even now their bards sing national songs which tell of the glorious deeds of those who fell at Kossovo,[20] and call upon the Serbs of to-day to spare neither "land, nor gold, nor son, nor wife, nor limb, nor life" in upholding the freedom of their race.

Amidst the high Alps a pistol shot may start an avalanche high on the snowy mountains. Slowly it moves at first; soon it gathers speed, and at last it comes crashing down with terrible force upon the quiet homesteads in the valley. So did the pistol-shot of a schoolboy in far-off Bosnia start an avalanche which has swept down upon Europe, leaving death and destruction and untold misery in its train.

Austrian soldiers on the bank of the Danube, opposite to Belgrade.
By permission of the Sphere.

CHAPTER II.

THE SEETHING WHIRLPOOL.

The scene shifts to Vienna,[21] the capital of Austria, the largest city of Austria-Hungary and the heart and centre of the Austrian Empire. It is one of the most attractive cities in all Europe, and has long been renowned as the favoured home of art, music, and gaiety. You will find the city by the side of the Danube, where the river leaves the Bavarian highlands and enters the great plain. Most of it is modern, and in the Ringstrasse you may see some of the finest buildings in the world, such as the Opera House, which seats 3,000 people; the University, which contains one of the most famous of medical schools; the Parliament House of Austria; and the chief law courts of the country.

Vienna, the capital of Austria, heart and centre of the Austro-Hungarian Empire.

The city is surrounded by the Danube and its canals, and has several parks and numerous shady avenues of trees, beneath which the gay Viennese love to stroll or sit at the tables of outdoor cafés listening to the bands. You can scarcely walk half a mile in Vienna without hearing music. The gipsy bands which are often heard in Vienna play their national airs with a dash and fire that sets even the most sluggish pulse dancing.

- 14 -

One of the finest of all the public buildings of Vienna is the Imperial Palace, or Hofburg, which contains a library of a million volumes. The great chamber in which the books are housed is said to be the most splendid library hall in the world. Its floor of red and white marble is adorned with noble statues, and its vaulted dome, which rises 193 feet above the pavement, is covered with beautiful paintings.

In the palace are preserved the crown, sword, and sceptre of Charlemagne,[22] the great Emperor of the West, who gave laws to nearly the whole of civilized Europe, and is renowned in song and story as a prince of knights, and the champion of the Christian religion. To this day he lives in the hearts of the German peoples both of Germany and Austria. They say that he still watches over them, and every autumn comes riding over the Rhine, across a bridge of gold, to bless their vineyards and cornfields with increase.

In the heart of the city stands the old cathedral of St. Stephen. For more than six hundred years this magnificent pile has lifted its towers to the sky. It has seen the Crusaders halt within its shadow on their way to free the Holy Land from the infidel, and it has looked down on great hordes of conquering Turks striving to capture the city. Vienna was the high-water mark at which the progress of the Turkish flood was stayed. The Turks beat upon its ramparts in vain; they were flung back from its walls like ocean waves from the cliffs of a rocky coast. In the old cathedral you may see a huge bell cast out of cannon captured from the Turks in the last of their sieges. For centuries Vienna has been the frontier city between the Eastern and Western peoples of Europe.

On the very day of the murders at Sarajevo the Emperor Franz Josef left Vienna for his summer holiday at the beautiful watering-place of Ischl,[23] in Upper Austria. What a difference between the reception of the old Emperor by the citizens of Vienna and that of his heir by the citizens of Sarajevo! At the station the mayor and members of the city council met the aged sovereign and told him how greatly they rejoiced at his recovery from a recent sickness. The Emperor was deeply touched by their words of affection and loyalty, and as his train steamed out of the station loud cheers were raised and the national anthem was sung.

A few hours later the terrible news from Sarajevo was flashed to him across the telegraph wires. You can imagine the anguish of the poor old man when he knew that fate had dealt him yet another crushing blow. When, sixteen years ago, he learned that his Empress had been murdered, he cried in his grief, "Then I am spared nothing." How true! Fate seemed again to have replied to his despairing cry, "Nothing." Long ago his mother said of him, "God has given him the qualities needed to meet all turns of fate." From every one of his former blows he had rallied, and prayed the Almighty for power to fulfil what he had been called upon to perform. Now he was fain to cry, with Elijah, "It is enough; now, O Lord, take away my life."

I have already told you that the peoples of Austria-Hungary are divided by wide and deep differences, and that they have little in common, but that they are all united in their reverence for their aged sovereign. They regard him with the same sort of affection which the people of this country used to feel for Queen Victoria. She was more than a queen; she was the mother of her people, high above all the quarrels of parties and sects. So it is with Franz Josef, and you can therefore imagine the bitter anger and the eager desire for revenge which took possession of the Austrian people when they learnt of the murder of his nephew. They showed their sympathy with the Emperor very clearly when he returned to Vienna to take part in the funeral ceremonies, and still more when thousands of them passed through the Hofburg Chapel, where the Archduke and his wife lay in state.

Every government in Europe sent messages of deep sympathy with the Emperor in his hour of sorrow, and that which was tendered by Mr. Asquith, our Prime Minister, was one of the most sincere of them all.

The children of the Archduke and Archduchess were living in a castle in Bohemia[24] when the sad news came to them that they were orphans—bereft of father and mother in one dread day. The German Emperor and his wife sent the following message to them: "We can scarcely find words to express to you children how our hearts bleed at the thought of you and your inexpressible grief. To have spent such happy hours with you and your parents only a fortnight ago, and now to think that you are plunged in this immeasurable sorrow! May God stand by you, and give you strength to bear this blow! The blessing of parents reaches beyond the grave."

Meanwhile the Austrian people had begun to fasten the blame for the murders on Servia. While the funeral procession was passing through the streets, crowds gathered in front of the Servian minister's residence with shouts of "Hurrah for Austria!" and "Down with Servia!" The sight of the Servian flag, to which a streamer of crape had been attached, only made them more angry still; the flag was burnt, and stones were thrown at the police. The newspapers now began to declare openly that the plot had been hatched in Servia, and that high officials in the Servian government had encouraged it. The Council of Ministers met and inquired into the question, and then came a lull of three weeks.

For a time the Austro-Servian question sank out of sight, and it was thought that at the worst there would only be another Balkan War. No one suspected for a moment that the other Powers of Europe would be dragged into the quarrel, and that the schoolboy's pistol-shot at Sarajevo would be the signal for Armageddon. Had any one suggested in the early days of July that in three weeks all the Great Powers would be at war, he would have been laughed at. But all the while a great whirlpool was seething, and slowly but surely Russia, Germany, France, and Great Britain were being drawn into the centre.

Before I tell you the further history of the quarrel between Austria and Servia, and show you how the chief Powers of Europe became mixed up with it, let me tell you of a very fortunate event which happened at home. On Saturday, the 18th of July, our King went down to Portsmouth to visit his Fleet, which had been assembled at Spithead. Every boy and girl knows that we live on an island home, and that the sea which surrounds us has been a great source of blessing to us.

"Thy story, thy glory,
The very fame of thee,
It rose not, it grows not,
It comes not save by sea."

Shakespeare tells us that the encircling sea serves us

"In the office of a wall,
Or as a moat defensive to a house
Against the envy of less happier lands."

King George V. in the uniform of a British admiral.
Photo, W. and D. Downey.

This "defensive moat" has always proved a barrier against foreign attack, but it has not preserved our islands from invasion. Celts, Romans, English, Danes, and Normans have in turn conquered England; but never since it became the home of a united nation with a strong Navy has any foreign invader landed in strength on our shores. For more than eight hundred years no hostile army has dared to invade us, and our people have never been forced to lay down their tools and snatch up their weapons to drive away the invader. No other land in Europe can make this boast. We owe this long reign of security to our Navy.

Not only has our Navy kept us free from invasion, but by winning for us the mastery of the sea it has enabled us to build up a great foreign trade, by which we have grown rich and great, and to found colonies and hold possessions in every continent on the face of the globe. At the present time it does even more than this—it secures for us the means whereby we live and move and have our being. So many of our people are now engaged in mines and quarries and factories, on railways, and in offices, that we do not grow enough food for our needs. There is never enough food in this country to last our people for more than a couple of months or so. We draw our food supplies from all parts of the world, and were a foreign foe to destroy our Navy and cut off our food ships, the great bulk of us would soon perish of starvation. So you see that "Britannia *must* rule the waves," if we are to exist at all and remain the greatest trading and colonial nation of the world, as we are to-day. Every sensible man understands this, and all agree that our Navy must be very strong and very efficient. It must be able to command the seas, for, as Raleigh told us long ago, "Whosoever commands the sea commands the trade; whosoever commands the trade of the world commands the riches of the world, and, consequently, the world itself."

H.M.S. Colossus firing a salute. *Photo, Cribb.*

The sure shield of Britain—a scene at the Naval Review. *Photo, Cribb.*

Never has the British Navy been so powerful and so well equipped both in ships and guns and men as at present. The "wooden walls" in which Blake and Nelson fought have long since disappeared, and our bluejackets now fight behind bulwarks of steel. Steam has taken the place of sail; the old muzzle-loading guns have been superseded by huge weapons, the largest of which can hurl nearly a ton of metal for twelve miles with deadly aim. Our modern warships are filled with costly machinery quite unknown and even undreamt of in the days when Britain fought and won the greatest sea fights of her history. But though the ships have changed out of knowledge, the officers, bluejackets, and marines who man them possess all the old fighting spirit and all the courage and daring of their forefathers.

"Ye mariners of England,
That guard our native seas;
Whose flag has braved, a thousand years,
The battle and the breeze!
Your glorious standard launch again
To match another foe!
And sweep through the deep
While the stormy winds do blow—
While the battle rages loud and long,
And the stormy winds do blow."

When the King went down to Portsmouth on the 20th of July there appeared to be no foe to fight; there was no sign of any war in which we could possibly be engaged, yet in less than a fortnight the Navy had cleared for action, and our sailors were standing at the guns watching and waiting for the battleships of Germany to appear.

Gray skies were overhead, and a cold easterly wind was sweeping over the seas as His Majesty led out to sea the largest and most powerful fleet ever seen in British waters. When the royal yacht anchored, no less than twenty-two miles of warships passed in procession before it. First came four battle-cruisers, headed by the *Lion*, and followed by the *Queen Mary*, *Princess Royal*, and *New Zealand*. Then in stately order, two by two, came the latest of our battleships, led by the *Iron Duke* and the *King George*. Marines and bands were paraded on the sides of the ships nearest to the King's yacht, and their scarlet uniforms ran like a ribbon of bright colour along the edge of the great gray monsters. Just as each ship reached the stern of the royal yacht, the sailors, with the smartness of a machine, removed their hats, held them at arm's length, and waved them to the roar of British huzzas. At the same moment the bands struck up the National Anthem, and the marines presented arms. The King and the Prince of Wales stood on the bridge of the royal yacht, saluting the ships as they passed.

Behind Sir George Callaghan's flagship came the four First Fleet battle squadrons, including twenty-nine vessels of the vastest power in the whole world. In the first and second squadrons were eight Dreadnoughts, in the third squadron eight of the great ships that were built before the all-big-gun ships became the first line of our Navy, and in the fourth squadron were three more Dreadnoughts and the *Agamemnon*.[25] Following these were the smart cruisers of the First Fleet—swift, armed ships that act as the fighting scouts of the seas. In their wake passed fifty-six torpedo destroyers, moving in sections of fours. By the time the last of the First Fleet ships had passed the King's yacht, the leading vessels were far away on the horizon.

A slight pause, and then the Second and Third Fleets began to appear, led by the *Lord Nelson* and the *Prince of Wales* respectively. When these ships had saluted their sovereign there still remained the cruisers attached to these fleets. Never had such an array been seen before in the history of the world—twenty-two miles of warships in endless columns, gliding slowly through the water, every one of them a tower of strength and a mighty engine of destruction. Not only was every type of warship represented, but the new powers of the air were visible. Scores of seaplanes and aeroplanes flew over the King's yacht like huge birds of prey.

Such was Britain's display of naval strength at the moment when the issue of war or peace was hanging in the balance. It was a sign to the world that, whatever might befall, Britain was ready, aye ready, to guard her own with the strong arm of ancient renown:—

"Come the four quarters of the world in arms,
And we shall shock them."

"It's a long, long way to Tipperary," sing our soldiers on the march, and it's a long, long way from Spithead to the Servian capital, Belgrade, whither we must now wend our way. On a bright, sunny morning, when the train has clattered across the iron bridge which spans the Danube, and the city comes into view, it looks very attractive. Belgrade in the distance well deserves its title of the "White City." A poetically minded person has described it as "shining like a pearl through the silvery mists of sunrise."

Prince Albert, the King's second son, as a midshipman. This photograph was taken during the King's inspection of the Fleet.
Photo, Ernest Brooks.

In the 'seventies Belgrade was a miserable, dirty, and comfortless town; its main thoroughfare was a sea of mud; its buildings were poor; and it was no better than a tumble-down Turkish fortress. But since those days Servia has become an independent kingdom, and she has made Belgrade a really fine city, with broad, tree-fringed streets, electric trams, and fine hotels. Only two of the ancient landmarks remain—the cathedral, and the citadel, over which flies the national flag. Through modern Belgrade runs a fine street more than a mile long, overtopped about the middle by the golden domes of the new palace. Here are the principal hotels, private houses, and shops, the latter of which blaze with electric light in the evenings. The people of Belgrade sometimes call their town "Little Paris," and they strive to make it as gay as the French capital itself.

The city of Belgrade. *Photo, Exclusive News Agency.*

While the British fleet was unfolding itself before our King, there was no gaiety amongst the high government officials in Belgrade. They were getting very anxious. The Council of Ministers in Vienna was inquiring closely into the part played by them in the Sarajevo murders. It was rumoured that the Austrians had traced the arms and explosives with which the murderers were provided to certain Servian officers and officials of the government who were members of a National Union for making Slav power supreme in the Balkan Peninsula. It was also said that these same officers and officials had secretly passed the murderers into Bosnia, and had helped them in various other ways to do their deadly work. If Austria could prove all this, she would be able to say that Servia had been playing the part of a secret enemy, and rightly deserved punishment of some sort.

The King and Crown Prince of Servia. *Photo, Topical.*

On the evening of the 23rd of July the Austro-Hungarian ministers in Belgrade handed the Note to which your father referred when he read his newspaper at the breakfast table. You know that every European country sends officials to live in the capitals of other countries, and that these officials represent the powers by which they are sent. They are always treated with the greatest possible respect, and their houses are supposed to be bits of their own land planted down in a foreign country. Sometimes these representatives are called ambassadors, sometimes simply ministers. When the government of one country wishes to communicate with the government of another country, it sends and receives messages through its ambassadors or ministers.

In Belgrade there was, of course, an Austrian minister, and it was he who handed the Note to the Servian Prime Minister. This Note was of such grave importance that I must tell you what was in it. First, it began by telling Servia that for a long time past she had been stirring up her people against Austria; that she had allowed men connected with the government to plot against her; and that she had taken no steps to punish those who had assisted the murderers at Sarajevo. The Servians were greatly to blame, and upon them must fall much of the responsibility for the wicked deeds that had been done in Bosnia.

Then followed a list of ten things which Servia was to do to make up for the mischief which she was said to have caused. She was to print on the front page of the government newspaper a statement that she would no longer permit her people to work against Austria, either by word or deed; she was to express regret that Servian officers and officials had spoken or acted in an unfriendly manner against Austria; and she was to remove from their posts all who had done so. The whole army was to be told that such conduct would no longer be permitted, and the National Union was to be broken up. Two officers, mentioned by name, were to be arrested, and all who had in any way helped the murderers of Sarajevo, either by giving them arms or helping them to get into Bosnia, were to be brought to trial. Austrian officials were to take part in the punishment of the wrongdoers, and in putting an end to the bad feeling between the two countries.

The Note ended as follows:—

"The Austro-Hungarian Government expects the reply of the Servian Government at the latest by six o'clock on Saturday evening, the 25th of July."

The Czar of Russia and President Poincaré.

This photograph was taken on board the Czar's yacht when President Poincaré visited Russia in the middle of July. (*Photo, Record.*)

This was very short notice indeed, and it clearly meant that if the Servian Government did not immediately agree to the Austrian demands war would be declared. In a few hours the full text of this letter was known to all the world. Your father read it, and called it "very harsh." Certainly it was very severe, and the Austrians meant it to be severe. They knew very well that they were asking for some things which no state could possibly yield and still call itself independent. For instance, if the Servians had agreed to remove officers and officials from their posts at the bidding of Austria, and had allowed Austrians to take part in the police work of the country, they would be confessing to all the world that they were no longer masters in their own house, and that they were nothing more than the tools of Austria. The Servians were prepared to punish any officers who were proved guilty, and were quite willing to give way on nearly all the points in the Note, because they wished to stave off war with their powerful neighbours; but they were not ready to acknowledge the Austrians as their overlords. Do you blame them? I don't.

So they handed in their reply to the Austrians, and in it they said that they would agree to all Austria's demands; but they asked for delay in order to make new laws by which they could carry out her wishes. They also asked for an explanation of the way in which Austrian officials were to take part in their police and law-court work. This ought to have been enough; but Austria had all along meant war, and she had drawn up the Note, with the knowledge, and perhaps the help, of the German Ambassador at Vienna, in such a way that the Servians were bound to refuse some of its terms. Immediately the reply was handed to the Austrian minister he rejected it, and asked for a safe conduct back to his own country. When a minister does this he clearly indicates that his country means to fight. The same evening the Austrian minister left Belgrade, and on the 28th Austria declared war. The next day fighting began, and the Austrians bombarded Belgrade.

Now we are to understand how Russia came into the quarrel. Russia has always regarded herself as the protector of the Slav races, and especially of the little Slav races. When, therefore, Russia saw that Austria was bent on conquering Servia, she began to call her troops together, and to prepare them for war. When a nation does this she is said to mobilize her forces. Russia is such a vast country and her troops are so widely dispersed that she cannot mobilize so quickly. She only partly mobilized, and by doing so meant to show Austria that she was not going to allow Servia to be swallowed up, or even to be badly beaten, especially after Servia had shown such willingness to meet Austria's demands.

For Fatherland.

This beautiful picture, which hangs in the Luxembourg Palace in Paris, illustrates the sacrifice which Frenchmen are always ready to make for their dearly loved native land.

Now I must break off my story for a few moments to explain to you that Germany and Austria, as far back as 1879, made a treaty by which they promised to stand by each other if either of them should go to war. Italy joined Germany and Austria three years later, but on the understanding that she would fight only if one or other of the three partners should be attacked. This agreement is called the *Triple Alliance*.

Ever since 1870, when the Germans invaded France, and in less than five months utterly overcame her, tore from her two provinces, and fined her two hundred million pounds, there has been ill-feeling between France and Germany. Frenchmen have longed for the day on which they might win back the lost provinces and pay off old scores. Germany is too rich and powerful and has too big an army for France to be able to meet her on equal terms, so she has formed an alliance with Russia. This is known as the *Dual Alliance*. France and Russia have agreed to help each other if either of them should be attacked.

During the lifetime of our late King Edward VII., who was very fond of France, we were brought nearer and nearer to our friends across the Channel. For centuries they have been our foes; we have fought them off and on since the days of William the Conqueror. Our great admiral, Lord Nelson, used to say to his midshipmen, "Your duty is to fear God, honour the King, and hate the Frenchman." King Edward was a man who loved peace, and he did much to bring the French and the British people together, and make it easier for our statesmen to come to an understanding with French statesmen. This understanding was that if the coasts of France should be attacked by the fleet of an enemy, our Navy would help the French Navy. Now, when we came to an understanding with France we also came to an understanding with the ally of France—that is, with Russia. For a long time we had only an understanding with these countries, but not long ago we turned this understanding into an alliance. So you see that in July last there were two triple alliances in Europe—Germany, Austria, and Italy on the one side, and Great Britain, France, and Russia on the other. Later on, when I tell you something about Germany, you will understand why this new triple alliance was formed.

CHAPTER III.
THE BEGINNINGS OF PRUSSIA.

About forty years ago a German boy, accompanied by his tutor and other attendants, was spending a holiday at a seaside resort in the south of England. One morning this boy went down to the beach and amused himself by throwing stones at the bathing machines. The son of the owner of the machines, a boy of about his own age, saw him so engaged, and, going up to him, told him to stop throwing. Now the German boy had been brought up to believe that he could do as he pleased, without anyone daring to take him to task. So he drew himself up proudly, and said, "Do you know who I am?" "No," replied the English boy, "and I don't care either. I only know that I'm not going to let you damage our machines."

Thereupon the German boy hit out and knocked the speaker down. In a moment the English boy was on his feet again. He pulled off his coat, put up his fists, and a fight began. Just when the German boy was getting the worst of it his tutor arrived, separated the fighters, and put an end to the combat.

That German boy is now the Kaiser[26] Wilhelm, the man who has plunged Europe into this terrible war. From the story which you have just read you may learn something of his character when he was a boy. Later on I shall tell you what sort of a man he became; but first you must learn something of the history of the land over which he rules.

The Kaiser Wilhelm and the Emperor Franz Josef.

Photo, Topical Press.

On a lofty, lonely crag, amidst the wilds of Swabia,[27] stands the picturesque castle of Hohenzollern, the cradle of the family from which the rulers of Prussia are descended. On this high rock the eagles formerly made their home, hence the crest of the Prussian royal family is the eagle—the boldest and fiercest of all the birds. About the middle of the twelfth century the lord of this castle, a man named Conrad, took service with the great Emperor of what was called the Holy Roman Empire—that is, with the overlord of nearly all Western Europe. Conrad served the Emperor so faithfully that as his reward he was made governor of the city of Nuremberg[28] in Bavaria. If you were to visit Nuremberg you would be charmed with the castle, now a royal palace, the ancient walls and towers, the grand old buildings, including churches which are full of priceless pictures and carvings, and the art galleries, which contain some of the best paintings of the great masters. The chief trade of Nuremberg to-day is the manufacture of toys, scientific instruments, motor cars, cycles, and beer.

About the beginning of the fifteenth century the Hohenzollern who was governor of Nuremberg was a man named Frederick. He had been very loyal to the Emperor, who rewarded him by making him ruler of the Mark of Brandenburg. The greatest day in the history of the Hohenzollerns was April 17, 1417, the day on which Frederick received from the hands of the Emperor the flag of Brandenburg, and swore to be faithful to him.

If you look at a map of Germany you will see in the middle of the North German plain the city of Berlin, the capital of the German Empire. Round about Berlin, in the valleys of the Middle Oder, and its tributary the Warthe, and in the valley of the Elbe, extends the province of Prussia, known as the Mark of Brandenburg. It was one of the first districts of Germany to be peopled by men of German race when they came advancing from the east in the twelfth and thirteenth centuries, but it was by no means a land flowing with milk and honey. Parts of the country were marshy or heavily wooded, and in many places the land was so thickly covered with sand that it was known as the "sandbox of the Holy Roman Empire." Thin crops of rye and oats alone could be raised on this thankless soil; nevertheless the colony prospered greatly under Frederick and his successors.

Map of Modern Germany.

The Hohenzollern prince who really founded the greatness of his house was Frederick William, who began to reign in the year 1640. He is known as the "Great Elector."[29] If I were to show you a coloured map of Germany as it was when this prince began to reign, you would say that it looked like a patchwork quilt of many colours. From the Baltic Sea to the Alps there were no fewer than three hundred states of all sorts and sizes, the smallest of them consisting only of a single town or village.

Frederick William was a very able man, and so well did he fight, and so skilfully did he plot and plan during what is known as the Thirty Years' War, that he added several of these small states to his own, and thus became master of the largest state in all Germany. Brandenburg under his rule spread out a little to the west, but a great deal to the north-east, and included a stretch of coast-line on the Baltic Sea. The present Kaiser has always revered the memory of the Great Elector. He once said: "Of all my predecessors, he is the one for whom I feel the greatest enthusiasm, and who from of old has stood before me as the example of my youth."

When the Great Elector died he was succeeded by his son Frederick, who was very eager to be called king. He attained this great object of his life in the year 1700; but, because he was a spendthrift and a lover of empty display, he did nothing to advance the interests of his country. After him reigned another Frederick William, who had some talents and did the business of his state very well, but was a thoroughly wicked fellow, and was, indeed, next door to a madman. Nevertheless he was the first Prussian king to set himself the task of making his kingdom strong enough to take its place among the European Powers. Carlyle calls him the "drill-sergeant of the Prussian nation."

Statue of the Great Elector in Berlin.

The present Kaiser is devoted to the memory of his ancestors, and does everything in his power to make the Prussians believe that they owe everything to the Hohenzollern sovereigns. Berlin is full of statues to these princes. In one of the avenues of the chief park there is a row of statues to all the rulers of Prussia. Of the Great Elector, who was the real founder of Prussia, and whose statue is shown above, the Kaiser has said, "He has stood before me as the example of my youth." He is also a great admirer of Frederick the Great, and has imitated some of the worst features of that monarch.

Photo, Exclusive News Agency.

This Frederick William stinted himself and his family of food and clothing, in order to keep up an army of 60,000 men, and he drilled them so well that they were the best troops of the time. The great desire of his heart was to possess a brigade of giants, and his agents scoured all the countries of Europe to find big men. He would pay almost anything for men over six feet, and it is said that he gave £1,200 for an Irishman who was more than seven feet high. These Potsdam[30] Guards were his passion; he hoarded his money like a miser on most things, but he spent it lavishly on buying tall men for his army.

Some day he hoped to send these huge fellows into the field, and see them drive the whipper-snappers of other nations before them. But he was so proud of his giants that he hated the thought of risking their lives in battle, and while he lived they never saw any harder service than sham fights in the fields round Berlin.

When King Frederick was gathered to his fathers, his son, one of the most remarkable men who ever lived, came to the throne. When you are grown up you will, if you are wise, read his life as Thomas Carlyle[31] wrote it. Here I can only touch very lightly on his character and the work which he did for his country. He is known to history as Frederick the Great.

One of the Potsdam Guards.

Probably no boy had ever so hard an upbringing as Prince Frederick. Macaulay tells us that "Oliver Twist in the parish workhouse and Smike at Dotheboys Hall were petted children when compared with this wretched heir-apparent of a crown." This is, perhaps, an over-statement; but there is no doubt that the boy spent a very hard and loveless boyhood. His father was a rough, bluff man, who thought that the whole business of life was to drill and to be drilled. He loved to drink beer, smoke strong tobacco, play cards, hunt wild hogs, and shoot partridges by the thousand, and he despised all the arts and graces which make life sweet and beautiful. Carlyle tells us that the young prince was nourished on beer soup, and that every hour of his life he was taught to be thrifty, active, and exact in everything that he did. His very sleep was stingily meted out to him. "Too much sleep stupefies a fellow," his gruff old father used to say. So little sleep was the boy allowed to have that the doctors had to interfere for the sake of his health. He had no money of his own until he was seventeen, and then he was provided with eighteenpence a month, and made to keep an exact account of all that he spent.

His father was determined to make the boy a soldier from his youth up. He thought of nothing else but soldiering; to him it was the only work fit for a man. A hundred and ten lads about the age of the young prince, and all sons of noble families, were formed into a tiny regiment for little Fritz, and when he had learnt his drill he took command of them. "Which he did duly, in a year or two; a little soldier thenceforth; properly strict, though of small dimensions; in tight blue bit of coat and cocked hat; miniature image of Papa (it is fondly hoped and expected), resembling him as a sixpence does a half-crown." Later on a little arsenal was set up for him, and in it he learnt to mount batteries and fire small brass guns.

His governess was a very clever woman, and she had taught him to read and enjoy French, and had given him some instruction in music. In the brief intervals which he could snatch from his soldiering he loved to read French books and to play on the flute; but when his father discovered how he spent his leisure there were terrible scenes. The flute was broken, the French books were sent out of the palace, and the Prince was kicked and cudgelled and pulled by the hair. At dinner the plates were hurled at his head, and sometimes his only fare was bread and water. Once his father knocked him down, and would have strangled him if the Queen had not interfered. At last the unhappy boy was driven to despair, and he tried to run away to the court of his uncle, George II. of England. At this the old tyrant his father was roused to madness. The poor boy was an officer, and he had committed the basest crime that the King could imagine—he had deserted. A young lieutenant who was trying to help him to get out of the clutches of his father was seized, and the King forced his son to look on while this friend was hanged.

The boy himself would have been shot, had not the kings of Sweden and Poland and the Emperor of Germany pleaded for his life. As it was, he was sent to prison; but he found his cell happier than his home. His gaolers were kind to him; he had wholesome food and plenty of it; he could read his French books without being kicked, and play his flute without having it broken over his head. Nevertheless, in less than a fortnight after the death of his friend he was ready to promise the King that he would not misbehave in the future. He was released from prison, but for some time was not restored to his old position in the army.

At length he became a man, and was allowed to set up a home of his own. He married a wife, and amused himself in his country retreat by laying out gardens and growing rare fruits and flowers. The friends whom he gathered around him were all French, and amongst them he set up a brotherhood called the Order of Bayard, after the name of the great French knight who was "without fear and without reproach"—the noblest hero of the Middle Ages.

Early in the year 1740 "Old Fritz" lay on his death-bed, and was able to say, as he put his arms round the Prince's neck, that he was content to die, knowing that he was leaving behind him so worthy a son and successor. Thus Frederick became King of Prussia in his twenty-eighth year. His subjects thought that he would prove a gentle and easy-going king; but imagine their surprise when they found that, like Prince Hal, he bade farewell to his companions and completely turned over a new leaf. "No more of these fooleries," he said, and at once flung himself into the work of making his army as strong and efficient as possible. The men were drilled without mercy, and the officers frequently beat them with canes; but in spite of this treatment they were full of spirit, and in after years showed great valour on the battlefield. Frederick was soon looking about for an opportunity of testing them in war.

A few months after he came to the throne, Charles VI., the Holy Roman Emperor, died, and there was no son to succeed him. He left his great dominions—Austria, Hungary, Bohemia, parts of the Netherlands, and parts of North Italy—to his daughter, Maria Theresa,[32] and before his death he had persuaded the sovereigns of Europe to support her as Empress. Amongst those who faithfully promised to do so was Frederick; but I am sorry to say that, very shortly after Maria Theresa ascended her throne, he suddenly assembled his army and marched at its head into her country. He broke his plighted word; he fell upon a state which he thought was unable to defend itself; and he plunged Europe into a long and terrible war, simply because he was eager to increase his power and make people talk about him. You cannot think of a baser crime than this. Frederick used to say: "He is a fool, and that nation is a fool, which, having the power to strike his enemy unawares, does not strike and strike his deadliest."

It was the depth of winter when Frederick set his armies in motion. Poor Maria Theresa was taken unawares; town after town yielded, until, before the end of January 1741, Frederick was master of Silesia,[33] and was able to return to Berlin, where he was received with joy by his subjects. Then some of the other greedy sovereigns followed Frederick's bad example, and soon all Europe was in arms.

Maria Theresa and the Hungarian Nobles.

When Frederick the Great was about to invade Silesia, Maria Theresa, holding her young son in her arms, begged the Hungarian nobles to fight for her. With one accord they drew their swords and cried, "Let us die for our *king*, Maria Theresa!"

Frederick had been brought up as a soldier, but up to this time he had seen nothing of actual war, and had never commanded great bodies of men in the field. In his first battle his cavalry was put to flight, and he spurred his English grey out of the battle, and ran away! He took refuge in a mill, and late at night the news was brought to him that, thanks to an old field-marshal, his army had won a great victory. When he realized that he had been running away while his men had been winning a battle for him, he was filled with shame. This was the turning-point in his career. In the next battle he showed great courage, and so diligently did he study the art of war, that he soon became renowned as one of the greatest generals who ever lived.

Frederick the Great visiting his People.

(From the picture by von Menzel.)

I cannot tell you here of all the long and cruel warfare which Frederick the Great waged. He gained many victories, chiefly by making cat-like leaps before his enemy expected an attack; but he had many defeats too, for several nations joined together to fight him. He would have been hopelessly beaten but for the British king, George II., who was also Elector of Hanover,[34] one of the German states. George II. sent him men and money, and enabled him to meet his foes on the battlefield. For seven years Frederick held his ground against the three great military Powers of the time—France, Austria, and Russia. In the year 1761 the British refused to help him any further, and it seemed as if he must be forced to give up the struggle for want of means to carry it on. But fortune favoured him; the new Emperor of Russia wished to make peace, and thus Frederick was freed from one of his powerful enemies. One by one his other foes dropped off, and in 1763 peace was made.

In some of his battles so many of his men were killed, and so terrible was the condition of his country, that more than once he thought of committing suicide as the only escape from the evils which he had brought upon his kingdom. But when peace came Prussia was a great Power, respected for her military strength by the whole of Europe. Thereafter, Frederick devoted himself to building up his country anew. Before his death he had increased his territories to an area of 75,000 square miles, and his people numbered 5,500,000. He had made Prussia great, but he had done it by craft and cunning and violence, and at the cost of untold misery and suffering.

Before I conclude the story of Frederick the Great I must tell you of another piece of wickedness which he did in the latter years of his life. I have already mentioned the Poles as a Slav race, and have told you that they now live partly in Austria, partly in Germany, and partly in Russia. There is no country of Poland now, but there may be one again when this war is over. In the reign of the English king, Edward III., Poland was an important and flourishing kingdom. Its capital was the old city of Cracow,[35] now in the Austrian province of Galicia.[36] If you were to visit its cathedral church, which stands high on a rocky hill to the south-west of the town, you would see the tombs of many of the Polish kings, patriots, and poets who have made Poland so famous amongst the nations. Amongst them you would see the last resting-place of John Sobieski,[37] who was the noblest warrior of them all. He it was who drove back the Turks from the walls of Vienna and saved Europe from the infidel.

In the year 1772 Poland was too weak to defend herself. Her nobles quarrelled fiercely amongst themselves, and the land was torn with disunion and strife. Then the cruel, crafty King of Prussia made an agreement with Russia and Austria, whereby they were to seize part of Poland. This was done, and the three sovereigns, like robbers in a cave, divided the spoils between them. Frederick took a big slice, and so did Russia, while Austria was given Galicia. This was the first mouthful. Twenty-one years later the same three Powers gobbled up poor Poland completely; and now, like the Jews, the Poles have no land which they can call their own. But they still love Poland, and yearn for the day when it will be a kingdom once more. When the present great war broke out, the Czar of Russia sent a message to the Poles saying that if they would help him to win he would set up the old kingdom of Poland again, and let it have a king of its own, under his protection. This was great, glad news to the Poles, and they eagerly agreed to help him.

CHAPTER IV.

THE GREAT WAR LORD OF EUROPE.

The noblest street in all Berlin is called the Unter den Linden, which simply means "under the lime trees." In this fine, tree-shaded avenue stands a splendid monument to Frederick the Great, the man who laid the foundations of Prussia by means of force and fraud. His successor, Frederick William II., was a weak man, who squandered the public money on favourites. Under his rule Prussia grew poorer every day; instead of being the best governed state in Europe, it rapidly became one of the worst, and a clever Frenchman at his court declared that no country was nearer to ruin. The army, however, was still kept up in the old way, though it had lost much of its fiery spirit. Frederick William was just as eager for war as Frederick the Great; but he was no general, and when he did fight, was badly beaten. Then, as you will soon hear, he made peace with his victorious foe, and had to give up a part of his country. It was in his time, however, that further slices were taken from Poland and added to Prussia.

The Kaiser and his Troops in the Unter den Linden.
Photo, Exclusive News Agency.

Three years after Frederick William II. came to the throne, one of the greatest events in all history took place. For hundreds of years the kings and nobles of France had ground down the people in all sorts of harsh and cruel ways.

At length the people rose in wrath and began to upturn the government and try to set up a new state of things. In July 1789 a Paris mob stormed the state prison and set free the prisoners; whereupon the peasants all over the country rose in rebellion, murdered the nobles, and burned their castles. The king dared not interfere; all power was taken from him, and a sort of Parliament began to pass laws sweeping away all the old abuses. The Revolution, or great upturning of the government, had begun.

The Attack on the Bastille. *From a contemporary print.*

The leaders of the people grew more and more violent, and thousands of nobles and gentry fled the country. The king and his family tried to escape, but were caught and brought back as prisoners. Those who had managed to get out of France went to the courts of the various kings, and begged them to declare war against the country which was so cruelly treating them and their king. At length the kings of the other European countries began to perceive that their own thrones were in danger, and that they must unite to protect themselves. Leopold II., Emperor of Austria, and Frederick William of Prussia prepared to fight. At the head of 50,000 of his own men and 30,000 Austrians, Frederick William crossed the eastern frontier of France. At this the Paris mob was filled with fury. They burst open the prisons in which their nobles and gentry were confined, and killed many of them. The same dreadful scenes took place in several other towns of France.

French nobles and gentry waiting the call to execution.

The French got together an army which was little better than a rabble, but was full of fiery zeal. It entered Belgium, and called on the people to rise against their government and set up a republic. Another French army advanced to the Rhine to meet Frederick. The anger of the French was now so great that they resolved to hurl at the kings of Europe the head of a king. On January 21, 1793, they cut off the head of their king, and a few months later that of the queen. A thrill of horror ran through the courts of Europe, and Great Britain, Holland, Spain, Austria, and Prussia united to make war on France. In the summer of 1793, during the six weeks of what was called the Reign of Terror, the French put to death more than 1,400 of their nobles and gentry, and some of the most bloodthirsty scenes in all history took place.

During this terrible time the French raised army after army, though they had scarcely the means of feeding and clothing and arming their men. These armies fought with wonderful spirit, and they attacked all the nations opposed to them. On the other hand, the Allies were jealous of each other, and were slow to mass their armies. The Prussians, with whom we are specially concerned, were beaten, and so were the Austrians. Then Frederick William II. deserted his fellow kings, and made peace with the French

Republic,[38] giving up to it the whole of the left bank of the Rhine. He died two years later, and was succeeded by Frederick William III. At the end of the year 1795 France held the upper hand in Europe.

Every boy and every girl who reads these pages must have heard the *Marseillaise*,[39] the great French war song. Here are the words of it, and on the next page you will find the music:—

"Ye sons of France, awake to glory!
Hark, hark! what myriads round you rise!
Your children, wives, and grandsires hoary—
Behold their tears and hear their cries!
Shall hateful tyrants, mischief breeding,
With hireling hosts, a ruffian band,
Affright and desolate the land,
While peace and liberty lie bleeding?
To arms! To arms! ye brave.
The avenging sword unsheathe.
March on! March on!
All hearts resolved on victory or death!
"Now, now the dang'rous storm is rolling,
Which treach'rous kings confed'rate raise;
The dogs of war let loose are howling,
And lo! our fields and cities blaze.
And shall we basely view the ruin,
While lawless Force, with guilty stride,
Spreads desolation far and wide,
With crime and blood his hands embruing?
To arms! To arms! ye brave, etc.
"With luxury and pride surrounded,
The vile insatiate despots dare,
Their thirst for pow'r and gold unbounded
To mete and vend the light and air.
Like beasts of burden would they load us,
Like gods would bid their slaves adore;
But man is man, and who is more?
Then shall they longer lash and goad us?
To arms! To arms! ye brave, etc.
"O Liberty, can man resign thee,
Once having felt thy gen'rous flame?
Can dungeons, bolts, and bars confine thee,
Or whips thy noble spirit tame?

- 43 -

Too long the world has wept, bewailing
That Falsehood's dagger tyrants wield;
But Freedom is our sword and shield,
And all their arts are unavailing.
To arms! To arms! ye brave, etc."

THE MARSEILLAISE HYMN.

Ye Sons of France awake to glory!
Hark, hark! what myriads round you rise!
Your children, wives, and grandsires hoary;
Behold their tears, and hear their cries!
Behold their tears and hear their cries!
Shall hateful Tyrants, mischief breeding,
With hireling hosts, a ruffian band.
Affright and desolate the land,
While peace and liberty lie bleeding?
To arms! to arms! ye brave!
Th'avenging sword unsheath,
March on! March on! all hearts resolv'd
On victory or death! March on!

March on! all hearts resolv'd
On victory or death!

It will interest you to learn that this splendid marching song, which is the French national anthem, was composed during the years when France was fighting with almost all the other nations of Europe. In April 1792, when war was declared on Austria, a young captain of Engineers named Rouget de Lisle[40] was in Strassburg[41] with his company, waiting the order to advance. He was fond of writing verse and composing music, but up to this time he had written and composed nothing worthy of special mention. His heart and mind were fired with the thought of giving freedom to all the world; to him it seemed that the armies of France were engaged in a holy crusade.

Food was scarce in Strassburg at this time, and many of the officers and soldiers would have gone hungry but for the mayor, who did everything he possibly could to supply them with food. Every evening he asked a number of the officers to sup with him, and one evening Rouget de Lisle was invited. During the meal the mayor said that he wished some one would compose a new war song which would stir up the young soldiers about to march on Austria. A major who was one of the company turned to Rouget and said, "You are a poet and a musician; can't you compose something that will do?"

Rouget was a very modest young fellow, and at once he said that a war song was quite beyond his powers. Some of the other men seated at the table joined in the request, and Rouget at last began to think that he would try. He retired to his chamber, and as he thought of his beloved France and of the great battles which she had to fight, he became greatly excited. Then the words flowed from his pen, and as he wrote them a tune sprang into his mind which seemed to suit the words exactly. By seven o'clock in the morning he had composed both words and music. At once he hastened to his friend the major, and said, "Listen to this, and tell me what you think of it." The major listened and was delighted, and some hours later carried him off to the mayor's house. Here Rouget sang his song, while one of the mayor's nieces accompanied him on the piano. Every one who heard it was thrilled. It seemed to call forth all the fighting spirit in them.

Rouget de Lisle singing "The Marseillaise."

(*From the painting by Pils, in the Louvre Gallery. Photo by Mansell.*)

The same day the song was published, and next day one of the military bands played it. Immediately it became all the rage. Through Alsace to the south of France it spread like wildfire; but the people of Paris knew nothing of the song until they heard the volunteers from Marseilles[42] chanting it as they marched through the streets. They had sung it in every town and village through which they had passed, and everywhere it had been greeted with loud cries of delight. Because it was first sung in Paris by the men of Marseilles, it was called the *Marseillaise*.

Such is the story of the great French war song which all Europe learned to know and fear in what is known as the War of the Revolution. It worked like a charm: men marched and fought and suffered and died to its strains. At the present time French soldiers are singing it as they swing along the roads to engage the enemy, and you and I sing it in this country because the French are our friends and allies, and their cause is ours.

Napoleon at School.

When Napoleon was a boy at a French military school he was jeered at by his fellows, who called him a surly Corsican.

Out of the bloodshed and terror of this time arose the figure of Napoleon, the greatest war lord that the world has ever known. He was a Corsican,[43] who first proved his ability by forcing the British to give up Toulon.[44] Thereafter he rose rapidly in the service of the Republic, and in 1796 was placed in command of the army of Italy. In two campaigns he completely overthrew the Austrians, and was hailed by his countrymen as the greatest general of the age. As he rose in power and fame he began to dream of making himself the master of France, and then of all Europe. Before long Great Britain alone stood against him. On sea the British were then, as now, supreme, and our great Admiral Nelson, and others worthy to be mentioned with him, defeated his fleets again and again. Nevertheless he won so many great victories on land that in the year 1801 the continental nations were obliged to make peace with him. You already know that Prussia had done so six years before, and had been forced to give up the whole of the left bank of the Rhine. Next year Britain made peace with him too.

Napoleon at Austerlitz.

On May 18, 1804, Napoleon put an end to the French Republic, and made himself Emperor of the French. He now planned a great scheme for turning all Europe into one vast empire, with kings and princes over the various nations, but himself as the head of all. He sent an army into Hanover, and overran it; but Prussia did not interfere, because she hoped that Napoleon would hand over that state to her if she remained quiet. Great Britain now persuaded Austria, Russia, and Sweden to join together against France, but Frederick William III. would not unite with them. He allowed Napoleon to do as he pleased in Germany, because he thought that Austria would be beaten, and that the conqueror would reward him with some of the spoils. The Emperors of Austria and Russia begged him to desert Napoleon and join them, but he would not listen to them. When Napoleon won the famous battle of Austerlitz, at which the three great emperors of Christendom were present, Frederick William received his reward—Hanover was handed over to him.

Napoleon was now master of all Europe except Great Britain. In the next year sixteen of the German princes separated themselves from the German Empire and joined him, and he turned many of the provinces which he had won into kingdoms, and placed his relatives and his generals on their thrones. As for Prussia, Napoleon had no respect for her, and very soon showed that he was going to seize her too. Louisa, the beautiful Queen of Prussia, had alone seen what the end of her country would be, and had begged the king to draw the sword against the conqueror. When Napoleon took one of the Prussian fortresses she again besought her husband to fight. The Emperor of Russia visited him, and joined his entreaties to hers, and at last, in 1806, he took the field against the great war lord.

Napoleon with King Frederick William III. and Queen Louisa at Tilsit.

From the picture by von Gros.

Napoleon struck swiftly. At Jena[45] he held the Prussians in check till his cavalry came up, and when they dashed down on the foe all was over. The Prussian horse and foot fled in panic; 20,000 Prussians were killed or taken, as well as 300 guns and 60 standards. After the victory Napoleon treated the Prussians very harshly. He said many bitter things about the old Duke of Brunswick, who had fought so bravely against him, and he overran his states. He insulted the queen, and he told the nobles that he would make them so poor that they would be obliged to beg their bread. He quickly subdued the whole country, and made Prussia pay him some millions of money. Then the conquered states were divided into four parts, over which he set commanders.

Leaving 60,000 French to hold beaten Prussia, he now turned on Russia, and in February 1807 marched 100,000 men into Poland, where he met the Russian army and the remnants of the Prussian army. On a field covered with snow a battle was fought during the short hours of a winter day. The slaughter was horrible, and the battle was drawn. In the following May the armies met again, and this time Napoleon was victorious. A week later he and the Czar met on a raft moored on the river Niemen,[46] and made plans for the greatest scheme of robbery ever known to history: they agreed to divide Europe between them.

Great Britain still struggled against Napoleon, and her fleet was the only force which prevented him from becoming the unchecked master of the whole world. Napoleon now tried to bring Great Britain to her knees. Some years before he had gathered fleets of flat-bottomed boats at Boulogne,[47] and had prepared a huge army for the invasion of Britain, but could not obtain that twelve hours' mastery of the Channel which would enable him to cross the "silver streak." Now he tried another plan. He ordered the harbours of the Continent to be closed against the British, so that they could not carry on trade or sell their manufactures. In this way he hoped to make Great Britain so poor that she would be unable to hold out against him.

By this time the Czar was tired of being Napoleon's underling, and he now said that he would not close his ports against the British. Napoleon was furiously angry, and marched a great army towards the Russian frontier, which was crossed on June 23, 1812. The Russians did not attempt to fight; they fell back, and lured him on, meanwhile wasting the country over which he had to pass. Soon the French found themselves short of food, and thousands died of hunger. Napoleon's line of march was marked by the dead bodies of thousands of men and horses.

At last the Russians stood firm, and a great battle was fought some seventy miles from Moscow. One hundred thousand men lay dead or wounded on the field, but Napoleon was not checked. A week later his troops entered Moscow[48] with shouts of delight. To their dismay they found it as silent as a city of the dead. All the people had left it, but before doing so had set fire to the place. Soon after the French marched in, flames began to shoot up from a thousand different points. The fire burned for five days, and the city lay in ruins. Then want of food and shelter compelled Napoleon to retreat. When he left Moscow his army had dwindled to about 100,000 men. The Cossacks[49] hung upon their flanks and rear, and cut off all stragglers. Soon the snow began to fall, and the cruel Russian winter set in. Thousands perished daily of cold and hunger.

Napoleon's starving and frost-bitten army soon became a rabble. As he approached the river Beresina[50] he learned that the Russians were waiting to oppose the passage. A battery of guns commanded the bridge, and as the French tried to cross thousands of them were mowed down, and heaps of dead and wounded blocked the way. A miserable, crushed remnant of 20,000 men was all that struggled back to Germany. The downfall of Napoleon had begun.

The Retreat of Napoleon from Moscow.
(*After the picture by Meissonier.*)

CHAPTER V.

HOW THE GREAT WAR LORD FELL.

This unexpected blow seemed to the enslaved peoples of Europe a sign that their hour of deliverance had struck. Everywhere they began to take fresh courage, and ere long there was a general rising of the nations against Napoleon. Berlin was still in the hands of the French; but when the King of Prussia called upon his people to rise against the common enemy, every able-bodied man was ready to throw off the hated yoke. The news reached Napoleon's ears; but he only exclaimed, "Pah! Germans can't fight like Spaniards." However, he got together another French army, and many of the German princes were so terrified that they let their troops join him. Prussia stood almost alone.

Her people, however, were filled with new hope and energy. The whole country became an armed camp. Youths scarcely more than boys, old men with gray hair, fathers of families, doctors, lawyers, tradesmen, even women in men's clothing, snatched up guns and grasped swords. Never was a nation more united. A large army sprang into being, the Tsar sent help, and Napoleon was defied. But once more the great war lord conquered, and in two fierce battles Prussia was beaten to the ground.

The Emperor of Austria now tried to act as a peace-maker, and sent Metternich,[51] his chief minister, to talk the matter over with Napoleon. As soon as he arrived, the French emperor said, "Well, Count Metternich, how much money have you been bribed with by England to take this part?" So saying, he threw his hat down on the floor to see if Count Metternich would stoop to pick it up. The minister looked at the hat and then at Napoleon, but did not stoop. Seeing this, Napoleon turned his back on him, and Metternich knew that war would be declared on his country.

Napoleon had now to fight Prussia, Russia, Austria, and Sweden. It may perhaps surprise you to find Sweden amongst Napoleon's foes, especially when you learn that the Prince of Sweden had been a French general, and had fought for Napoleon. But he, too, was tired of Napoleon's yoke, and was ready to help in throwing it off. Three armies were gathered together—a northern army, a second in Bohemia, and a third in Silesia, the last being under the command of Marshal Blücher,[52] of whom we shall hear again.

On August 23, 1813, a battle took place between the French and the northern army at a place called Gross-Beeren.[53] The Swedish king was supposed to be in command of this army, but he and his Swedes looked on without fighting. It was a battle of untrained men against a trained army. The Prussian peasants rushed on the foe, beat down whole battalions of them with the butt-ends of their muskets, and captured 2,400 prisoners. Three days later Marshal Blücher also won a success in Silesia. Having lured the French across the river Neisse, he drove them back into the stream, which was then swollen by heavy rains. The muskets of his men were wetted, and so were of no use for firing; but Blücher drew his sabre and dashed forward, shouting, "Forward!" The Prussians clubbed their muskets and beat thousands of the French to death. Many others were drowned or bayoneted, and the victory was complete. The French general escaped almost alone, and galloped to Dresden,[54] where Napoleon then was. "Sire," he said, "your army no longer exists." Marshal Blücher was made a prince, and thenceforward was known as "Marshal Forward."

While his generals were thus suffering defeat, Napoleon himself gained a victory near Dresden. But when his army learned that elsewhere his forces had been beaten, the Germans under his command began to waver, and the outlook was black indeed. Napoleon knew that his end was drawing near, and for several days he could not make up his mind whether to fight or to return to France. At last he determined to fight, and then took place what is known as the "battle of the nations," because soldiers of so many different nations were engaged in it. This battle was one of the longest and fiercest that had ever been fought up to that time. It lasted four days, and at the end of it Napoleon was defeated. He lost no less than 78,000 men; but the Allies, though victorious, lost very heavily too.

Napoleon was beaten at last, and Germany was full of rejoicing. The yoke of French bondage was broken, and many nations were free once more.

The Prussians fighting their way through the village of Planchenoit to reach the field of Waterloo.

(From the picture by Von Udolf Northen.)

I can tell you the rest of Napoleon's story in a very few words. He struggled hard with the remnants of his army, but in vain, and on March 31, 1814, the Allies entered Paris, where the French people received them with shouts of joy. They had been devoted to Napoleon while he was victorious; now that he was defeated, they remembered all the sorrow and suffering that he had caused them, and cried, "Down with the tyrant!" The Allies forced Napoleon to give up his throne, and sent him to reign over the little island of Elba.[55] For eight or nine months he lived on this island, and Europe thought that the last had been seen of him. But he was biding his time, watching and waiting for the chance to become Emperor of France once more. The king to whom his throne had been given was a selfish, stupid man, and he soon disgusted the army and the people. At the moment when they were ready to rise, Napoleon suddenly appeared on the south coast of France, and as he travelled north to Paris his old soldiers flocked to him. The troops sent against him deserted and went over to his side. When he entered Paris, on the 20th of March, the king had fled.

The Allies now bound themselves to put more than a million men into the field against him, and never to rest until they had subdued him for ever. Napoleon, however, gathered an army, and marched into Belgium, where the Duke of Wellington had a mixed force of British and Belgians, and Prince Blücher an army of Prussians. I cannot now tell you fully the story of the great fight which followed. Napoleon's general, Ney, attacked the British at Quatre Bras,[56] but was beaten. On the same day, at Ligny,[57] Napoleon met

Blücher, and defeated him, but not so badly that he was unable to fight again. The Prussians were obliged to retreat, and Wellington was forced to fall back to the field of Waterloo,[58] at which place Blücher promised to meet him next day.

On the 18th of June the great battle took place. All day the British held their ground, though they were fiercely assailed again and again. At eight o'clock in the evening, just when the last desperate charge had been driven back, Blücher and his Prussians appeared. Then the French army turned and fled. Napoleon put spurs to his horse and rode through the summer night to the coast, where he tried to escape to America. Failing to do this, he gave himself up to the captain of a British man-of-war. "Last scene of all to end this strange eventful history," Napoleon was banished to the lonely Atlantic island of St. Helena,[59] where he was kept prisoner like a caged tiger for nearly six years. He died on May 5, 1821. So much had he passed out of history that a great Frenchman said his death was not an event, only a piece of news.

Why did we fight so hard and so long against Napoleon? First, because he was a tyrant, bent on making himself master of Europe and ruling it as he pleased; secondly, because he wiped out or trod underfoot many of the smaller nations; and thirdly, because we were determined not to allow him to gain possession of the Netherlands. Look at a map of Europe, and you will see that the Netherlands, which now consist of Holland and Belgium, are opposite to our east and south-east coasts. These two countries are small, but they are very fertile, because they are mainly formed of the rich soil brought down by the Rhine, the Meuse, and the Scheldt.

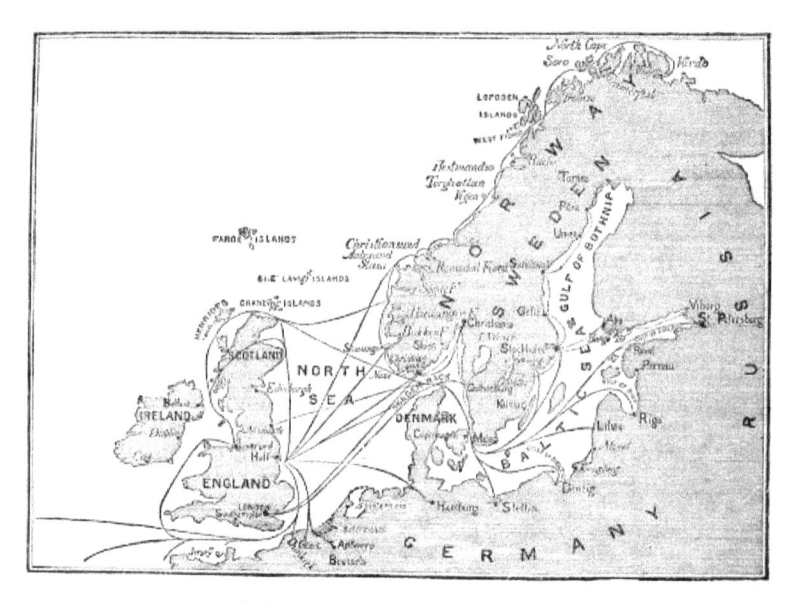

Map of Northern Europe.

The thick lines show the chief trade routes.

Thanks to the rivers, the Netherlands have some of the best ports in the world, and through them passes much of the sea-borne trade of Northern Europe. Antwerp, on the Scheldt, is opposite to the mouth of the Thames, and is one of the great ports of the world. Rotterdam, at the mouth of the Rhine, and Amsterdam, near the Zuider Zee,[60] are also very important seaports. If an enemy held these ports, and was able to drive our navy from the North Sea, he might invade us very easily. Napoleon used to say that Antwerp was a pistol held at the heart of England. We should have been very blind and very foolish if we had allowed him to be master of the Netherlands, and permitted him to point the pistol at our heart. As master of the Netherlands he would not only have gained greatly in strength, but he would have been better able to carry out an invasion of our shores than he had ever been before. When we pressed him very hard to give up the Netherlands, he refused, and said that he would rather surrender the French colonies than Antwerp. His overthrow removed a great danger from our very doors.

The last days of the man who tried to make himself Master of the World.

This picture, which is by the famous French artist Paul Delaroche, shows Napoleon at St. Helena.

Before we part from Napoleon I want you to learn a lesson from his fate. He was one of the greatest soldiers who ever lived, and a man of wonderful powers of mind. His ambition was boundless, and he tried to make himself master of Europe, and therefore of the world. For many years he succeeded, but from the first his doom was sealed. The nations of Europe will never permit one man, however great, to be their master. While many of the nations of the Continent were forced to yield to him, we British never did. We fought him by sea and by land, and we were always ready to send men and money to those nations who stood up against him. The contest was very long; but the British people never wavered. They held on with the courage of a British bulldog, and in the end, by destroying his fleets at Trafalgar[61] and defeating his army at Waterloo, they brought the tyrant low.

Preparing the famous signal at Trafalgar. *From the picture by Thomas Davidson.*

Just before the battle began, Nelson ordered the famous signal to be made: "England expects every man to do his duty."

The story of how Britain saved Europe from the tyranny of Napoleon should steel our hearts and animate our minds at this time, when we are trying to lay a would-be tyrant low. The British people by their courage and doggedness overthrew the most powerful man and the most powerful nation in the world, and what they did then they can do now. Our forefathers struggled with wonderful patience and courage for long, weary years, but in the end they were victorious. We shall be victorious too if we are but worthy of our sires.

CHAPTER VI.

THE MAN OF BLOOD AND IRON.

When Napoleon was safely imprisoned on St. Helena the Powers met to make peace, and to rearrange the map of Europe. A large part of the left bank of the Rhine which Napoleon had reft from Prussia was given back to her. An arrangement was made that thirty-nine states of Germany should join together into a *Bund*,[62] or bond, and that each state should be represented in its ruling body. Saxony,[63] Wurtemberg,[64] and Bavaria,[65] which had been turned into kingdoms by Napoleon, were allowed to keep their kings, but the brothers and field-marshals whom he had placed on other thrones were dismissed. The only one of his marshals who retained his throne was the King of Sweden.

When peace reigned once more, a German prince said, "I have slept seven years; now we will forget the bad dream." But the "bad dream" was a good dream for the peoples of Europe. Though they had suffered so terribly in the wars, the French Revolution had made men very disinclined to allow kings to rule them as they pleased, and had encouraged them everywhere to ask for more freedom to govern themselves. In Germany the people had only two duties—to pay and to obey. Now they asked for many rights which they had never possessed before, and in some of the states they obtained them; but the King of Prussia held out to the last, and only gave his people a Parliament when he could resist the demand no longer.

During this time, when the people were crying out for more freedom, one very good arrangement was made. Germany, as you know, consisted of a large number of states, some small and some large, but all of them with their own rulers, and armies, and customs officials. It was possible to pass through several of these states in the course of a day's ride. All of them took toll of goods passing through them, and all of them had to have guards at their frontiers, to see that the goods did not pass through without paying toll.

You will get some idea of what this meant if you suppose the English counties to be separate states, and that a wagon-load of goods is being sent, say, from Birmingham to Carlisle. Suppose the wagon to reach the border of Staffordshire: it would be stopped there by customs officers, who would estimate the value of the goods in it, and make the owner pay a certain sum before he was allowed to proceed. When the wagon came to the Cheshire border, there would be another search and another payment; and the same business would be repeated on the borders of Lancashire, Westmorland, and Cumberland. I am sure you will say in a moment that this was not only a great nuisance, but it must have interfered with trade a great deal, and made goods very expensive to the purchaser. This is exactly what happened in

Germany. Of course, men tried to get out of paying toll whenever they could, and smuggling goods from one state to another became a regular business.

If I were to ask you to suggest a way out of the difficulty, you would say: "Let all the states join together into a group, and take toll once and for all when the goods enter the group. The money so received can be divided up amongst the states afterwards." This is just what was done. A Customs Union, or Zollverein, was formed by Prussia and several of the neighbouring states, and each state sent a member to represent it in a sort of Parliament known as the Bund Diet.[66]

When the German people began to see the advantages of joining together in this way so as to make trade easier, they would soon come to perceive that a union for other purposes would be good too. In the year 1848, six hundred representatives from the German states met at Frankfort,[67] and did away with the old Bund. They said that they wished all the German states to be united into one empire, with one Parliament and one set of laws. They asked the King of Prussia, Frederick William IV.,[68] to be emperor; but he refused, because he was not going to be dictated to by the people. "They forget," he said, "that there are princes still in Germany, and that I am one of them." Then there were many risings, especially in the south of Germany; but they were all put down, and the kings and princes seemed to have gained the upper hand. As a matter of fact, the people had gained much; they had aimed at unity, and though many years were to pass before they obtained their desire, unity was bound to come. In May 1851 the old Bund was restored, and once more held its meetings at Frankfort.

Now let me introduce to you the man who brought about the union of the German states into an empire. His name was Otto von Bismarck, and he was born in the year of Waterloo. The title *von* shows you that he was of what is called gentle birth. His father was a Brandenburg squire, and young Bismarck spent his childhood on the flat stretches of his father's estates. As a boy he had a great reverence for kings, and thought that those who rose against them were wicked men. For example, he believed that William Tell,[69] whose story you are sure to remember, was a rebel and a murderer.

Otto von Bismarck.

(*From the picture by Franz von Lenbach.*)
This portrait shows Bismarck at a time when he was practically ruler of Prussia.

In 1832 he was sent to a university, where he was more renowned outside the classroom than in it. He was a big, burly man, of great strength, with a large, firm chin, and a look of confidence and self-control. It is the custom for German students to fight duels as a pastime. When they do so they protect their bodies and heads and eyes, and leave only the face exposed. The foolish young fellows slash at each other's faces, and are very proud of the scars which remain when their wounds have healed. Bismarck was a great duellist; he fought and won while he was in the university no fewer than twenty-seven duels.

He was the son of a soldier, and was very proud of the fact that his ancestors had fought in all the great Prussian wars. Rough and bluff in his manner, and homely in his speech, he greatly admired strong men who could force others to do their bidding. For people who were turned from their purpose by feelings of pity or kindness he had nothing but contempt. He had few friends outside his own family, but he was very fond of his dogs. Above all things he was a Prussian, and he was ready to do anything and everything to make Prussia not only the greatest state of Germany, but the leader of all the German states as well. By nature he was honest and straightforward; but he did not stick at deceit if he thought that thereby the interests of his country might be advanced.

In the year 1847 we find him attending the Bund Diet as the member for Prussia. He soon showed that he was a king's man, and that he had no belief in the rule of the people. Prussia, he knew, had been created by the power of the sword, under the sway of kings who did pretty much as they pleased, and allowed the people to have no part or lot in the government. No doubt his father had often told him of the black day when Napoleon beat the Prussians at Jena, and of the sad years when his beloved land was beneath the Corsican's yoke. It was in those days that the great Baron Stein[70] did his great work. At the peace of Tilsit Napoleon said that Prussia might have a standing army of 42,000 men. Stein set his wits to work to use this army as a means of training all the men of the nation. When 42,000 men were drilled they were dismissed, another 42,000 were called up, and so on. In three years Prussia had 180,000 well-drilled men and 120,000 reserves. With these troops Prussia played a large part in overthrowing Napoleon. Remembering all this, Bismarck felt that parliaments had done nothing; strong men and a strong army had done everything, and it was by similar means that Prussia might be made the great overlord of Germany. Such was Bismarck's fixed belief.

Though he had made no mark at college, he possessed the biggest brain of his time, and he now began to set it to work. Soon he was a marked man, and the king made him ambassador, first at St. Petersburg and then at Paris. In 1862 he was recalled to be the first minister of King William I., brother of Frederick William IV., who had died insane. From that day down to the year 1890 he was the foremost man, first of Prussia, then of Germany, and finally of Europe.

At that time Prussia's great rival for chief power amongst the German states was Austria. It was Austria who had forced the Prussian king to set up the old Bund again, because in it she had the chief power. When Bismarck went to the Bund in 1862, he plainly told Austria that Germany could never be united until she ceased to interfere with German affairs, and that she had plenty of work to do in looking after her own business. He also told the Bund that the unity of Germany could never be brought about by parliaments, but only by "blood and iron." By this he meant a European war. He firmly believed that the German states could only be welded together when their soldiers fought and died side by side on the battlefield.

But first of all he had to build up an army so strong that it could strike respect or fear into all the German peoples, and make them regard Prussia as their leader and chief. You already know that when the Prussians beat Napoleon in 1813, all the men of military age in the country had been passed through the army. Bismarck determined that the new army should be formed in the same way. Most of the people objected, but Bismarck still persisted, and his old college friend von Roon[71] began to plan an army on these lines. The Prussian Parliament would not agree to the new army law, and at last the king said he would resign his throne. Bismarck, however, would not give way, and one day, after he had made a bold speech in Parliament, the king said, "Over there, in front of the Opera House, under my windows, they will cut off your head, and mine a little while afterwards." Bismarck, however, was not frightened. He succeeded in getting the king to take no notice of Parliament, and the army was created.

The Coronation of William I. of Prussia in the Cathedral of Königsberg on October 18, 1861.

(*From the picture by Adolf von Menzel.*)

CHAPTER VII.
CLEARING THE PATH.

The new Prussian army was trained by a great soldier named von Moltke,[72] whose nephew was chief of the German staff[73] when the war in which we are now engaged broke out. When this new army was strong enough, Bismarck meant to go to war with Austria; but until that time arrived he intended to keep the peace with her. In the year 1863 the King of Denmark died, and when the new king came to the throne a dispute arose about the two duchies of Schleswig and Holstein,[74] which you will see on the map to the south of Denmark. I cannot explain here to you all the rights and wrongs of this dispute. An English statesman of the time said that only two men understood it—one was dead, and the other was in a lunatic asylum. Both these duchies were subject to Denmark; but the people of Holstein were Germans, while those of Schleswig were Danes. There were constant quarrels between the Danes and the Germans in these duchies, and Bismarck thought that the time had come for Prussia to seize them. So, like the far-sighted man that he was, he made preparations, and took care that none of the other nations would interfere. He made a treaty with Russia on the eastern border, and asked Austria to join him in fighting the Danes. The idea of joining these duchies to Germany was very popular in all the German states, and Austria felt bound to take part in their conquest. If she had not done so, Prussia would have stood forward as the leader of Germany, and this was the very thing that Austria was determined to prevent. You now begin to perceive what a wily man Bismarck was.

To make a long story short, the two giants, Prussia and Austria, attacked the little kingdom of Denmark; and, though the Danes fought like heroes, they were crushed, and the two duchies were seized. But what was to become of them?—that was the question. Prussia soon showed that she meant to have them both. To this Austria would not agree, and thus the robbers fell out over the division of their booty. Before they came to blows, King William made Bismarck a count, and thus addressed him: "In the four years which have elapsed since I summoned you to the head of the State Government, Prussia has gained a position which is worthy of her history, and which promises a fortunate and glorious future."

During the spring of 1866 von Moltke was rapidly preparing his army, and studying his plan of campaign. He had a surprise in store, not only for Austria, but for all the world. What that surprise was you shall now learn.

Chief of the Staff General von Moltke (nephew of the great General who trained the Prussian Army for the wars against Denmark, Austria, and France).

He is here seen with the Kaiser Wilhelm watching the manoeuvres of German troops.
(*Photo, Oscar Tellgmann.*)

In the year 1806 a Prussian boy, named John Nicholas Dreyse, finished his apprenticeship as a locksmith. The battle of Jena[75] had just been fought, and Dreyse wandered on to the battlefield, where the Prussians lay thick on the ground, with their muskets beside them. He picked up one of these guns and examined it carefully. He was a clever and inventive lad, and he soon saw that the musket was a poor weapon, and that his countrymen had been beaten because Napoleon's army had a much better gun. Thereupon he began to dream of inventing a gun for his country that should be the best in the world. He found his way to Paris, and obtained employment in the workshop of a Swiss gunmaker who was trusted by the Emperor Napoleon.

The clever, hard-working Prussian boy soon gained the confidence of his master, who one day told him that he was going to make for the Emperor a gun that would be loaded at the breech. Dreyse had never thought of this before. All the guns that he had ever seen were muzzle-loaders—that is, they were loaded by pouring powder into the barrel and ramming home a bullet. The new idea filled his mind, and night and day he thought of ways in which such a quick-loading gun might be made. When Napoleon heard how he was occupied, he encouraged him to further effort by promising him a gift of money and the Cross of the Legion of Honour.[76] Before, however, the gun was made, Napoleon was sleeping his last sleep under the willow-tree on the island of St. Helena.

Cross of the Legion of Honour.

At length, in 1835, after thirty years of thought and trial and disappointment, Dreyse made a breech-loading gun which was fired by the prick of a needle. At once he offered his gun to the Government of his own country. It was tried against the Danes, and proved so successful that the Prussian Government set up a large factory in which to manufacture it.

By the month of June 1866, many of the Prussian soldiers were armed with this needle-gun, and had learned how to use it. Then when all was ready war began.

On the 23rd of June three Prussian armies entered Bohemia[77] by different routes, with orders to drive back the Austrians and gather in force near Sadowa.[78] These armies had to advance through the passes in the wall of mountains which forms the natural rampart of Bohemia. What the Austrians should have done was to fling themselves against the Prussians as they issued from the passes; but, as of old, the Austrian generals were slow to move, and before they did anything the Prussians were all in Bohemia. At Sadowa, or Königgrätz,[79] as the Germans call it, a terrible battle took place. The Austrians were posted in a strong position, and they had good artillery, with which they caused many losses in the Prussian ranks. After three or four hours' fighting, it seemed as if the Austrians had driven off their foes. Suddenly, however, the second army, under the Crown Prince,[80] arrived on the field of battle. Regiment after regiment of Prussians in their dark-blue uniforms advanced, all armed with the needle-gun. Then a rapid and deadly fire burst upon the Austrian army. Nothing so terrible had been known before. The Austrians held their ground for an hour, suffering fearful losses; but they were obliged to give way at last, and the battle was won. Thirty-two thousand Austrians were killed, wounded, or missing; the Prussians had lost only nine thousand men.

The defeat was so crushing that Austria could no longer resist. The Prussians marched on Vienna, and peace was made. Austria had to pay the Prussians a great deal of money; she had to give up her claim to the duchies, and agree to let the German states form a union, from which she was excluded. The whole campaign had only lasted seven weeks. At the end of it Prussia stood without a rival in Germany. She was now a large, compact state of nearly thirty millions of people, stretching over the whole of North Germany from Frankfort in the south to Kiel[81] in the north. Not only had Prussia become the greatest state of Germany, but she had cleared away the great obstacle that stood in the path of a united German Empire of which she was to be the head.

Place de la Concorde.

CHAPTER VIII.

PREPARING FOR WAR.

The finest of all the squares of Paris is the Place de la Concorde.[82] Let us stand in the middle of this square and look around. To the west we see a long avenue of chestnut trees, the Champs Elysées;[83] to the north we catch a glimpse of the Madeleine,[84] one of the most famous of all the Parisian churches; to the south, across the river, is the noble building in which the French Members of Parliament (Deputies) meet; and to the east we see the terraces and trees of the Garden of the Tuileries,[85] leading by the pond on which children sail their toy yachts to the Louvre Museum. If we stroll in the park of the Champs Elysées, we shall be sure to see roundabouts and swings, and hear the squeak of our old friend Punch, whom the French children call Guignol.[86]

The Place de la Concorde is very bright and gay now, and does not in the least suggest sad scenes to your mind. But it was here in January 1793 that the guillotine[87] was set up, and hundreds of the nobility and gentry of France were executed. Louis XVI. and his queen, Marie Antoinette, here saw the light of the sun for the last time before the cruel axe descended, and all was over. The square was then known as the Place de la Révolution.

As you glance round the square you will see a number of statues. Each of the following towns has its own statue—Marseilles, Lyons,[88] Lille,[89] Rouen,[90] Brest, Nantes, Bordeaux,[91] and Strassburg. You can look these places out for yourselves on a map of France. It is the statue of Strassburg to which I wish to direct your special attention. Up to the end of July in the year 1914, it was draped in black, and mourning wreaths were placed on it. As soon as the war broke out, the students of Paris tore away the black drapery, and replaced it with the French flag. They also removed the mourning wreaths, and put bright, fresh flowers in their place.

Perhaps you wonder why the statue of Strassburg remained in mourning from the year 1871 to the end of July in the year 1914. By the time you have read the next two chapters you will understand.

Now we must return to the story of Germany. In the former chapter I told you how Austria was overthrown, and how Prussia became the leading power amongst the German peoples. Thus, by means of "blood and iron," the first step towards German unity was taken. After the Austrian War the German states north of the Main[92] were united into a Nord-Bund, with Prussia at their head. The states south of the Main remained outside the combination, and had still to be brought into it. Bismarck knew that this could only be done by means of war. I will now tell you how this war came about.

The Battle of Magenta (June 4, 1859).

This picture represents the second attack by the French soldiers known as Zouaves on the town of Magenta, 15 miles west of Milan, in that part of N. Italy known as Lombardy. A French officer carrying the flag of his regiment is seen leading his men on to victory.
(*From the picture by Yvon. In the Versailles Gallery.*)

In the year 1852 France had once more an emperor, who was a nephew of the great Napoleon,[93] but was by no means a man of the same military genius. His throne was not secure, and he believed that he could make it so by restoring the old martial glory of his country. His troops fought along with us in the Crimea[94] against the Russians, and in 1859 he sent them to the help of the Italians, who were then throwing off the yoke of Austria. In the course of a few weeks he took a leading part in winning three victories, and returned to Paris in triumph, where he was hailed as the saviour of Italy.

For centuries the French had kept a jealous eye on Germany, and had done everything they could to keep it from becoming a rival. Louis XIV. had taken away from Germany the two provinces of Alsace and Lorraine, which you will see on the map between the Moselle and the Rhine. Napoleon I., as you know, stole a good deal of Germany, and gave it away to his marshals and to the members of his own family. After his fall, the Germans began to grow in power by good government and by peaceful industry, and France regarded this growth with a very unfriendly eye. When Prussia beat Austria and made herself head of the North German Bund, the French began to think that the time had come for clipping Prussia's wings.

Soon a quarrel arose, as quarrels always do if you seek for them. The King of Spain died, and Bismarck put forward a German prince as a candidate for the vacant throne. The French people were much alarmed at the prospect of a German king ruling Spain, and there was great excitement in all parts of France. The German prince was withdrawn; but this did not satisfy the French people, who were eager for war.

At this time King William of Prussia was at Ems,[95] enjoying a holiday, and his chief ministers were away on holiday too. The French ambassador went to Ems and demanded that the Prussian king should apologize, and give a promise never to put forward a German candidate for the Spanish throne again. King William refused to do this, and sent a telegram to Bismarck, giving him an account of the interview. Bismarck, you will remember, wanted war in order to unite North and South Germany into an empire. He saw his chance, and cut out part of the telegram so as to make it read in a way that angered both the French and the Germans. Then he published it, and almost at once the French declared war.

On July 16, 1870, the North Bund met, and agreed to fight. Three days later, to the great surprise of Napoleon, the South German states held a meeting, and declared that they would join with the North states in making war against France, under the leadership of the King of Prussia. This was a great triumph for Bismarck, who now saw clearly that if the united German armies could beat France, their comradeship in arms and their common joy in victory would make a German Empire very probable.

The united armies of North and South Germany were far greater than those of France, and the Germans were also far stronger than the French in another important way. For years past they had prepared for war. All their plans had been made. They had all the stores, and guns, and ammunition, and railway trains they needed, and the whole system was arranged like clockwork. On the other hand, the French were very badly prepared. The Minister of War said he could place 400,000 men on the frontier. He also said that everything was in order; that there were huge stores of clothing, and that not even a "gaiter-button" was missing. There were enough cartridges to kill all the Germans twice over, and the army had a new machine gun[96] that would prove more deadly than the needle-gun which the Prussians had used against the Austrians. But all this was mere boasting. The French people had been living in a fool's paradise. They were as ill-prepared for war as they possibly could be.

When the Emperor joined the army at Metz,[97] prepared to lead his eager troops across the Rhine to Berlin, he found to his dismay that he had but 220,000 men in place of the 400,000 promised. The men of the reserve[98] joined the colours very slowly, and when they appeared it was discovered that they had not been drilled in the use of the breech-loading rifle, and that they would not be ready to take the field for weeks. It was discovered, too, that the officers who had learned how to handle the machine guns had been drafted off to other duties, and that those who were in charge of these terrible new weapons knew nothing about them. There were huge stores of food in two or three depots, but there were no means of bringing it rapidly to the army. The transport wagons were stored in one place, while their wheels lay elsewhere at a distance, and wheels and wagons could not be brought together for weeks. The artillery[99] were without horses, and the guns could not be moved until horses were borrowed from the cavalry.[100] The only maps which were provided were those of Germany.

While everything was at sixes and sevens on the French side, the Germans were massing their armies in a perfectly wonderful way. The boast of the French minister was true as regards them: the Germans were prepared to the last gaiter-button. Every detail had been thought out; every difficulty had been foreseen and provided for. By night and day railway trains followed each other to the frontier, laden with soldiers, horses, and guns. In fourteen days 450,000 Germans, well trained, well armed, and well fed, were ready to give battle to the ill-prepared armies of France.

Belgian Soldiers of to-day. *Photo, Sport and General.*
Notice the dogs drawing the machine guns.

CHAPTER IX.

"THE COCKPIT OF EUROPE."

Before I tell you the story of the great struggle between France and Germany in 1870-71, I must ask you to look for a little time at Belgium. You know that it lies between Holland and France, and is one of the smallest countries in the world. The five northern counties of England cover a greater area than the whole of Belgium.

The coast is low and sandy, and is fringed with dunes. There are only two important harbours on the coast—Nieuport, which is the same word as our English "Newport," and Ostend, which simply means "East-end." The eastern part of the country contains a few low ranges of forest-clad hills, but elsewhere the surface resembles that of Holland.

Let us climb to the top of the belfry which happily still remains in the fine old town of Bruges.[101] Looking westwards, we see the North Sea; southwards and eastwards and northwards the country is as flat as the sea, and only just above its level. As you glance across the plain your eye lights upon other towers similar to that upon which you are standing. About twenty-five miles to the south-east you make out the belfry of Ghent,[102] and you might see, if the weather is clear, the ruins of Ypres,[103] an old cloth-working town, far to the south. Bruges, Ghent, Ypres, and the other towns which you see, were rich and flourishing for centuries, and they prove very clearly that the Belgian plain has long been famous for manufactures and trade.

We now proceed to Ghent, and climb its belfry, which is higher than St. Paul's Cathedral. Looking around, we notice that the towns within view are even more numerous than those which we saw from the belfry at Bruges. Below us are two large rivers, the Scheldt[104] and the Lys,[105] which unite and wander away eastwards in a broad, full stream. If we look at the map, we see many other broad and deep rivers, all tributaries or sub-tributaries of the Scheldt.

As we travel eastwards to Brussels, the capital, the flat land begins to get tumbled and uneven. There are no real hills yet, but you feel that you are rising to higher land.

As we proceed eastwards from Brussels we shall ascend higher and higher, until we reach a point from which we can look down a deep valley, through which flows a broad, clear river. This is the Meuse,[106] and you notice at once that it is quite unlike the rivers of the east of Belgium. The Meuse runs everywhere between steep hills, and where it enters Belgium from France it flows through a narrow gorge. From this gorge we can row for a long day down the river between the deep, silent forests covering the hills, which rise hundreds of feet on both sides of us. As we proceed, the hills sink in height, the stream becomes broader, and the towns upon its banks become larger and more frequent. We pass the beautiful town of Dinant,[107] and later on the larger fortified town of Namur,[108] where the river is joined by the Sambre.[109] Still further down the river, near the German frontier, is the great industrial town of Liége,[110] the "Belgian Birmingham."

Beyond the Meuse we find the third and final division of Belgium. It is quite unlike the rest of the country. The hills are lofty and are covered with woods, which on the south are known as the Forest of the Ardennes.[111] Where there are no forests, this part of the country consists of heaths and moors.

If you look at an ordinary map of Belgium you will see a number of crossed swords showing you the position of battlefields. So many battles have been fought in Belgium that it has been called the "Cockpit of Europe." Now why has Belgium been the scene of so many battles? You see that the country stands between England and France and Germany, and I must tell you that before Napoleon I. conquered Holland and Belgium they belonged to Austria. If Germany should go to war with France, and Great Britain should join in, their armies naturally meet in Belgium. An army from North Germany and an army marching north from France would come into contact somewhere on the rolling land between Brussels and the Meuse, where you see so many crossed swords. The French would find a shorter way into Germany, and the Germans into France, across the Ardennes and the high land, but an army with its food and baggage trains always avoids hill country if it can. The reason why the British have fought battles in this district is also clear. They had to meet their allies as rapidly as possible after crossing the sea, and the most convenient meeting-place was the rolling country between Brussels and the Meuse.

You can easily understand that when these armies entered Belgium to fight their battles, the Belgians were sure to suffer. Their fair fields would be trodden down, their industries would cease, food supplies would be seized, houses and public buildings would be destroyed, and many innocent townsfolk and peasants who had no part or lot in the war would be killed by stray shots, or put to death because they gave information to the enemy. The plight of Belgium, when her big neighbours quarrelled and fought out their quarrels on her soil, was always terrible, so in the year 1839 the five great European Powers—Great Britain, France, Russia, Austria-Hungary, and *Prussia*—made a solemn treaty, by which they promised faithfully that they would never again trespass on Belgian soil in time of war. This is what we mean when we talk about the neutrality[112] of Belgium.

Now what has all this to do with the war between France and Germany in 1870? We shall soon see. When there was no doubt that Germany and France were going to fight, the British Government sent a message to each of them, saying that it would declare war against that Power which broke its plighted word with regard to Belgium. Bismarck replied by telegraph that she had no intention of invading Belgium, and France gave her answer in the same strain. Thus Belgium was spared untold suffering. A new treaty was made renewing the old one, and this treaty up to the beginning of the present war was Belgium's charter of freedom from foreign invasion.

The Belgian people were very much relieved when they knew that they were to be left alone during the war, and the town council of Brussels sent a beautiful letter of thanks to Queen Victoria. It ran as follows:—

"The great and noble people over whose destinies you preside have just given another proof of its benevolent sentiments towards this country. The voice of the English nation has been heard above the din of arms. It has asserted the principles of justice and right. Next to the unalterable attachment of the Belgian people to their independence, the strongest sentiment which fills their hearts is that of an imperishable gratitude to the people of Great Britain."

CHAPTER X.

A TERRIBLE STRUGGLE.

Now we must hark back and pick up the threads of the story which we dropped at the end of Chapter IX. Look at the map of the French frontier which you will find on the next page. If you trace the present boundary line between France and Germany, you will see it running south from the little state of Luxemburg,[113] in front of Metz, then turning south-east, and proceeding to the Vosges[114] Mountains, along the ridge of which it continues to the border of Switzerland. In July 1870 the French frontier ran eastwards from Luxemburg to the right bank of the Rhine, and continued south along that river to Basel.[115] France, you will observe, then possessed the two frontier provinces of Lorraine and Alsace.[116] The most important town in these provinces is Strassburg, on the left bank of the Rhine.

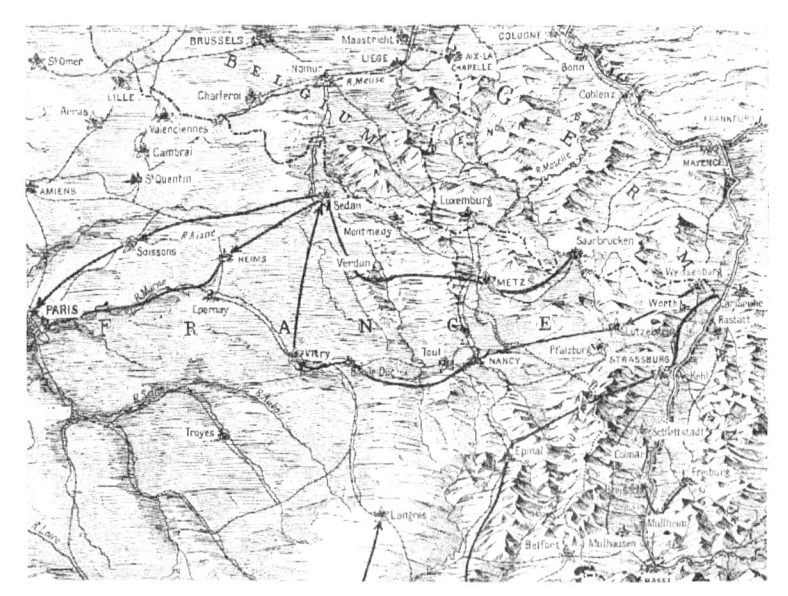

Now look closely at the province of Lorraine, and find Metz. You see that it is marked with a star, which indicates that it is a fortress. It stands on a fertile peninsula, formed by the confluence of the Seille[117] and the Moselle, and is surrounded by low-lying meadows, which are now rich market gardens. There is hill country to the west and hill country to the east and south, so that it is naturally a strong place and capable of resisting attacks. At the time of which we are speaking it was the strongest fortress of France.

Let us suppose that we have the invisible cloak of the fairies, and are thus enabled to enter unseen the long dining-room of the Hôtel de l'Europe in

Metz during the closing days of July 1870. The first figure to catch our eye is that of the Emperor Napoleon III. We observe that he is a grave, dreamy man, with nothing of the first Napoleon's power and determination. We guess that he is seriously ill, and our guess is true; for he is suffering from an incurable complaint, which will soon render him incapable of directing the affairs of the army and the country. Ever since he was a child the great Napoleon has been his ideal, and he has long dreamed of founding an empire just as great as his uncle's, but far more lasting. By his side you see a boy of fourteen, the Prince Imperial,[118] his only son. Before another month is over this boy will receive his baptism of fire, and will bear himself on the battlefield with a coolness far beyond his years. He will, however, never wear the crown of France, and nine years later will receive his death-wound while fighting for Britain in South Africa.

At a glance you perceive that Napoleon and the staff officers about him are full of anxiety; and well they may be, for not half the expected number of soldiers have mobilized, and the reserves are coming in by driblets. Telegrams arrive every few moments from the generals, beseeching the Emperor to send them transport, horses, and camp equipment. The army is utterly incapable of advancing, and it is very clear that the great dash across the Rhine must be put off. Meanwhile the German armies are moving like a well-oiled machine. Three great masses of men are assembling on the Rhine, ready to invade France. Their plan of campaign has been thought out long ago; it is now being followed to the letter. On the other hand, Napoleon and his generals are powerless to move, and are chopping and changing their plans every day. The Parisians are beginning to growl: "We ought to be across the Rhine by now. Why does the Emperor wait? On to Berlin! to Berlin!"

On the 2nd of August something had to be done to allay the impatience of the French people, and Napoleon ordered an advance on Saarbrücken,[119] where a Prussian detachment of 1,300 lay. After a fight of three hours the Prussians were driven back; but they retired in good order, and were not pursued, neither was Saarbrücken occupied. Shortly afterwards the tide of German invasion began to roll across the frontier. It consisted of three armies, and comprised 447,000 men. Behind these armies was a first reserve of 188,000 men, ready to be sent forward later; and behind them, again, a second reserve of 160,000 men. In addition, there were 226,000 men to fill up the gaps caused by the killed and wounded. Von Moltke's plan was that the three armies should march into France separately, and then unite to give battle.

At Weissenburg,[120] which you will see on your map almost directly east of Metz, the 3rd German army came in contact with the French. MacMahon,[121] the French general, had no idea of how the German armies were disposed, and he had sent but a single division to Weissenburg. This division had to meet a whole German army, and though it struggled gallantly for five hours, it was crushed by overwhelming odds. The Emperor and his staff now lost their heads completely; all was confusion and dismay.

The victorious Germans marched southwards towards Wörth,[122] where Marshal MacMahon was striving to draw his scattered forces together. A careless watch was kept, and early in the morning the marshal was painfully surprised to find himself attacked by a force which greatly outnumbered his own. He was well and strongly posted, and had with him a number of fine Algerian troops;[123] but the enemy attacked with such fierceness that, in spite of the desperate bravery of his men, they could not hold their ground. Under cover of darkness the remnants of the French army escaped.

The same day another calamity befell the French. The 1st and 2nd German Armies had by this time crossed the Rhine, and were marching on Saarbrucken. When the advanced guard reached that place, about nine on the morning of the 6th of August, it discovered that the French, under General Frossard,[124] were strongly entrenched on a plateau with steep wooded sides. Almost immediately the French guns opened fire, and the German troops at a distance from the battlefield marched "to the sound of the guns." As each regiment arrived it was hurried into action, and one of the fiercest and most deadly battles of the war began. The French ought to have won. There were enough of their troops in the neighbourhood to beat back the Germans, but the commanders had not been trained to act together, and the consequence was that several divisions of the army never came into the fight at all.

When darkness began to fall, Frossard fell back, and the Germans had won a victory of which they were hardly aware. The poor, distracted Emperor sent a telegram to Paris announcing this double defeat, and doubtfully declaring, "All may yet be regained."

All the three German armies were now on French soil. The 3rd Army, which formed the German left, was commanded by the Crown Prince, afterwards the Emperor Frederick; the 1st Army, on the right, was under old General Steinmetz;[125] and the 2nd Army, forming the centre, was under King William's nephew, Prince Frederick Charles of Hohenzollern, called by the soldiers the "Red Prince," because of his fondness for wearing the red jacket of the famous Death's Head Hussars. The aged King William held supreme command of these armies, and with him as chief of the staff was von Moltke.

So great was the anger of the Parisians at the French defeats that the Emperor hurried to the capital, leaving Marshal Bazaine[126] to command the "Army of the Rhine." From Paris he ordered Bazaine to retreat on Châlons,[127] the French Aldershot, and there join the remnant of MacMahon's army and a reserve army which was being formed.

At once Bazaine began blundering. While the Germans were sending out their cavalry to scout in all directions and to pick up information as to the movements of the French, Bazaine made no such use of his mounted men, and was quite ignorant of the doings of the Germans. He ought to have retired on Metz with all speed, but he wasted much time. Only part of his army was across the Moselle when the Germans attacked his rearguard at a place called Colombey.[128] After a fight of seven hours, darkness ended the battle, and the French claimed a victory. Both sides had lost heavily, and Bazaine was wounded for the sixth time in his long career, during which he had fought his way up from private to field-marshal.

Napoleon III.

(From the painting by J. H. Flandrin at Versailles.)

The Emperor now joined his victorious army, and Bazaine continued his retreat, which was to be by way of Verdun[129] to Châlons. There were four roads by which Bazaine might have marched through the chalk downs to Verdun, but he had ordered his whole army, 150,000 strong, to march by a single road until they reached the village of Gravelotte,[130] which stands seven miles west of Metz. I think you can form a good idea of what this meant. The road was hopelessly cumbered with guns and wagons, mounted men and foot soldiers, and this caused great confusion and delay. So long was the column that it took two days and nights to pass a given point. While it was slowly plodding up the sloping road to Gravelotte, the Emperor lay in a little inn near the village, and Bazaine went to see him. The old marshal was doubtful whether, after having been wounded, he was fit to command the army. "It is nothing," said Napoleon. "You have won a victory. You have broken the spell. Bring the army to Châlons, and all will yet be well."

The Germans at Gravelotte.   *From the picture by E. J. Hünten.*

That was the difficulty—to bring the army to Châlons. I am sure you do not suppose that the Germans were idle while the French were slowly moving along the crowded road to Gravelotte. As soon as King William heard of the fight at Colombey he ordered his 2nd army to cross the Moselle at a point nine or ten miles south of Metz, from which the Roman road runs by way of Verdun to Châlons. When the army reached the river it discovered that the bridges had not been destroyed, and was therefore able to cross unmolested and hasten forward to cut off the French retreat. Not a moment was wasted. On the morning of Tuesday, August 16th, the French army left Gravelotte, and found before it two roads, both running across the downs to Châlons, the one a few miles to the north of the other. One column travelled by the northern road, the other by the southern road.

Napoleon and the Prince Imperial sped along the more northern road in their carriage, and soon after bidding them farewell Bazaine learnt that great masses of Prussian troops were rapidly advancing northwards to cut him off. He halted some of his troops, and rode on towards the first village on the road—Rezonville.[131] At that time the leading cavalry of the French were at the village of Mars-la-Tour, some miles farther along the same road. One German corps struck at the left of the French line, while another tried to turn its flank at Mars-la-Tour. The battle was long and fierce, and both sides claimed the victory. Bazaine telegraphed to the Emperor: "The enemy left us masters of the battlefield;" while Moltke sent the following message to King

William: "Our troops, worn out by a twelve hours' struggle, encamped on the victorious field, opposite the French lines."

The fight was largely between cavalry, and there were several magnificent charges. Two German cavalry regiments made a charge that day which is remembered in the Fatherland as we in Great Britain remember the charge of the "Six Hundred" at Balaclava. They dashed down on the French guns, and sabred or rode down all the gunners save one. Then they charged through a line of infantry, and turned to return. Out of 600 men who rode in that "death-ride," only 194 ever came back.

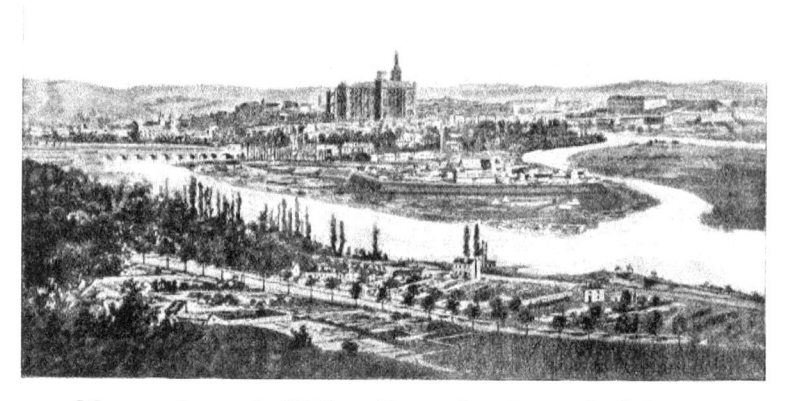

Metz as it was in 1870. *From the picture by Meyret.*

Next day the French retired to a line of hills lying north of the road from Gravelotte to Metz. Here they dug trenches and threw up embankments, and thus fortified themselves in a strong position. The Germans attacked this position, but again the battle was indecisive. The hardest fighting was near the village of St. Privat,[132] on the French right wing, where the line was fiercely bombarded for several hours. Attack after attack was made at this point, but none was successful until the French defenders ran short of cartridges. Even then they fought most stubbornly with the bayonet in and around the village, but were overcome at last, and the left wing was turned. This meant that the whole French army had to retire for protection to the forts of Metz.

Visitors to this battlefield need no guide to show them the line of heights which the Germans stormed so desperately and the French held so stubbornly on that day. All along the ridge are monuments and mounds marking the graves of the dead. Beneath some of the mounds hundreds of bodies lie buried. "They rise like green islands out of the growing corn or the ridges of the cultivated ground." A gigantic bronze statue of St. Michael,[133] leaning on a long sword, has been erected on the summit within a few hundred yards of the present frontier between France and Germany. This statue was unveiled by Kaiser William II., who said that he wished it to be a memorial not only to those who fought and died for the German Fatherland but to those equally brave men who gave their lives for France. In this terrible fight the loss of the French was 7,850 killed and wounded; that of the Germans, 19,640.

Advance of the German Grenadiers at Nuits.

(From the picture by G. Emelé.)
[This battle took place near Dijon, in December 1870.]

When Bazaine reached Metz with his army he discovered that the railway running north had been cut, and that he was surrounded. Two German armies, numbering 160,000 men, were left to hem him in and wait until starvation drove him to surrender. Two other armies were sent to meet MacMahon, who was supposed to be at Châlons. The cavalry, however, soon discovered that Châlons was deserted; MacMahon had marched north, with what purpose could only be guessed. The cavalry hunted the country for him, and at last found him trying to reach Metz so as to relieve Bazaine. Had he pushed on with all speed he might have relieved Metz, and, with the troops in that city, have formed a strong army which could have faced the German legions once more. But he had wasted ten precious days on the road, and this gave the Germans time to catch him up. They came upon him unawares, for his watch had been carelessly kept, and his men were cooking their dinners as the advance guards of the enemy burst upon them. MacMahon found to his dismay that the Germans were between him and Metz and that he was obliged to retreat. They drove him northwards to the town of Sedan,[134] which you will find on the Meuse, in a corner of the country from which there was no escape unless he crossed the Belgian border. He might have done this and avoided the onslaught of the Germans; but, as you know, the French had promised that they would not trespass on Belgian soil, and they kept their word, though it cost them dear.

Through the dark night, amidst a heavy downpour of rain, the men toiled along the heavy roads in great confusion, and reached Sedan at nine next morning. The Emperor, who was following MacMahon's army, arrived late at night, without baggage or escort, and walked almost alone from the railway station to the little town. Next day MacMahon tried to restore some sort of order in his ranks and prepare his forces to meet the enemy; but by nightfall the two German armies had so completely hemmed them in that he could neither hope to break through nor escape if defeated. His army was massed under the walls of Sedan in a valley known as the Sink of Givonne,[135] in a sort of horse-shoe line, concave to the enemy.

At five the next morning, on all the hills around, appeared the dark masses of the German troops. Two hundred and fifty thousand men were in a circle on the heights round the Sink of Givonne. They had come as stealthily as serpents. They were there when the sun rose, and when the French saw them they knew that all was over. The German guns commanded every part of the crowded valley, and when they opened fire the result was a massacre. One of the first to fall was MacMahon, who was struck down by a bursting shell, and was carried from the field. Another commander took his place, but no general, however great, could save the French army, which was now a helpless, beaten mob.

That night the miserable Emperor, worn out by fatigue and suffering, sent an aide-de-camp to the King of Prussia with a note containing this message: "Not having been able to die in the midst of my troops, it only remains for me to place my sword in the hands of your Majesty.—I am, your Majesty's good brother, NAPOLEON."

Next day the fallen Emperor and Bismarck met in a weaver's house upon the banks of the Meuse. Chairs were brought out, and they talked in the open air. It was a glorious autumn morning. The Emperor looked careworn, as well he might. He wished to speak with the King of Prussia before the terms of surrender were drawn up, but William refused to see him. When, however, terms had been arranged, the king visited the Emperor, who had taken refuge in a country house, and showed him much kindness. The next day the royal prisoner was sent to a palace in Germany, where he remained until the end of the war.

Thus, on September 2, 1870, 80,000 French soldiers yielded, and were marched as prisoners into Germany.

But what of Bazaine, who was shut up in Metz with 170,000 men? Several times he tried to break through the ring of steel surrounding him, but in vain. Famine and fever struck down his soldiers every day, and after ten weeks he too was obliged to yield. On the 27th of October he handed over the fortress, 170,000 prisoners, including three marshals of France, and more than 1,500 guns. From this second great blow France could not recover.

As soon as MacMahon's army had yielded at Sedan, the Germans without loss of time began their march on Paris. When the news of the disaster arrived, the Parisians deposed the Emperor and set up a republic. The new government at once determined to defend Paris to the last. Meanwhile, the Germans had entirely surrounded the city, and had begun to starve it into submission. They did not fire on the city. There was no need to do that, for hunger and disease were far more deadly weapons. During four months the Parisians held out. When all the meat in the city was consumed, they slaughtered the animals in the Zoological Gardens, and at length were so short of food that a sewer rat was a delicacy. From time to time balloons were sent up, and men and letters thus found their way to the outer world. Carrier pigeons were also used to carry messages, which were tucked into quills and concealed beneath their wings. The new French Government, which had its headquarters at Tours, called out every able-bodied man in the country, and strove with all its might to relieve Paris. But the new soldiers, though full of heroism, could not stand against the well-drilled and well-tried armies of Germany. One by one the new French armies were defeated, and all hope of relieving the capital vanished. At length Paris could hold out no longer. On January 30, 1871, she yielded, and the hosts of Germany marched through the streets in triumph and took possession of the city. The ruin of France was complete.

At this point let us pause a moment to notice with what great rapidity the French were overcome. On the 4th of August the Germans crossed the frontier; by the 22nd of the same month Bazaine was shut up in Metz; and on the 2nd of September Napoleon and 80,000 men surrendered at Sedan. Thirteen days later the siege of Paris began. Bazaine surrendered at Metz on the 27th of October, and when Paris fell on the 30th of January all was over. The whole campaign, from the moment the first gun was fired to the day Paris fell, lasted only six months. As we shall see later, the Germans believed that what they did in 1870-71 they could do again in 1914.

The Defence of Paris. *From the picture by J. L. Meissonier.*

[This picture does not represent an actual scene, but is intended to illustrate the heroism of the defenders who freely gave their lives for their city and country. France is shown in the centre of the picture as a female figure. The angel of destruction, attended by a carrion crow is seen on the upper corner on the left.]

CHAPTER XI.

FRANCE UNDER THE HARROW.

Before Paris fell, Bismarck's hour of triumph had arrived. The headquarters of the German armies around Paris was at Versailles,[136] where King William held his court in the palace of the French emperors. Early in December King Ludwig of Bavaria proposed that a German empire should be established, and that the King of Prussia should be its first emperor. All the leading states gladly agreed, and on January 18, 1871, an imposing ceremony took place in the great gallery of the palace at Versailles. Every regiment around Paris sent its colours in charge of an officer and two non-commissioned officers, and all the chiefs of the army were present. A chaplain read a special service, and then the king, ascending a dais, announced himself German Emperor, and called upon Bismarck to read a proclamation addressed to the whole German nation.

Proclaiming the German Emperor at Versailles, January 18, 1871.
From the picture by Anton von Werner.
1. Duke Ernest of Saxe-Coburg-Gortha. 2. Crown Prince, afterwards Frederick II. 3. William I. 4. Grand Duke of Boden. 5. Bismark. 6. Molke.

The Crown Prince, as the first subject of the empire, came forward and kneeled before his father in homage. The Emperor raised him, and clasped in his arms the son who had toiled and fought and borne so great a share in bringing about that unity which the German peoples had so long desired.

On the 24th of February terms of peace were arranged, and on the 15th of March peace was signed. Before I tell you how France was punished by her conqueror, I wish to introduce to you two men who fought in this war—the one a Frenchman, the other an Englishman. If you were to see the Frenchman to-day you would find him a sturdy, thick-set man, with a heavy white moustache, huge eyebrows, and teeth that flash when he speaks. His head is massive, his neck is short and thick, and he gives you the idea of a trustworthy watch-dog. He is General Joffre,[137] Commander-in-Chief of the French army.

General Joffre, Commander-in-Chief of the French Armies.

He was a lad of eighteen, a cadet at a military school, when the Franco-German War broke out. At once he was promoted second lieutenant and attached to a regiment of artillery. During the siege of Paris he fought his gun bravely against the Germans. Since that time he has seen much fighting, and his countrymen know him to be strong and silent—"a great soldier and a great man." He now commands the armies of France against the foe with whom he fought as a boy of eighteen. France and her soldiers have laid to heart the lessons of those terrible days, and the present war sees them no less brave, but far better prepared to meet their old enemy.

When the war began, an English boy of twenty, a cadet of the Royal Military Academy at Woolwich, was staying with his father in Brittany. Without waiting to consult his father or his masters at Woolwich, he enlisted in the

French army as a private, and joined the 2nd Army of the Loire. An attack of pneumonia put an end to his services, but not before he had realized the terrible peril which a nation runs when unprepared for war. One of his experiences with the French army was a perilous ascent in a war balloon; forty-three years later he made his first aeroplane flight.

That boy is now Field-Marshal Earl Kitchener,[138] the British Secretary of State for War, the man whom we all regard as our organizer of victory. Since the days when he fought against the Germans in France he has seen warfare in many lands, especially in Africa. In 1898 he overcame the Mahdi[139] in the Sudan, and it was largely due to him that the Boers were forced to make peace after the long war of 1899-1902. A German general who was with him in the Sudan said: "Lord Kitchener was cool and perfectly calm; he gave his orders without in the least raising his voice; he always made the right arrangements at the right moment. He seemed to be absolutely indifferent to personal danger, and never did anything out of bravado. Acting is out of the question with him; he is always perfectly natural." Such is the man who is the Secretary for War at this time of national stress and anxiety. The Germans were his first foes. Let us hope that they will be his last.

France paid dearly for her defeat. Germany demanded £200,000,000, and ordained that a German army should remain on French soil until this huge sum was paid. It seemed at first sight quite impossible for France to find the money; but so rich is her soil, and so thrifty are her peasants, that the whole of it was paid by the end of the year 1874. To most Frenchmen this was by no means the heaviest blow which France suffered. When Germany took back Eastern Lorraine and Alsace, which, you will remember, had once been her own, there was the deepest shame and sorrow throughout the land, and thousands of Frenchmen swore they would never rest until these provinces had been recovered. Though forty-three years have come and gone since that black day, Frenchmen have never forgotten the shame which they then endured. They have mourned without ceasing for Alsace and Lorraine, and that is why the statue of Strassburg in the Place de la Concorde has been draped in black for so many years. Every patriotic Frenchman believes that, when the present war is over, the tricolour will once more wave from the towers of Alsace and Lorraine.

Field-Marshal Lord Kitchener, British Secretary for War.

Most of the people in Alsace were French by descent and by sympathy, and they were greatly distressed when they found that they must become subjects of Germany. When the Germans tried to force the German language on them, they were reduced to despair. I think the best way to explain to you their feelings is to ask you to read the following pathetic little story, which was written by a great French novelist, named Alphonse Daudet.[140] It is entitled—

"THE LAST FRENCH LESSON."

"This morning I was late in going to school, and I was very much afraid of a reprimand, as Mr. Hamel had said he would question me on the participles, and I had not prepared a single word. For a moment I thought of playing truant; the day was warm and bright, the blackbirds were whistling, and the Prussian soldiers were at drill in the park. I managed to resist all these attractions, however, and hurried on to school.

"In passing the mayor's house, I saw that a new notice was posted up on the board, which every one stopped to read. Many a sad notice had been posted up there during the last two years—news of battles lost, and orders for men and money for the war. As I passed on, the blacksmith, who was standing there, called to me, 'Don't hurry, my boy; you will be at your school soon enough to-day.' I thought he was making fun of me, and ran on.

"When I reached the playground, I did not hear that buzz of noise which I had counted on to enable me to get to my place unnoticed. Everything was quiet. You may imagine how frightened I was at having to open the door and enter in the midst of this silence. But Mr. Hamel only looked at me, and said in a kindly voice, 'Hurry to your place, my little Franz; we were about to commence without you.'

"When I was seated at my own desk, I had time to notice that the master had on his handsome green coat, his finely-embroidered shirt-front, and his black silk skull-cap, all of which he wore in school only on examination days and at the distribution of prizes. But what surprised me most was to see the benches at the end of the room, which were usually unoccupied, filled by the old people of the town, all sitting silent like ourselves.

"Mr. Hamel took his seat, and in a grave, sweet voice he said, 'My children, this is the last time I shall teach you. The order has come from Berlin that nothing but German is to be taught in the schools of Alsace. The new master will come to-morrow. To-day is your last lesson in French. Be very attentive, I pray you.'

"Now I understood why he had put on his fine Sunday clothes, and why the old men were seated at the end of the room. My last French lesson! Why, I could hardly write. How I regretted the time I had wasted in bird-nesting and in sliding on the Saar! My books, that I had found so wearisome, now seemed old friends that were about to leave me.

Alsace.

(*From the picture by Henriette Browne.*)

"I heard my name called. What would I not have given to be able to recite all those rules of the participles without a blunder! But I could only stand silent, with a swelling heart, not daring to look up.

"'I will not scold you, my little Franz,' said Mr. Hamel, in a sad tone; 'you are punished enough. Every day you have said, 'I have time enough—I will learn to-morrow;' and now what has happened? This putting off instruction till to-morrow has been the fault of us all in Alsace. Now the invaders say to us, 'How can you pretend to be French, when you cannot read and write your own language?'

"Mr. Hamel went on to speak of the French language, saying that it was the most beautiful, the most polished, and the richest language in the world, and that we must now watch over each other and see that we never forgot it; for even when a people become slaves, while they keep their own language it is as if they held the key to their prison.

"Then he took up a grammar, and went over our lesson with us. I was astonished to find that I could understand it quite easily. I had never listened so eagerly, and the master had never explained so patiently. It seemed as if he wished to make all his knowledge enter our heads at once.

"Next we passed to writing. He had prepared an entirely new exercise for us, to be written in round hand: 'France, Alsace; France, Alsace.' How eagerly each one applied himself! Nothing could be heard but the scratching of the pens upon the paper. A butterfly entered, but no one stopped to watch it.

"Mr. Hamel sat silent in the chair he had occupied for forty years. To-morrow he would leave the country for ever; even now we could hear his sister in the room above packing the trunks. Yet he had the courage to go through the school work to the end.

"Suddenly the clock struck noon. At the same time the bugles of the Prussian soldiers sounded under our windows, where they had come to drill.

"Mr. Hamel rose, pale, but full of dignity.

"'My friends,' he said in a low voice—'my friends, I—' But he was not able to finish the sentence.

"He turned to the blackboard, and with a piece of chalk wrote, in letters that covered the whole board, '*Vive la France!*'

"Then he stopped, leaned against the wall, and without saying a word, he waved his hand as if to say, 'The end has come; go!'"

CHAPTER XII.

THE BOYHOOD OF THE KAISER.

I must now redeem the promise which I made to you at the beginning of Chapter III., and tell you the story of the present Kaiser. His father was that young prince whom we saw clasped in his father's arms at the great moment when the German Empire was proclaimed at Versailles. His mother was Princess Victoria, the eldest child of our own Queen Victoria and the Prince Consort. So you see that the Kaiser and King George are first cousins.

Princess Victoria was a clever, sprightly girl when the Crown Prince came to woo her at Balmoral, and Queen Victoria in her *Journal* gives the following charming account of how the two young people plighted their troth:—

"*September 29, 1855*.

"Our dear Victoria was this day engaged to Prince Frederick William of Prussia, who had been on a visit to us since the 14th. He had already spoken to us on the 20th of his wishes; but we were uncertain, on account of her extreme youth, whether he should speak to her himself, or wait till he came back again. However, we felt it better he should do so, and during our ride up Craig-na-Ban this afternoon he picked a piece of white heather (the emblem of 'good luck'), which he gave to her; and this enabled him to make an allusion to his hopes and wishes as they rode down Glen Girnock, which led to this happy conclusion."

The Princess was a little more than seventeen years of age when she thus became engaged, and her lover was twenty-four. At this time his uncle, Frederick William IV., was King of Prussia, and his father, afterwards the first German Emperor, was Crown Prince. The happy pair were married at Windsor with great pomp and circumstance on January 25, 1858. Three years later the bridegroom's uncle died, his father was crowned King of Prussia, and he became Crown Prince.

Prince William (afterwards Emperor William I.) with his wife and family at the Castle of Babelsberg.

[The little boy with the sword afterwards became the Crown Prince and the father of the present Kaiser.]

When the young bride arrived in Berlin her youth and happy disposition won her many friends; but Bismarck was not among them. He did not like her—first, because she was British, and secondly, because she was clever, and had a great influence over her husband. He thought with the present Kaiser that women should give all their attention to *Kinder, Küche, Kirche*,[141] and not meddle in matters of State. The Princess had come from a land where her mother reigned as queen, and she naturally expected to be something more than the mere mistress of a household. Bismarck did his best to keep her in the background, and no love was lost between them. As time went by, the Princess was much misunderstood.

Her first child—the present Kaiser—was born on January 27, 1859. When Queen Victoria heard the news, she telegraphed, "Is it a *fine* boy?" It was a fine boy, for an old field-marshal who saw him when he was but a few hours old declared that he was as strapping a recruit as one could ever wish for. There is a story told that when the little prince, still in long clothes, was shown by his proud father to a group of princes and generals and statesmen, one of them took out his watch to amuse the baby. Instantly the little fellow grabbed the prize, and would not let it go. "You see, gentlemen," said the father, "that when a Hohenzollern once gets hold of a thing he does not easily let it go."

Though the child was a fine boy, he had one defect—his left arm was shorter and weaker than his right, and even to this day he cannot raise it to his shoulder, though he can use it in driving or playing the piano. This withered arm has always been a great source of bitterness to him.

As a baby he had an English nurse, and his mother devoted herself to him. His early upbringing was far too English to suit many of the Germans, and all sorts of stories were told about the harshness of the Princess to her children. There was not a word of truth in them. The Princess loved her children greatly, and spared no pains to bring them up in the best possible way.

The boy was reared amidst wars and the rumours of wars. He was only a few months old when King William and Bismarck were struggling with the Parliament over the army law, which you read about on page 79. He was only five years old when the war broke out with Denmark, and seven years old when the Austrian War began. In his tenth year, according to the custom of his House, he was made second lieutenant of the 1st Foot Guards. A little more than a year later his regiment marched away to the war in France, and the little lieutenant was eager to accompany them. When his father told him that he was too young, he burst into tears. Many years later he said that he well remembered the day on which war was declared.

Views in Potsdam.

1. Palace of Sans-Souci. 2. Castle of Babelsberg. 3. Brandenburg Gate. 4. The Orangery. 5. The New Palace.

"It was at Potsdam. We were about to take our places at table for dinner, when my father, pale and much overcome, came suddenly into the room. 'It is all over,' he said, in a broken voice, as he embraced us. 'France wishes for war. Ah, my children, what a frightful misfortune!'"

I do not think that the children would be able to understand what their father meant when he spoke of the frightful misfortune of war. At Potsdam, the beautiful country place near Berlin where they lived, they saw only the bright and dashing side of war. Little William loved to strut with drawn sword by the side of his regiment, and try to keep pace with the long-legged guardsmen as they performed the high and prancing step in which the German army indulges. Especially did he love to be with his regiment when the king came to review the troops. His grandfather would pass in front of his soldiers and say, "Good morning, Uhlans, or Cuirassiers," as the case might be, and then would come a noise like thunder, as every man in the regiment shouted at the top of his voice, "Good morning, your Majesty!" How the boy's eyes flashed, and how his heart leaped within him at all this martial parade! One day, perhaps, he would command the German army, and then—.

Cannot you imagine how the boy swelled with pride as the story of victory after victory came to his ears? When they told him that his grandfather was now German Emperor, he could not fail to remember that some day he would be German Emperor too.

His grandfather had added great glory to the House of Hohenzollern. When his turn came to sit on the throne, he would give it even greater glory.

On his twelfth birthday he received as a present a wonderful panorama of the Franco-German War. He delighted in this toy, and no doubt it made him long more than ever to be a leader of armies and a victor in battle.

By this time it was clear to his parents and tutors that he was a very clever boy. He was exceedingly quick, and he took the greatest possible interest in his sports and studies. He desired to shine in them all. His mother determined that he should be brought up as an English boy, and that he should live an outdoor life, and learn to play outdoor games. A number of other boys were chosen as his playmates, and he and his brothers spent many merry hours in the park at Sans-Souci. He became a good fencer, a good shot, a good rider, a good swimmer, and a good oarsman. On horseback he accustomed himself to hold the reins with his weak left arm, so that he might have his sword-arm free.

His younger brother Henry was to become a sailor, so masts and rigging were set up in the park, and many a mimic battle was fought round this ship on dry land. Better still, on the lake there was a complete frigate mounted with guns, which the boys loved to fire. A little steam tender was provided to tow the frigate home in case the wind should fail, and a party of bluejackets was always on duty to look after the vessels.

This is what his English tutor wrote about him at this time:—

"After an experience of teaching many hundreds of English boys of the same age, I do not hesitate to say that Prince William could read English as well, and knew as much of English history and English literature, as boys of fifteen at an ordinary English public school. Since then I have given hundreds of lessons to many hundreds of boys, but a more promising pupil than Prince William, or more gentlemanly, frank, and natural boys than both Prince

William and his younger brother I can honestly say it has never been my lot to meet."

When the Prince was fifteen he was sent to a German public school, where he was made to study very hard. This was the kind of day which he spent. He rose before six in the morning, and prepared his lessons until it was time to go to school. At twelve he returned home for lunch, and then went back to school until five. Bedtime was at nine. The rest of his time was taken up with lessons in French, English, music, shooting, and in riding or taking walks. Sometimes he and his brother were allowed to play with their schoolfellows, and this was a great treat to them. On their birthdays, and on the birthdays of their near relations, they were usually taken to a theatre. By way of pocket-money, Prince William received five shillings a week and Prince Henry two shillings and sixpence.

Though William was a clever and diligent lad, he was not a brilliant pupil. When the time came for him to leave school for the university he had to pass an examination; he was tenth out of seventeen candidates, and his certificate was marked "satisfactory." Shortly afterwards he was sent to a university.

The Prussian Guard, the flower of the German army, and the pride of the Kaiser.

Photo, Record Press.

At the University of Bonn he was accompanied by an aide-de-camp, who did everything in his power to foster the young man's already keen interest in soldiering. At this time he also received instruction from the three men who, more than any others, had made German history—the Emperor William, Bismarck, and Moltke. The Emperor taught him to reverence the name and fame of the Hohenzollerns; to believe himself chosen specially by God for his high office; to do his duty without fear or favour, and not to be turned from his path by the wishes of his people if he thought them wrong. Bismarck deeply impressed upon him the policy of "blood and iron;" taught him how to manage Parliament and the people; and how to deal with foreign countries, so that the name and fame of the Fatherland might grow in greatness. Moltke instructed him in the art of war.

The Crown Prince himself had none of the high and mighty notions of Bismarck. He had no desire to prevent the people from obtaining freedom to rule themselves, and many Germans believed that his wife had taught him that the British way of governing was the wisest and best. The upper classes in Germany, and especially the great land-owning nobles, hated these ideas of liberty for the people. They believed that the whole duty of the middle and working classes was to pay and obey, and they grew more and more angry with the Princess, who was supposed to be leading the Crown Prince astray. Meanwhile Bismarck was doing his best to teach Prince William that he must be a man of blood and iron. How well the young man learnt the lesson we now know—only too well.

While he was at Bonn he joined the "crack" fencing club, and proudly wore its colours and its white cap. He attended its beer-drinking bouts and "sing-songs," and watched his companions fighting duels. Though he did not fight himself, he greatly admired seeing others do so; and in later years, when he was old enough to know better, he hoped that the students would always take delight in handling the duelling blade, because it made them strong and courageous.

CHAPTER XIII.

CROWN PRINCE AND KAISER.

In the autumn of 1878 Prince William paid a visit to his royal grandmother at Balmoral. As he passed through London he met Princess Victoria of Schleswig-Holstein, who happened to be staying with her uncle in England, and on February 27, 1881, he married her. Bismarck approved of the marriage, for the bride's father had all along claimed Schleswig-Holstein[142] as his own, and had continually objected to Prussia's action in seizing these provinces. The marriage put an end to the Duke's claims, and was, in Bismarck's words, "the concluding act of joy in a drama otherwise rich in strife."

The Germans were specially pleased that the young Prince had chosen a German bride, and they cheered the happy pair to the echo. After the wedding the Prince and Princess made their home in the Marble Palace at Potsdam, and there, on May 6, 1882, their first son, the present Crown Prince, was born. When old King William heard the news, he cried, "God be praised and thanked! Four generations of kings!"

Prince William now threw himself with energy into his military duties. He became colonel of the famous Hussar regiment, the Garde du Corps, and was speedily renowned as a brilliant and dashing cavalry officer. When he led his regiment for the first time before the old Emperor at a review, his uncle, the famous "Red Prince," who was a man very difficult to please, said, "You have done very well; I should never have believed it."

Not only did the Prince give his nights and days to the study of war, but he also began to study the business arrangements of the Empire, and to make himself acquainted at first hand with the work of the Foreign Office. Old Bismarck watched his progress keenly. He believed that the young Prince would prove an emperor after his own heart; that he would care nothing for parliaments, and stand up for his imperial rights like a rock of bronze. So popular did he become, and so much was he admired, that the people began to overlook his father, the Crown Prince, altogether. Military men had never regarded the Crown Prince with favour, and he was now almost eclipsed by his strong-willed, eager, gifted son. The ruling classes of Prussia saw in him the man who would surely lead them on to military glory.

In the spring of 1887 a growth appeared in the Crown Prince's throat. It increased so rapidly that soon he could only speak in a strained, husky voice. He gradually grew worse, and an English doctor was summoned by the Crown Princess to examine him. She was much blamed for putting her faith in an English doctor rather than in German doctors, and many bitter things were said about her. When the old Emperor heard of his son's affliction he was overwhelmed with grief. "I have only one wish," he said, "which I should like to be gratified before I die, and that is to hear my poor son Fritz speak as clearly as he used to do." Alas! this was a wish never to be realized. The poor Crown Prince had lost his voice for ever.

At the first sign of his father's serious illness all eyes were turned to Prince William, who began to appear on all sorts of public occasions, and make speeches about the military glories of his house, and its bulwark, the Army. At this time there was some trouble with France and Russia, and the German army was increased by more than half a million men. Bismarck, who had made a secret treaty with Austria as far back as 1879, went to Parliament and explained the situation in what is thought to be his greatest speech. He thus concluded: "We Germans fear God, and nothing else in the world." There was no more delighted listener in the assembly than Prince William. This defiant speech exactly suited his temper of mind. He was all for military glory, and though in after years he constantly declared himself the friend of peace, and more than once strove to preserve it, we now know that towards the end of the year 1913 he was ready to stake all upon a war which would make him master of Europe.

"Four Generations of Kings."

The old Emperor William I. is seated, nursing his great-grandson, the present Crown Prince, who was born in 1882. On the left stands the Crown Prince, who became the Emperor Frederick III. on the death of William I. in 1888. On the right stands his son, the baby's father, Prince William, who became Emperor on the death of his father, after a brief reign of eighty-four days (1888). When the old Emperor learnt that a great-grandson had been born to him, he cried, "God be praised and thanked! Four generations of kings!" He could not, of course, foresee the present war, which may bring about the ruin of his house and make his prophecy false. You will learn something of the present Crown Prince later on.

The sands of the old Emperor's life were now fast running out. He was ninety-one years of age, and he had felt his son's affliction very keenly. It was Prince William who watched over the last few years of the old Kaiser's life.

It was to him that the aged monarch gave warning and counsel for the future. He advised his grandson to be patient and dutiful during his father's reign, which could not last long, and he begged him to be "considerate" to Russia, for he had always feared to make an enemy of that great Power. He knew full well that if ever Germany should come to blows with Russia, France would attack her, and thus she would have to fight two wars, one on each frontier, at the same time. Then the old man begged Bismarck to remain in office, no matter what should befall; and a few days later he died, full of years and honour, leaving the imperial crown to his poor afflicted son. His dying words were, "Fritz, lieber[143] Fritz."

William was now Crown Prince, and he knew that he would soon be Emperor. His poor father was a doomed man. He reigned eighty-four days, and bore his sufferings with the greatest fortitude. He once wrote to the Crown Prince: "Learn to suffer without complaint, for that is all that I can teach you." With his broken-hearted wife and some of his devoted servants kneeling round him, he breathed his last on June 15, 1888, and the Crown Prince in his twenty-ninth year became Kaiser as William II.

How he received the news of his father's death we do not know, but in less than half an hour he called out a squadron of Hussars in their red jackets, and sent them clattering to the Palace where the dead Emperor lay. They surrounded the building, and behind them came a company of infantry at the double. The place was thus sealed up, and no one was allowed to go in or come out. Before his poor mother had recovered from her first transports of grief the home in which her dead husband lay was in a state of siege.

The Emperor Frederick III.

(*From the picture by Heinrich von Angeli.*)

The late Emperor had issued his first proclamation to his people, and his second to his Army, but the new Emperor reversed the order. On the day of his father's death he sent messages to the Army and Navy, and kept his people waiting three days before they received their proclamation. To the Army he wrote as follows:—

"I and the army belong to one another; we are born for one another, and we will stand together in an indissoluble bond in peace or storm, as God may will. I swear always to remember that the eyes of my ancestors look down upon me from the other world, and that one day I shall have to give an account to them of the honour and glory of the army."

Then he proceeded to bury his father, but there was none of the military pomp which had been seen at the Emperor William's funeral. It looked as though the new sovereign thought lightly of his own father because he was a peace-loving monarch, and had determined to follow the example of the "War Lord" who had brought France to her knees, and by doing so had created the German Empire.

In the passage quoted above the Emperor spoke of the bond which united him with the Army. Let us see what this bond is. As King of Prussia he is supreme over the Prussian army; he can declare peace or war as he pleases, though, of course, his people must vote him "the sinews of war"—that is, money, before he can set his armies in motion. In ordinary times the Prussian army forms about two-thirds of the whole German army, so you see that as King of Prussia the Kaiser is a very powerful "war lord" indeed.

As German Emperor his position is quite different. He is the leader of the five-and-twenty sovereigns and free cities which are united into the German Empire, and before he can declare war he must call together the representatives of all these states, and obtain their consent. Each of the states has to send to the German army a certain number of troops, according to its population. In peace time the Kaiser has the right to inspect them, and to see that they are properly trained and ready to take the field. As soon as war is declared, he takes the supreme command, not only of the Prussian soldiers, but also of all the other German troops.

I cannot now tell you the Kaiser's story in detail. I can only dwell on a few incidents that reveal his character. When he first opened the Prussian Parliament in state he declared, amidst a perfect storm of applause, that he should be guided by the maxim of Frederick the Great—that the King of Prussia was but the first servant of the state. To do him justice, he has devoted himself unsparingly to the duties of his high office; and though he has made many mistakes, and has brought his Empire to the edge of the precipice over which it bids fair to topple in utter ruin, he has always laboured, according to his lights, to make Germany overwhelmingly strong in war and prosperous in peace. But from the first he meant to do this in his own way. He clearly told the Prussian Parliament that, while he had no desire to take away such liberties as the people had, he would never yield one jot or tittle of his rights as king. British sovereigns know that they derive all their power from their people, but the Kaiser has always held that he holds his throne directly from God. Some years later he said:—

"The German people are the chosen of God. On me, on me as German Emperor, the Spirit of God has descended. I am His weapon, His sword, and His viceregent. Woe to cowards and unbelievers!"

"There is only one master in this country. I am he, and I shall suffer no other beside me."

"There is only one law—my law, the law which I myself lay down."

Four years ago, at Königsberg, he repeated his claim to "divine right" in the following words:—

"It was on this spot that my grandfather placed the royal crown of Prussia on his head, [144] *insisting once again that it was bestowed upon him by the grace of God alone, and not by Parliaments and meetings and decisions of the people. He thus regarded himself as the chosen instrument of Heaven. I consider myself such an instrument of Heaven, and shall go my way without regard to the views and opinions of the day."*

The Kaiser Wilhelm II. opening his First Parliament.

(*From the picture by Anton von Werner.*)

Now to you and me such statements as this seem to be the ravings of a madman, and we wonder why the Prussians permit one man to lord it over them in this fashion. The explanation is that the Prussians have never known any other condition of things; that though every man over twenty-five has a vote, matters are so arranged that a hundred rich men have more voting power than two thousand poor men. The nobles and the officials dislike popular liberty, and they do their utmost to prevent any further rights being granted to the people. Then, again, as every Prussian must be a soldier for one or more years, the nation has been well drilled into submission. All Prussians know that the Empire was founded by the sword, and they believe that it can only be maintained in the same way. The majority of them, therefore, regard the Emperor as their commanding officer, and are prepared to obey him with unquestioning obedience.

William had not been long on the throne before he quarrelled with Bismarck, the wily old Chancellor who had served his grandfather so long and so faithfully, and had taught the young Emperor all the tricks of government. The fact was, that while Bismarck remained Chancellor, William could not truthfully say, "There is only one master in this country. I am he." All the Prussians who were not jealous of Bismarck knew that he was the chief maker of the German Empire, and they, therefore, held him in the greatest honour and esteem. The old man was very strong and self-willed; so was the young monarch, who was extremely vain as well, and quite confident that he could do everything he turned his hand to better than anybody else. William therefore determined to dismiss Bismarck, and treated the old man in such a manner that he resigned office. When the Chancellor went to the Palace to give up his seals he still thought that the Emperor would give way. He was soon undeceived. After listening to the Kaiser for some time, Bismarck said, "Then I am in your way, sir?" To which William replied, "Yes." He had already got rid of Moltke.

In the early part of his reign William had treated his mother very harshly, probably because he thought this would be pleasing to those of his subjects who hated Britain. He now began to behave better to his mother, and then suggested to his grandmother, Queen Victoria, that he should pay her a visit in England. She agreed, and he came amongst us for the first time as German Emperor. He was present at a naval review, and the Queen made him, to his great delight, a British admiral. In return, he made the old Queen colonel of one of his regiments. Thereafter he professed great friendship for our country. When Queen Victoria died he walked behind her coffin along the streets of Windsor, side by side with his uncle, King Edward VII., and showed great grief.

King Edward VII. and the Kaiser following the coffin of Queen Victoria through the streets of Windsor.

On his return to Germany the Emperor shone in the full blaze of the limelight as the one only man in the whole land. He made many speeches, declaring over and over again that he was the chosen of God, and assuring his subjects that all who would help in his great task would be heartily welcomed, but those who attempted to oppose him would be dashed in pieces. Of course there were many Germans who greatly disliked the acts and speeches of their boastful and meddlesome sovereign. On one occasion he told these critical persons that if they were dissatisfied they should "shake the dust of Germany from their feet." A newspaper pointed out that if all those who were dissatisfied in the German Empire were to emigrate, his Imperial Majesty would be left entirely alone, and then he also would be dissatisfied and would leave too!

At various times during his reign the Emperor has tried hard to win the favour of the peoples who have been forcibly included in the German Empire. He went to Alsace, and made a gracious speech in Strassburg; but later on, at Metz, he harshly told the people of Lorraine, "German you are, and German you will remain. May God and our German sword help us to effect this." These words were meant to crush any hopes that the people might entertain of one day being reunited with France. He also went amongst the Poles,[145] who have never been satisfied with German rule, and severely rebuked the nobles and the citizens. When he was leaving one of the Polish towns he said to the Mayor, "I hope that my words will be well borne in mind, for you know that I can be very disagreeable too."

Not content with being supreme in government, William now set up to be a judge of art and poetry in the Empire. He wrote a set of verses of pagan fierceness, and sent for an artist, and gave him the idea of the picture which you see on page 142. It represents the civilized nations of Europe standing in the midst of mountains, valleys, and cities, with the castle of Hohenzollern in the foreground. Confronting the nations is a sea of flames and clouds of smoke, which are twisted into the form of terrible faces, representing the Chinese and Japanese. Buddha[146] sits enthroned in the midst of this framework as the demon of destruction. The Archangel Michael with a flaming sword appears in front of the civilized nations, urging them to prepare for a terrific conflict. Underneath the original picture the Emperor wrote, "Nations of Europe, defend your holiest possessions." You will observe that in this picture, which is supposed to warn us of what is called the Yellow Peril,[147] Germany is the chief figure, and that clinging to her is her ally, Austria.

Early in the year 1895 the Kaiser began to turn his thoughts to the Navy. Already he had the finest and best-organized army in the world; now he desired to win the sovereignty of the seas as well. "Germany's future," he said, "is upon the waters." The navy which he proposed to build was out of all proportion to the number of merchant ships which Germany possessed, and from the first many people in this country rightly guessed that it was meant to be the means of overcoming Great Britain. The Kaiser also caused a canal to be dug through Schleswig-Holstein, so as to unite the North Sea with the Baltic Sea, in order that his warships might rapidly pass from one to the other. The work of enlarging and deepening this canal was only finished in June 1914, within six weeks of the outbreak of war.

All this time envy and hatred of Britain was growing in Germany. Thanks to hard work, great perseverance, and much thought, Germany had become a great manufacturing nation, the rival of Great Britain. She felt that she was marked out to be the head of a world-empire, yet there were many drawbacks in her way. If you look at a map of Europe you will see that Germany has a very poor sea coast, and but few good harbours. The bulk of the Baltic Sea, which fronts the greater part of her coast, is frozen up for months every year. Every day Germany feels the necessity of possessing ports on the open ocean; yet she can only secure them by conquest. She is surrounded by old-established nations: by France on the west, Russia on the east, Austria-Hungary on the south. Two small states, one of them neutralized by a treaty to which she was a party, lie between her and the North Sea, and both of them possess ports which rank amongst the world's finest havens. The bulk of her sea-borne trade must pass through Belgium, the more southerly of these states, and she has never concealed her eager desire to possess it. Holland has long been regarded by her as a "brave bit of the Fatherland."

Germany, therefore, cannot expand in Europe without conquest, and she has found many difficulties in the way of expanding overseas. When she was ready to make herself a world-power, all the best parts of the earth had been taken up by other nations. She found that she had been born too late. She managed to found several colonies in Africa; but, with the exception of Togoland and the Kamerun, they were unfruitful and thankless regions of sand and stones. In Asia she set up the colony of Kiao-chau, in North China, and thereby aroused the anger of the Japanese. When she tried to get territory elsewhere she found herself in conflict with one or other of the Great Powers. Then, too, she saw hundreds of thousands of her people departing for America or for the colonies of other Powers, and there becoming lost to her. All this has been very galling to the Germans, and the Prussian military class has never ceased to point out that Germany can only expand by means of warfare.

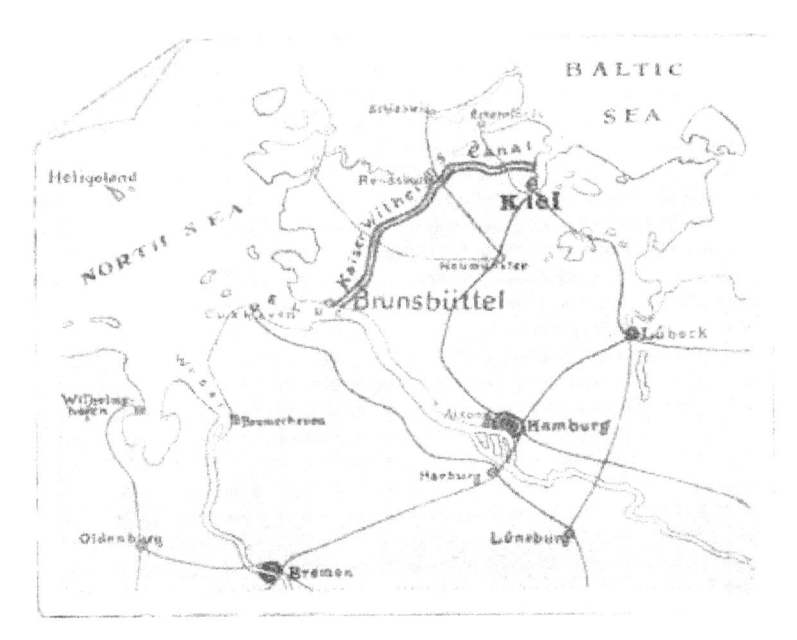

Kiel Canal.

Though the Kaiser has frequently declared himself the friend of peace, he has always made the most warlike speeches to his own subjects. When he addresses his Army and Navy he does so in a defiant and boastful manner, and is fond of talking about the "mailed fist" and "shining armour" of Germany. For many years past this kind of talk has been very irritating to the other nations of Europe. On the eve of the Boer War he sent a telegram to Mr. Kruger, the President of the South African Republic, which plainly showed that he was no friend to Great Britain. When the war went against us in its early stages he and his advisers thought that we should be beaten, and that the British Empire would fall to pieces. It was openly said by Germans that if they had then possessed a strong navy they would have been able to capture some of the British colonies. The Kaiser seized the opportunity to press his Parliament to give him a big grant for building warships. He plainly told his people that his navy was to be so strong that "the next greatest naval power"—that is, Great Britain—would not be able to attack it without grave risk. So a big navy, costing more than 300 millions of money, was built.

"Nations of Europe, defend your most sacred possessions."

(Painted by H. Knackfuss from a sketch by the Kaiser.)

I have already told you that for many years past Germany has been very envious of the British Empire. A great German historian was never tired of teaching that Britain was *the* enemy of Germany. She was, he said, a "robber state;" she had become mistress of one-fifth of the whole world by making cat's paws of other races; and she had no real right to all this territory. She could not even rule it properly. If ever she had been strong and warlike, that time had long gone by. Though she appeared to be strong, she was really very weak, and quite unable to hold her Empire against such a strong Power as Germany. The Germans have come to believe this teaching, and for years past they have looked forward to "the day" on which they would challenge the power of Great Britain, and, after having defeated her, would enter into her heritage. They have also been taught that there is nothing wrong in trying to seize the territory of other nations. Might, they believe, is right, and the spoils of the world are for the strongest.

Newspaper writers in Germany have constantly preached this doctrine to the people, and several Prussian officers have written books showing how Germany ought to go to work to beat down Great Britain, and tear her Empire from her. War has become the religion of Germany, and she has prepared for it with wonderful foresight and zeal. While she has grown to be a great manufacturing and trading nation, she has never for a moment neglected her Army nor ceased to build up her Navy.

She has also tried to win the mastery of the air. When Count Zeppelin, about the year 1899, invented a great airship which could travel for hundreds of miles and carry some thirty or forty men, the Kaiser saw at once that it might become a great weapon of war. Germany now possesses about thirty of these airships, and they are meant to play a large part in an invasion of Britain. On the opposite page you will see a picture of a modern Zeppelin, with a part of the covering removed to show you the framing of the interior, and the many separate gas chambers which it contains. It is said that even if half these chambers were destroyed the airship would still float and answer its helm. The outside covering is made of light metal known as aluminium. It costs some thousands of pounds to inflate a Zeppelin, and two hundred pounds a week to restore the gas lost by evaporation.

The *Victoria Luise*, one of the crack Zeppelins, has made some wonderful trips, and she could no doubt fly from Kiel or Hamburg over any part of the British Isles and back again. But fog and storm are her deadly enemies, and there are many other difficulties to be overcome before she could make a raid upon Britain, drop bombs on her cities, and return in safety.

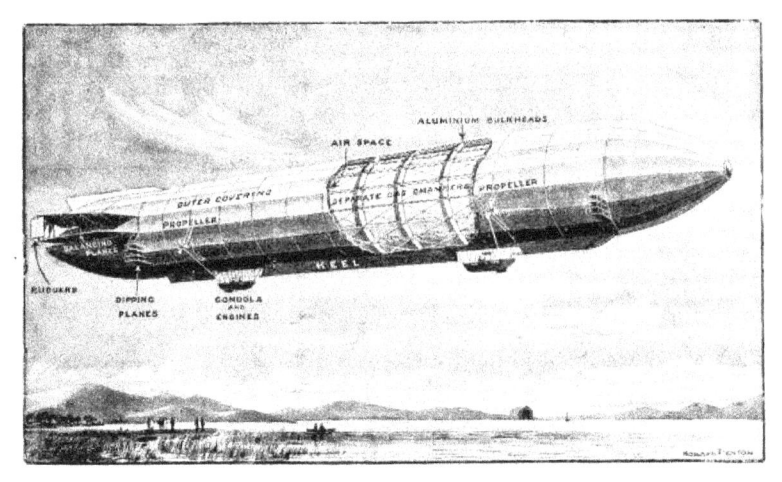

A Zeppelin with part of the covering removed to show the interior.

CHAPTER XIV.

THE DAWN OF "THE DAY."

The great instrument of the Kaiser's ambition is his army. Every male who is a German subject can be called upon to serve as a soldier from his seventeenth to his forty-fifth year. Though this is the law, men who are not strong, or have to support a family, or intend to be ministers of the Church, are excused from serving. Most German boys, however, know from childhood that they will have not only to learn a trade or prepare themselves for a profession, but become soldiers as well. As a rule, Germans begin their military training at twenty-one. If a young man has done well at one of the higher-grade schools, and can afford to keep himself, he need only spend one year with the colours; all others must be trained for two years if they are in the infantry, and three years if they are in the cavalry and horse artillery. When this time is over they go back to their work, and belong to the reserve. The two-year men serve five years with the first-line reserve, and the three-year men four years. Large bodies of the reserve are called up each year for exercise, but the same men are not called up more than once in two years, and, as a rule, their service amounts to two periods of about thirty days each. From the first-line reserve men pass into the *Landwehr*,[148] or second reserve, for five or six years if infantry, and for a longer period if cavalry. They, too, are called up from time to time for training, which lasts from a week to a fortnight. Finally, they pass into the *Landsturm*, and are only called up now and then for roll-call. Except in such special times of stress as the present war, the *Landsturm* are not required to serve in the field. Under ordinary conditions they leave the army altogether at the age of forty-five.

If you look at the diagram on page 150 you will see a comparison of the war strength of the great Powers of Europe. Germany has a population of 65,000,000, and her war strength is given as 4,500,000 men. As a last resource she can probably put into the field 7,500,000 men. Russia has a population of 141,000,000 in Europe alone; her war strength is given as 5,500,000 men, but as a last resource she can probably call to the colours about 15,000,000 men. You thus see that the great military Power which stands in the way of Germany's overlordship of Europe is Russia. Bismarck knew this well, and he constantly insisted that Germany should always keep on good terms with Russia. Since the Kaiser took the helm into his own hands, he has regarded the growth of the Russian army as a great menace to his power, and has come to the conclusion that unless something is done, and done quickly, to check it, he cannot realize his ambitions.

He and his advisers have always regarded Germany as the heir of Austria. For long it has been thought that Austria-Hungary would go to pieces on the death of Franz Josef, and that Austria would then be included in the German Empire. Now Austria, as you know, possesses Bosnia and Herzegovina, which would give Germany a footing in the Balkan Peninsula, and enable her to push her way southward to warm water ports on the Mediterranean Sea. Should Germany be able to capture Constantinople she would soon be mistress of Asia Minor, and would hold a very powerful position on the sea road to India. Her dreams of world-empire would then be likely to come true.

The Kaiser as a Yachtsman. *Photo, Record Press.*

Germany has already obtained a footing in Asia Minor. As far back as 1898 the Emperor and the Empress visited the Sultan at Constantinople, where they were received with all honour, and the Empress accepted from the Commander of the Faithful[149] a present of diamonds worth £25,000. Then the Kaiser and his wife visited the Holy Land, and entered Jerusalem to take part in the dedication service of a German church within the walls of the Holy City. At this service His Majesty was attired in the white uniform of the Garde du Corps, with a white silk mantle such as was worn by the Crusaders. Before him was borne aloft the German Imperial standard.

In the following year, thanks to the Kaiser, the Sultan gave a German company permission to build a railway line from Konieh[150] to the Persian Gulf, by way of Bagdad.[151] You can easily understand that a German railway through Asia Minor to the head of the Persian Gulf would practically make Germany master of all the resources of this part of the world. France was not willing that the railway should be entirely German, so she was allowed to provide some of the money for it. Great Britain pointed out that the proposed line would be the shortest route to India, and that it would end in the territory of a chief with whom she had a special treaty, and that, therefore, Britain ought to have a hand in it too. There was a great deal of debate over the question, and at last it was agreed that the Germans should own four-tenths of the line, and that the other six-tenths should be owned by Frenchmen, Austrians, Swiss, Italians, and Turks. The railway was to end at Basra,[152] and was not to be continued to the Persian Gulf without Great Britain's consent. The Germans have spent between £16,000,000 and £18,000,000 on this railway, which was begun in 1912, and is now half built. In addition to the Bagdad railway, Germany has other important undertakings in Asia Minor, which is rich in coal and copper, oil and timber. The Russians, it should be noticed, have also large business interests in the same part of the Turkish Empire.

What connection has all this with the present war? Let us see. You already know that the late Sultan of Turkey was the friend of the Kaiser, and that he had given the Germans some very valuable rights in Asia Minor. Since that time German soldiers have trained the Turkish army, German money has been lent to the Turkish Government, and German influence has become so strong that we may almost regard Turkey as a German province. In 1908 there was a revolution in Turkey, the Sultan was forced from his throne, and his younger brother was chosen to take his place. In the autumn of 1912 the Balkan States declared war on Turkey, and beat her very badly. When the war was over all that remained of her territory in Europe was a little country less than twice the size of Wales. Serbia had become very powerful in the Balkan Peninsula.

Now this did not suit Germany at all. The Kaiser saw very clearly that if Serbia became the chief power in the Balkan Peninsula, Germany would be crushed out, and her interests in Asia Minor would be in great jeopardy.

From the German point of view it was necessary that Serbia should be crippled as soon as possible.

You remember the murder of the Archduke Ferdinand, which I described to you in Chapter I. of this book. Austria was naturally very angry with Serbia, and was bent on making her pay dearly for her part in the crime. The Kaiser egged on Austria to fight Serbia, because he thought that a war would give him an excellent chance of reducing Serbia's strength, and of beginning that career of conquest on which he was now bent.

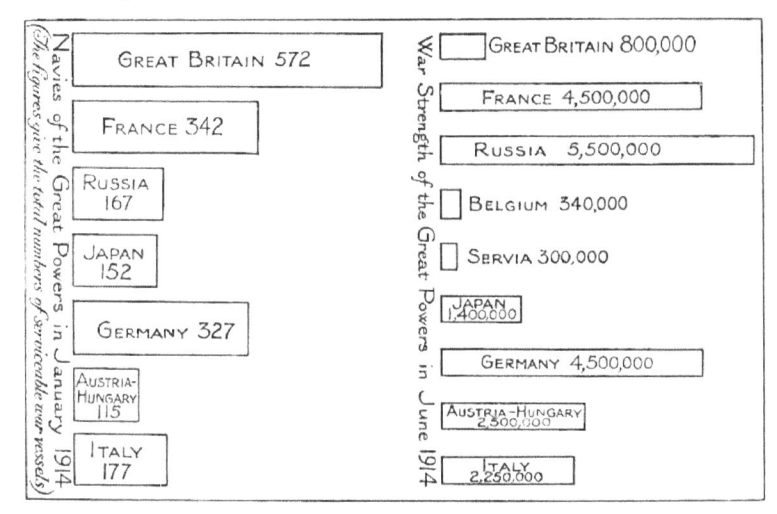

```
Navies of the Great Powers in January 1914    War Strength of the Great Powers in June 1914
(The figures give the total numbers of serviceable new vessels)

GREAT BRITAIN 572          GREAT BRITAIN 800,000
FRANCE 342                 FRANCE 4,500,000
RUSSIA 167                 RUSSIA 5,500,000
JAPAN 152                  BELGIUM 340,000
GERMANY 327                SERVIA 300,000
AUSTRIA-HUNGARY 115        JAPAN 1,400,000
ITALY 177                  GERMANY 4,500,000
                           AUSTRIA-HUNGARY 2,300,000
                           ITALY 2,250,000
```

The above diagram compares the armies and navies of the chief European Powers.

We know, from a French Yellow Book[153] which was published on December 1, 1914, why the Germans wanted war, and what preparations they made for it. From a dispatch written by the French Ambassador at Berlin, we gather that even in July 1913 the Germans thought war was "inevitable," for the following reasons. Since the Franco-German War the national pride of the Germans has been fostered to such an extent that they really do believe themselves to be the greatest, strongest, and most efficient nation of the world. They believe that they must have colonies in order to provide new markets and an outlet for their surplus population, and they are very sore at the failure of their attempts to win them. In this respect they are specially angry with us and with France, because they consider that we and the French gained a victory over them in 1911, when they tried to secure a part of Morocco,[154] and were prevented from doing so. They cannot bear to think that a country which they beat so badly in 1870 should dare to stand in their way. The great manufacturers of guns and armour plate, and the chief merchants, believe that war is "good business," and in this belief they are strongly backed up by the nobles and military class. The soldiers are naturally anxious for war because it is their profession, and because war brings that quick promotion which is impossible in time of peace. The nobles fear the growing power of the people, and believe that they will only be able to preserve their "rights" by means of a war which will turn the nation's thoughts away from plans of reform. Armed peace such as Germany has maintained for many years past is a crushing burden to the nation; it swallows up the money which might be expended on improving the condition of the people, and turns many of them into Socialists.

From a secret report to the German Government, which somehow fell into French hands in April 1914, we learn how Germany proposed to prepare for this "inevitable" war. Since 1906 she has increased her Army four times, and in 1913 she raised from her people a war levy of £50,000,000. Her object in increasing the Army and raising this money is clearly revealed in the course of the report—namely, to fortify and extend German power "throughout the whole world." In order to do this, the people were to be taught that Germany must begin a war because her foes were threatening her, and that such a war would make their burdens lighter, and give them many years of peace and prosperity. When the mind of the people was thus prepared, discontent was to be stirred up amongst the native peoples in the French and British possessions of North Africa and Egypt, as well as in Russia, so that these countries would be full of revolt when war was declared. As for the small states, such as Belgium and Holland, they must be forced to follow Germany, or be conquered. If Belgium should prepare to resist, she would be invaded, in spite of the treaty which guaranteed her neutrality. All this was arranged as far back as May 1913.

In November of the same year King Albert of Belgium[155] had an interview with the Emperor and General von Moltke. It was then very clear that the Kaiser had been won over by the war party. The French Minister suggests that the Kaiser was jealous of the popularity of his son, the Crown Prince, who was then the rising hope of the soldiers. If so, history had repeated itself. The Kaiser as a young man had played for popularity against his father; the Crown Prince had followed his father's example, and had tried to throw him into the shade. It is probable, too, that the Emperor was very angry with France, because she had strengthened her army by making her soldiers serve three years instead of two.

King Albert of Belgium.

Photo, Newspaper Illustrations Limited.

During this interview with King Albert the Kaiser and von Moltke threw off the mask. They told the King that the time had come to "finish" with France, and they assured him that the German army was bound to win. The object of this conversation was to show the King of the Belgians that he would be wise not to resist if war with France should arise. We shall see later on that King Albert was not moved from the path of honour either by threats or promises.

Meanwhile Germany was busy asking her ambassadors to find out what the other Powers would be likely to do if Austria and Germany were to join together to fight Serbia. Germany's agents at St. Petersburg[156] said that Russia would not stir; there were serious labour troubles in that country, and the Czar would be afraid to call his troops together for fear they would join with the strikers. From France came the news that the French army was not fit to fight. On the 13th of July a speaker in the French Parliament declared that the forts were weak; that there was not sufficient ammunition for the guns; and that the soldiers were without a sufficient supply of boots. If war broke out the men would have to take the field with one pair of boots, and only one reserve boot in their knapsacks, and that one would be thirty years old. Thus the Kaiser believed that Russia dared not fight, and that France could not fight, because, as in 1870, she was unprepared.

But what of Britain? The Kaiser had flooded the British Isles with spies, who kept him informed of every movement of our fleet and troops, and gave him full information about all our political affairs. These spies told him that civil war was about to break out in Ireland, and that the Government would have its hands so full at home that it could not possibly spare troops to fight on the Continent. The German ambassador in London did not believe all this talk about civil war, and he advised his Government not to rely upon it. The German Government, however, would not listen to him. The Kaiser knew better; he believed his spies.

Feeling sure, then, that Russia would not fight, that France could not resist, and that Great Britain would not interfere in what seemed to be a far-off quarrel, the Kaiser decided that "THE DAY," so long hoped for and prepared for, had come. In July of the present year he was ready to "let slip the dogs of war."

CHAPTER XV.

FATEFUL DAYS.

Every visitor to London knows Trafalgar Square, with its huge column guarded by four bronze lions. On the top of the column is a statue to the "little, one-armed, one-eyed hero of a hundred fights," our greatest seaman, Lord Nelson. South of Trafalgar Square is the broad, fine street known as Whitehall. On the right-hand side of Whitehall, just before you come to Westminster, is Downing Street, and on the left-hand side of Downing Street is the handsome pile of buildings known as the Foreign Office.

The head of the Foreign Office is the Foreign Secretary, that member of the British Cabinet who looks after British interests abroad. All letters sent by the British Government to foreign Governments are written and dispatched by him and his officials, and all communications from foreign Governments are received by him. He appoints and controls all the ambassadors and ministers and consuls who represent us in foreign countries. They are his agents and his eyes and ears in the countries to which they are sent. It is their duty to keep him well and promptly informed of all matters which directly or indirectly affect the British Empire in its relation to other Powers. So widespread is the British Empire, and so world-wide are its interests, that very little happens abroad that does not concern us in some way or other.

Our present Foreign Secretary is Sir Edward Grey.[157] He is the grandson of a famous statesman, and has been a member of Parliament since 1885, when he was twenty-three years of age. No Briton has studied foreign affairs more diligently than he, and all parties have the fullest confidence in him as a cool, prudent, far-seeing statesman. He is a great lover of peace, and it is due to him that the representatives of the warring nations of the Balkan Peninsula were induced to meet in conference and come to terms in May 1913.

Let me remind you once again of the murder of the Archduke Ferdinand at Sarajevo on the 23rd of June 1914.[158] When Sir Edward Grey heard the tragic news, he saw at once that it might lead to a great war. He was anxious to know what Austria proposed to do in the matter, but was kept in the dark. He spoke to the German Ambassador about it, and was told that Austria was certainly going to take some step, and that the outlook was grave. On the 22nd of July our representative in Berlin told him that the German Secretary of State[159] thought that Austria and Serbia alone were concerned in the quarrel, and that outsiders ought not to interfere. Next day Sir Edward Grey met the Austrian Ambassador, who explained to him what Austria was going to demand[160] from Serbia. He also informed him that Austria would fix a time limit within which Serbia was to reply in a manner satisfactory to Austria, and that if the reply was not satisfactory, war would be declared.

At once Sir Edward Grey pointed out that the time limit was really a threat of war, and that it might anger Russia, and make her get ready to fight against Austria. You can easily see what the result would be. If Russia joined Serbia against Austria, Germany, as Austria's ally, would fight for her; and if this came about, France would be sure to help her ally, Russia, so that a vast and terrible European war would arise—the vastest and most terrible conflict that the world has ever known. To this the Austrian Ambassador replied that it all depended on Russia; but Sir Edward Grey reminded him that it takes two to keep the peace, as well as two to make a quarrel.

As we already know, the Note was sent to Serbia with a time limit of forty-eight hours. As soon as Russia received a copy of the Note, she felt that it was meant as an indirect challenge to her. A Council of Ministers was held to consider the question. It was fortunate that the President of the French Republic was then paying a visit to the Czar, and that the two allies could take immediate counsel together.

On the 24th of July the Russian Minister for Foreign Affairs told the British Ambassador in Petrograd that Austria was trying to bring about war with Serbia, and that she would never have done this had Germany not been backing her up. He also said that France would stand side by side with Russia if war should break out.

During the forty-eight hours allowed by the Austrian Note Sir Edward Grey made three attempts to bring about peace. First, he tried to get the time limit extended, and Great Britain, France, and Russia united in urging Austria to give Serbia more time. He begged Germany to join with the other Powers in trying to persuade Austria to do this, but all that Germany would consent to do was to "pass on" the message to Vienna. Next, Sir Edward Grey tried to get Great Britain, France, Germany, and Italy—all of whom had no interest in Serbia—to unite in an attempt to bring Russia and Austria to a friendly agreement. All the Powers mentioned were ready to do this except Germany. She said that she had no objection to the course proposed if war should be threatened between Austria and Russia. Sir Edward Grey's third effort was to advise Serbia to do as much as possible to meet Austria's demands.

I have already told you that on the 25th of July Serbia accepted all Austria's terms, and only asked for delay in order to make new laws by which she could carry them out, and for information as to the way in which Austrian officials were to take part in Serbia's police and law-court work. Every one hoped that this would end the quarrel; but the same evening the Serbian reply was declared unsatisfactory, and the Austrian Minister left Belgrade, thus showing clearly that war would follow. Serbia at once ordered her troops to mobilize.

French Infantry. *Photo, Central News.*

[These soldiers are French regulars, who, unlike the conscripts, serve for more than three years in the army.]

Sir Edward Grey learnt what the Serbian reply was to be an hour or two before it was handed to Austria. At once he begged Germany to press Austria to accept it, but again Germany would only pass on his suggestion to Vienna. Directly afterwards the German Ambassador in Vienna told our ambassador that Serbia had merely pretended to give way, and that her promises were only a sham.

During the next four days—26th July to 29th July—Sir Edward Grey strove with all his might to bring Russia and Austria to agreement. On the evening of the 28th the German Chancellor[16] told our ambassador that he was trying to bring the Russians and Austrians to agreement. This was very good news to Sir Edward Grey, who now thought that he saw a chance of staving off the European war which was threatening. He had already proposed that the German, French, and Italian ambassadors should meet him in London, to try to bring about a settlement; but though France and Italy had agreed to this proposal, Germany had refused, and had said that it would be better if Austria and Russia could be persuaded to come to some agreement between themselves. Now that Germany declared that she was working for peace at Vienna and Petrograd, Sir Edward Grey sent a telegram to the German Government, on the afternoon of the 29th, telling them that he would agree to any method of bringing Russia and Austria together that might be proposed. All that Germany had to do was to "press the button in the interests of peace."

A strange reply came to this telegram. It came from Sir Edward Goschen,[162] our ambassador in Berlin, towards midnight of the same day. He had just seen the German Chancellor, who said that if Austria should be attacked by Russia, Germany would have to fight for Austria, her ally. He then made an amazing offer to Britain. If Great Britain would promise not to fight, Germany on her part would promise to take no part of France from her. "But what about the French colonies?"[163] asked Sir Edward Goschen. To which the Chancellor replied that he could give no such promise with regard to them. In answer to other questions, he said that the action of France might force Germany to invade Belgium.

Now this was very startling. For the first time we knew that Germany was about to invade France, and that she would probably march her troops through Belgium for that purpose. We also knew that Germany was so anxious to keep us out of the war that she was prepared to make a bargain with us. "What the German Chancellor asks us in effect," said Sir Edward Grey, "is to engage to stand by while French colonies are taken and France is beaten, so long as Germany does not take French territory as distinct from the colonies." What answer should you have given to Germany if you had been our Foreign Secretary? I think it would have been just the answer which Sir Edward Grey gave. He told Germany that we could not possibly accept such a proposal, nor could we permit Germany to break her solemn pledge to Belgium and advance through that country.

On July 31 there was a gleam of hope in the darkness. Russia offered to stop all her military preparations if Austria would agree that all the European Powers were now concerned in her quarrel with Serbia, and if she would strike out of the Note those demands[164] which would destroy Serbia's independence. Strange to say, Austria agreed to this proposal—to the very thing she had refused to do in the early days of the crisis—that is, to discuss the whole question of the Note to Serbia. Perhaps you wonder why Austria should give way at the last moment. The fact was that Austria had been assured by the German Ambassador that Russia would not and could not fight. She now discovered that Russia was quite prepared for war. She had been deceived and misled, and she was eager to draw back. You will soon see that no chance was given to her of doing this.

Just at the moment when men were beginning to breathe more freely, and to believe that war might yet be averted, the thunderbolt fell from the blue. On the very day when the horizon was brightening, the Kaiser sent an impudent message to the Czar, ordering him to cease mobilizing his troops within twelve hours under pain of war! No answer was returned, and at midnight on the 1st of August Germany declared war against Russia. Armageddon had begun.

CHAPTER XVI.

WHY BRITAIN WENT TO WAR.

Do you remember the week-end between Friday, 31st July, and Monday, 3rd August? It was the most anxious and exciting time that living Britons have ever known. On every tongue there was the same question: "Are we going to war?" Everywhere you saw people feverishly buying edition after edition of the evening papers, and gathering into little groups to discuss the situation.

London, as you know, is the chief money market of the world, and the effect of wars and rumours of wars in any country on the globe is felt at once in the City of London. When it was evident that the four greatest continental nations were setting their armies in motion, stocks and shares fell to such a low price that dealing in them became impossible. Many of the stockbroking firms failed, and business was suspended, not only in London, but on almost every exchange throughout the world. It was thought that there would be a shortage of gold, and from noon onwards on the 31st of July the court-yard of the Bank of England was crowded with people eager to exchange notes for gold. Nevertheless "the Old Lady of Threadneedle Street," as the Bank of England is sometimes called, remained perfectly calm, and inside the building business went on as usual. On the 1st of August the bank rate[165] rose to 10 per cent., and the Stock Exchange was closed.

Naval Reserves passing through Portsmouth to join their ships. *Photo, Sport and General.*

On Sunday, 2nd August, the Naval Reserves[166] were called up, and the War Office became very active. A number of the London Territorial[167] regiments were on their way to camp for their annual training, but they were ordered to return and remain within reach of headquarters. It was very clear to everybody that the issue of war or peace was hanging in the balance.

On Sunday, 2nd August, the first important act of war was committed. Look at the map on page 38, and find the river Moselle. Not far from its left bank you will see the city of Luxemburg, which stands in the little independent duchy of the same name, at the south-east corner of Belgium. This state is about as large as the county of Essex, and its population is less than that of the city of Edinburgh. It is a country of low ridges and meadow land, and more than a quarter of its surface is covered with forests. There are good deposits of iron, and many of the people are engaged in mining and smelting the ore. From 1825 to 1867 the state belonged to Germany, and down to 1872 its fortress was in the hands of the Prussians. In that year the garrison was withdrawn, the fortress was dismantled, and the state was neutralized. The army of Luxemburg only consists of 150 soldiers and the same number of armed policemen. Its Grand Duchess is Marie Adelaide, who is now in her twenty-first year.

I want you to notice especially that the Germans did not propose to invade France by the routes which they followed in 1870. In that year, you will remember, they crossed the frontier in the direction of Metz, and south of it. They had determined not to do this during the present war, because, as you will gather from the map on page 98, the country is hilly, and therefore difficult to traverse, and because the frontier is protected by a chain of very powerful fortresses. As we shall see later, they wished to enter France very quickly, and beat her as rapidly as possible. Time was all-important to them, and they could not afford to waste it in the long business of besieging barrier fortresses. They therefore decided to invade France by the easy route through Belgium, even though they would have to break a solemn treaty by so doing.

The frontier between Belgium and Germany is very narrow, only about forty miles in width. As this space is insufficient for the quick and orderly transfer of the huge armies which the Germans proposed to send into France, they determined to break another treaty, and enter through Luxemburg as well. This would give them another forty miles of line across which to advance, and would place them in possession of a town in which the whole network of railways uniting Germany, France, and Belgium forms a junction. Once in Luxemburg, they were in command of the whole system of roads and railways leading from North Germany into France and Belgium.

When the inhabitants of Luxemburg awoke on the hot Sunday morning of 2nd August, they were surprised to find that the Adolf Bridge, which leads to the city across the river Alzette, was in the hands of the Germans. A little later, armed motor cars, filled with German officers and men, were seen approaching the city. It was the vanguard of the 39th Regiment. A member of the Luxemburg Government met the invaders, and handed them a copy of the treaty guaranteeing the neutrality of the state. They told him that they knew all about the treaty, but that they had their orders. The Archduchess now drove up, and tried to block the path of the Germans with her motor car. She was told to go home at once; and, having no force behind her, was obliged to obey.

On and on came the Germans, and the people were greatly surprised to see amongst them many men who up to that time had been clerks in the offices of Luxemburg. These men, while pretending to be peaceful citizens, had made themselves thoroughly acquainted with the geography of the country, had carefully noted the best points for the Germans to occupy, and the places where they could procure provisions. Before nightfall the whole state was in their hands; the roads and railways were guarded by sentries; and houses, woods, and standing crops which might afford cover to the enemy were destroyed.

That same day German cavalry crossed the French border near Longwy,[168] and farther south, near Strassburg, they pushed across the frontier to the town of Cirey-les-Forges.[169] Still farther south, near the Swiss boundary, another raid was made. You will remember that the French had promised to keep their troops back from the border as long as there was the slightest chance of bringing Austria and Russia to agreement.

Monday, 3rd August, was the most remarkable Bank Holiday ever known in Britain. All Bank Holiday excursions were cancelled, for the railways were in the hands of the military authorities. Hundreds of thousands of persons, who would otherwise have spent the day at the seaside or in the country, were forced to remain in London. Great crowds gathered at Westminster to see the members of Parliament enter Palace Yard. It was known that a Cabinet Council had been held on the previous day, and that a very important statement was to be made that very afternoon.

Let us peep into the House of Commons on that memorable occasion. The Chamber, which is far too small to accommodate all the members of Parliament, is crowded to excess. All the green benches are filled, the side galleries are thronged, and there are rows of chairs in the gangways. It is evident that a matter of great pith and moment is now about to arise. There is some preliminary business to be got through, and the House is impatient to see the end of it. Then Sir Edward Grey rises, and amidst loud cheering advances to the table, and begins the most fateful speech that was ever made in all our long history. He is very grave, and his set face shows traces of the anxious and laborious days through which he has recently passed. He speaks without passion, and with no attempt at fine language; but every word that he utters is full of deep meaning, and the House listens with eager attention.

He tells his fellow-members that the Government has worked with a single mind, and with all the earnestness in its power, to preserve the peace, but that its labours have proved vain—Germany and Russia have declared war on each other. Then he goes on to speak of our friendship with France— that warm and cordial friendship, which has replaced the enmity of long ages. This friendship, he declares, entails duties upon us. The French fleet is in the Mediterranean Sea, because of the good feeling and confidence that has grown up between us, and the northern and western coasts of France are without defence. "My own feeling is," he says, "that if a foreign fleet, engaged in a war which France had not sought, and in which she had not been the aggressor, came down the English Channel and bombarded and battered the unprotected coasts of France, we could not stand aside." The loud cheers which immediately break forth show that the great majority of the members thoroughly agree with him. When the cheers have subsided, he proceeds: "We could not see this going on practically within sight of our eyes, with our arms folded, doing nothing, and I believe that would be the feeling of this country."

France, he says, is entitled to know at once whether she can depend upon British support should her northern and western coasts be attacked. He has therefore given an assurance to the French Government that, should the German fleet come into the Channel or through the North Sea to undertake hostile operations against the French coasts or shipping, the British fleet, if Parliament approves, will give all the protection in its power. The cheers that follow this statement clearly show that the House of Commons fully approves of the undertaking which he has given to France.

Then he turns to the all-important question of Belgium. He tells the House what you already know—namely, that in 1870 we made a stand for the neutrality of that little country, and were thus able to save her from the horrors of invasion. What we did then, we are trying to do now. France has given us her assurance that she will not enter Belgium if it is not invaded by another Power, but Germany refuses to reply. She has already asked King Albert to grant unopposed passage for her troops through his country, and has promised to guarantee its independence if he will consent to this course; but, at the same time, she has threatened to treat Belgium as an enemy if the request is refused. The Belgians are determined to resist the invasion of their land by every means in their power.

Our treaty with Belgium binds us in honour to take her part. If in a crisis like this we run away, we shall lose the respect of the nations—a respect which we can never regain. Though we might, by husbanding our resources, be able at the end of the war to prevent the whole of western Europe from falling into the hands of Germany, our moral position would be such———. The rest of the sentence is lost amidst a loud burst of cheering. Almost to a man the members of the House of Commons are convinced that we should sink to the lowest depths of dishonour were we to abandon Belgium in her dark hour of trial.

The cheers are renewed when Sir Edward Grey declares that our Fleet has been mobilized, and that our Army is mobilizing. Britain is ready to play her part, whatever that may be. Then the speaker points out the one bright spot in the whole terrible situation. Formerly, when Britain has been engaged in war, the Irish people have seized the opportunity to rise in revolt. At this time we have no such fear. Finally, he believes that, should war come, the Government will be supported, not only by the House of Commons, but by the determination, the resolution, the courage, and the endurance of the whole country. Amidst loud and prolonged cheers the speaker resumes his seat.

Then the Leader of the Opposition[170] rises and pledges the loyalty of his followers in this great and grave crisis. So, too, does the leader of the Irish Nationalists,[171] and only one voice is heard disapproving of the course which the Government proposes to take. In the face of national peril the vast majority of the men of every party, creed, and sect stand shoulder to shoulder—forgetting their differences of opinion, and only remembering that they are Britons, faced with the greatest danger that has ever threatened their land. When Lord Macaulay, in his ballad *Horatius*, wished to show us the Romans in their noblest aspect, he said,—

"Then none was for a party;
Then all were for the State; . . .
The Romans were like brothers
In the brave days of old."

So it is with Britons all over the world in these days of anxiety and peril. None is for a party, and all are for the State; and so it will be until the war clouds roll away, and peace once more smiles upon us.

Sir Edward Grey making his great Speech in the House of Commons on August 3, 1914.

"My own feeling is this, that if a foreign fleet, engaged in a war which France had not sought, and in which she had not been the aggressor, came down the English Channel and bombarded and battered the unprotected coasts of France, we could not stand aside [loud cheers] and see this going on practically within sight of our eyes, with our arms folded, looking on dispassionately doing nothing; and I believe that would be the feeling of this country [cheers]. ...If, in a crisis like this, we ran away [loud cheers] from our obligations of honour and interest with regard to the Belgian Treaty, I doubt whether whatever material force we might have at the end of it would be of very much value in face of the respect that we should have lost."

By permission of the illustrated London News.

That afternoon the King and Queen drove from Buckingham Palace along the Mall, and were everywhere greeted with the heartiest of cheers, especially when they passed the German Embassy.[172] His Majesty could not fail to understand the meaning of these cheers—the nation was one in heart and mind in the great task which lay before it. In the evening, thousands of people gathered outside Buckingham Palace, singing patriotic songs and cheering again and again. Just after nine o'clock the King, accompanied by the Queen and the Prince of Wales, appeared on the balcony above the entrance to the north side of the Palace. Then the cheers grew louder than ever. The King and Queen bowed again and again to the people, and the Prince waved his hand. By this time it was clear to all the world that the people of Britain were ready to face the future, as Sir Edward Grey had prophesied, with determination, resolution, courage, and endurance.

Next morning Sir Edward Grey telegraphed to Sir Edward Goschen, bidding him request an immediate assurance from the German Government that Belgium would not be invaded. Later in the day he telegraphed again, telling our Ambassador that Belgium had already been invaded, and asking for a satisfactory reply by twelve o'clock that night. If such a reply was not forthcoming, Sir Edward Goschen was told to ask for his passports, and say that Great Britain would do everything in her power to uphold those treaty rights of Belgium to which Germany was a party as well as Great Britain.

Sir Edward Goschen accordingly called upon the German Secretary of State, Herr von Jagow, about seven o'clock that evening, and delivered his message. The Secretary at once replied that he was sorry to say that he could give no such undertaking, for the German troops were already in Belgium. He then explained why his Government had been obliged to take this step, and, in so doing, revealed the German plan of campaign. They had to advance into France, he said, by the quickest and easiest way, so as to be able to strike a decisive blow as soon as possible. It was a matter of life and death to them; for, if they had gone by the more southern route, they would have had bad roads to cross and strong fortresses to take, and would, therefore, have wasted much time. This loss of time would mean that the Russians would be able to bring up their troops to the German frontier before the German conquest of France was complete. As Russia had an almost endless number of soldiers, they were bound to overthrow France as quickly as possible before the Russians could muster in full strength.

Sir Edward Goschen then asked if there was not still time for the Germans to draw back, and so avoid bringing Great Britain into the war. To this, Herr von Jagow replied that it was now too late. Thus there was nothing left for Sir Edward Goschen to do but to demand his passports. Before doing so, however, he went to see the Chancellor, the man next in authority to the Kaiser himself. Then followed one of the most dramatic interviews known to history.

Sir Edward Goschen tells us that he found the Chancellor much upset, and that he at once began a loud, angry speech, which lasted twenty minutes. He said that the step taken by the British Government was terrible to a degree. We were going to war just for a word—"neutrality"—a word which had so often been set aside in time of war. Just for a treaty—"*a scrap of paper*"—we were going to fight a kindred nation which desired nothing better than to be friends with us. What we had done was like striking a man from behind while he was struggling for his life against two foes. He should hold Great Britain responsible for all the terrible events that might happen.

Sir Edward Goschen strongly protested against this statement, and said that in the same way that the Chancellor and Herr von Jagow thought the violation of Belgium's neutrality was a matter of life and death to them, so it was a matter of life and death to the honour of Great Britain that she should keep her solemn engagements, and do her utmost to defend Belgium if she should be attacked. If Great Britain did not keep faith, what confidence would other nations have in her word for the future? To which the Chancellor replied, "Has the British Government thought of the price at which this compact will be kept?" Sir Edward Goschen replied that no fear of consequences could be regarded as an excuse for breaking solemn engagements; and he would have said more, but the Chancellor was so agitated by the news that Great Britain would fight for her honour, that he was incapable of listening to reason.

So the painful interview ended. A report of what had passed was drawn up and handed in at a telegraph office a little before 9 p.m., but was never dispatched.

You can now understand how the German Government regards its solemn agreements. When they stand in the way of its ambitions they are but "scraps of paper," to be torn into shreds. You can also understand how anxious Germany was to keep us out of this war. Up to the last she believed that we should not fight, and that she would be allowed to work her wicked will on Belgium and France, while we stood by without lifting a finger. We want no other charter of right for taking part in this war than the speech of the German Chancellor which you have just read.

By our action we had put a spoke in the German wheel, and it was soon evident that the Berlin crowds understood this, for they gathered before the British Embassy and hurled stones at the windows. Police were summoned, and the street was cleared; but large crowds assembled at the stations, and jeered at Sir Edward Goschen as he travelled to the Dutch frontier. Just before he left Berlin the Kaiser sent him a message, regretting what had taken place, and saying that he would no longer retain his rank as a British field-marshal and a British admiral.

Later on, the Chancellor made a speech in Parliament, and tried to explain why Germany had broken her plighted word with regard to the neutrality of Luxemburg and Belgium. He said, "We are now in a state of necessity, and necessity knows no law. We were compelled to override the just protest of the Luxemburg and Belgian Governments. The wrong—I speak openly—that we are committing we will endeavour to make good as soon as our military goal is reached. Anybody who is threatened as we are threatened, and is fighting for his highest possessions, can only have one thought—how he is *to hack his way through*." Thus Germany began the war by a confession of wrongdoing. Since the Chancellor spoke, nothing more has been said of the "wrong;" but attempts have been made to prove that Germany only invaded Belgium because Great Britain and France were about to do so, and she wished to be ahead of them. There is not a particle of truth in this excuse.

The Scrap of Paper.

This is a copy of the really important part of the treaty of 1839 which guaranteed the neutrality of Belgium. It is signed by the representatives of Britain, Belgium, Austria, France, Prussia, and Russia. The French words which are written above the seals may be translated as follows: "Belgium, within the limits indicated by Articles I., II., and IV., shall form an independent and perpetually neutral State. She will be bound to observe this same neutrality towards all the other States."

At 11 p.m. on the 4th of August Great Britain declared war on Germany.

The order for placing the British Army on a war footing was signed the same day, and immediately all the reservists of the Regular army and the Territorials were called to the colours. At once the country became an armed camp. Everywhere we heard the tramp of soldiers, the rattle of moving guns, and the rumble of baggage trains. The railways passed into the hands of the Government, and time-tables were suspended in order that the troops might be moved to and fro without loss of time. The Territorials took over the work of home defence, and guards were stationed at arsenals, reservoirs, bridges, and docks. The country was so full of German spies that it was feared attempts would be made to do damage to the railways and other important public works; but thanks to the careful guard kept by our citizen soldiers, no harm was done. Even the Boy Scouts, whose motto is "Be Prepared," were pressed into service. In a hundred different ways they proved useful, especially as messengers.

Next day Lord Kitchener was appointed Secretary of War, with the approval of the whole nation. Everybody felt that the right man was in the right place, and that he would see us through. It is said that, when he entered the War Office for the first time as Secretary, he asked the porter, "Is there a bed here?" "No, sir," replied the man. "Then get one," he said, clearly showing that he meant to spend his nights as well as his days in the laborious work of raising armies and fitting them for the work of war. At the same time Sir John Jellicoe[173] was appointed to command the Grand Fleet in home waters.

Sir John Jellicoe.

Our artist has here shown him as "the man at the wheel," for he is in supreme command of the Grand Fleet in home waters. He is fifty-five years of age, and has been in the Navy for forty-two years. He has the full confidence of every officer and man in the service, and Britons everywhere believe that he will uphold the fame of the great admirals who gave Britain command of the seas.

On the 6th of August the Prime Minister asked the House of Commons for a war vote of a hundred millions of money, and seized the occasion to reply to the question, What are we fighting for? In the first place, he said, we are fighting to keep our solemn promise—a promise which, had it been made between private persons in the ordinary course of life, would have been thought so binding in law and honour that no self-respecting man would have dreamed of setting it aside. In the second place, we are fighting on behalf of the little nations. When their safety has been guaranteed by treaty, we are determined that they shall not be crushed out of existence by any Power, however strong and over-mastering it may be. No nation, he said, has ever entered into a great war with a clearer conscience or with a more certain knowledge that it is fighting for the right. We are not battling for power or land or gold, not even for our own selfish interests, but we are struggling to maintain that good faith amongst the nations without which the world would sink back into barbarism.

The war vote was at once granted, and it was quickly agreed that the Army should be increased by half a million men. On the next day Lord Kitchener called for a first army of 100,000 men, and instantly recruits of high quality came flocking to the colours. Men waited in front of the London recruiting offices hour after hour for days together, in order to offer their services to the country. From the Colonies and from India came the most loyal of messages, and the most generous offers of men and money. The whole Empire was united as never before, in this the most righteous war that has ever been waged.

I have already told you that there was what is called a "run" upon the Bank of England at the prospect of war. In order that the nation should be steadied at this crisis, the Bank Holiday was continued for three days longer, and an order was made that no one need pay his business debts for a month. To keep gold in the banks for the service of the Government, paper money was introduced, and postal orders passed from hand to hand instead of coin. The newspapers were not allowed to print anything they pleased about the war, for fear that the enemy might gain important information. All war news was to be passed by what is called a censor before being printed.

CHAPTER XVII.

THE SUBMARINE THAT FAILED.

Meanwhile our Grand Fleet was watching and waiting for the German Navy to come out and fight. Our sailors seized many German merchant vessels on the seas, and those that were in our ports were captured; but the warships of the enemy were nowhere visible. We soon began to understand that the Germans did not propose to risk their ships in battle for some time to come. One of their military writers had recommended that they should try to reduce our Navy to the strength of their own by means of submarine[174] and destroyer[175] attacks before coming out to fight. On the second day after war was declared, we discovered that they had planned another method of sinking our ships without endangering their own.

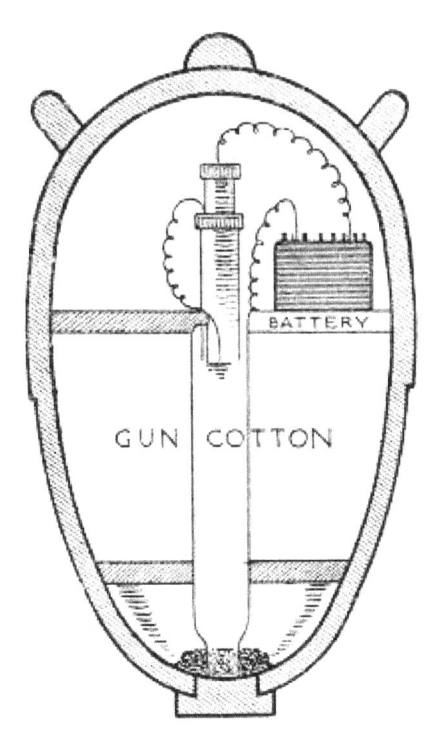

Floating Mine.

Here is a little picture of what is known as a floating mine. It consists of a hollow, pear-shaped case, containing an electric battery and a large amount of gun-cotton, or some other high explosive. This mine is thrown into the sea, and by means of an iron weight is made to float three or four feet below the surface. If the mine is struck hard, it will cant over sixty-five or seventy degrees. Then the mercury in a little cup would overflow, and by so doing would complete an electric circuit and explode the gun-cotton. So terrible is the explosive force of gun-cotton, that it will tear asunder the biggest ship, and either cripple it or send it to the bottom. Never before has any nation strewn the open seas with such floating mines, and their use in this way is against all the laws of war which are observed by civilized nations.

Sweeping up mines in the North Sea.

The Germans soon discovered that large mine-layers ran a great risk of being sunk by the guns of our warships, so they employed fishing-boats and other small craft to lay these deadly engines in the sea. Many of these ships flew the flag of a neutral Power, and thus pretended that they were engaged on lawful and peaceful business. The North Sea became a death-trap, and our Admiralty had to meet the danger by employing a large number of trawlers to sweep up the mines.

The work is done in the following way. Two trawlers sailing parallel with each other drag through the sea a steel hawser which is attached to each of them. The hawser drags the mines along, and they are then picked up. You can readily understand how dangerous this work is. The trawlers themselves may strike a mine, and be blown up; or two mines drawn along by the hawser may collide when they are near to the trawlers, in which case the same result follows. Many gallant smacksmen have lost their lives in trying to free the sea from this terrible peril. We ought to think of them as heroes of the best and highest type. Always remember that it is more glorious to save life than to destroy it.

On the 6th of August a flotilla of British destroyers, accompanied by the light cruiser[176] *Amphion*,[177] sighted a German vessel off the Dutch coast engaged in throwing out floating mines. The *Lance*, a British destroyer, at once attacked this vessel, and in four shots destroyed her bridge, tore away her stern, and sank her—all within the space of six minutes. Some fifty members of the crew were saved by the British boats. Though the mine-layer was at the bottom of the sea, she had done her deadly work, and was soon to achieve a victory. As the *Amphion* was steaming towards Harwich, and was about thirty miles off Aldeburgh, she struck one of the mines laid by the sunken ship, and was instantly blown up. The bow of the ship was shattered, and in less than twenty minutes she sank, with a loss of 131 lives. The captain, sixteen officers, and 135 men were saved; but twenty German prisoners confined in the bow were killed by the explosion of their own mine. Since the *Amphion* went down, many peaceful merchant ships and trawlers, both British and neutral, have been sunk by these mines, as well as two other British warships.

Here is a section of a submarine, a type of vessel which is now being used for the first time in warfare. You see that it is shaped like a rather fat cigar, tapering towards its after or tail end. In the centre of the top of the hull we see a small conning-tower. At the stern there is a propeller, and also a series of rudders which enables it to steer to and fro, or up and down. If you study the picture, you will see what the interior of a submarine is like. By means of tanks, which can be filled with water or emptied, the submarine can sink or rise at will. When she comes near an enemy, she sinks until only a short mast appears above the surface. This mast is a hollow tube fitted with a lens and mirrors, so arranged that images of objects outside the boat and above the surface are thrown on to another mirror, where they are examined by means of a magnifying glass. This "periscope," as the hollow mast is called, is the eye of the submarine. It enables her to see when her hull is beneath the waves. If she sinks altogether, or if the periscope should be carried away, she is blind and can see nothing.

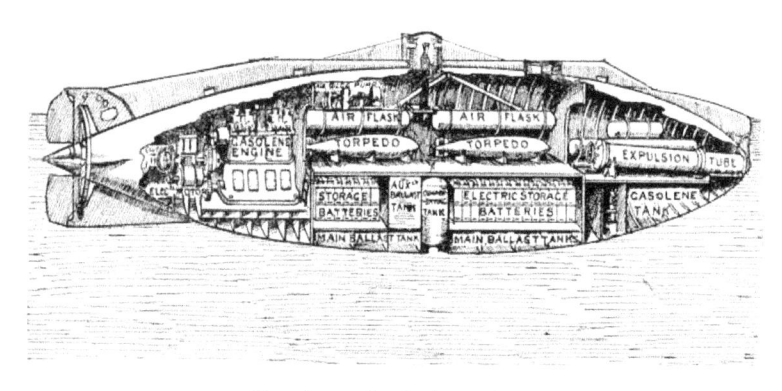

Section of a Submarine.

Some submarines have a gun on deck, but their real weapon is the torpedo. There is a picture of one on page 183. It is really a little warship in itself, with its own hull, propeller, rudders, engines, and a mass of gun-cotton in the place of guns. This explosive is stored in the head of the torpedo, which is provided with a striker-rod of steel. When this rod hits the target it is forced back and explodes a little charge, which in its turn explodes the gun-cotton which lies behind it. A torpedo is fired from a tube, and immediately it strikes the water its engines begin to work. It then rushes towards its target at the rate of forty or fifty miles an hour for a distance of three miles or more. By means of a very remarkable piece of apparatus, it is steered back to its line of fire if it should be turned out of its course. If the aim is sure, and the torpedo hits its mark, the gun-cotton explodes with such terrific force that it will sink or cripple the biggest ship afloat.

On ordinary warships a torpedo can be fired from a tube either above or below water. The tube can be moved just like a gun, and so a correct aim can be taken. The tubes of a submarine, however, are all below water, and they are fixed so that the submarine itself must be moved into the right position before it can discharge a torpedo with correct aim.

Submarines have been called, with good reason, "the deadliest things that keep the sea." With only the thin periscope showing above the waves, they can silently and secretly creep within range of a warship, and send off a torpedo on its deadly errand. To detect the thin periscope from the bridge of a warship is not easy, and during the present war several gallant ships have been taken unawares and sent to the bottom.

Now let me tell you the story of a submarine that failed.

On the 9th of August a flotilla of German submarines was in the North Sea. Their narrow gray bodies were furrowing the waves at a speed of about fifteen knots an hour. On the little deck of each of them stood a commander, sweeping the horizon through powerful glasses for signs of the enemy. Down below men were standing by the motors, examining the gauges, filling the compressed air chambers, and making sure that the torpedoes were "ship-shape."

Yonder is Submarine U 9. Suddenly her commander closes his glasses with a snap. He has sighted the funnels of British cruisers, and the hour of action has arrived. The long-expected signal rings out below, and the commander leaves the tiny deck and withdraws into the interior through a hatch, which is carefully closed behind him. He takes his place in the conning-tower, where, under his hand and eye, is all the apparatus needed for steering and controlling the boat.

A valve is opened, and air is allowed to escape from the water-ballast tanks in the bottom of the vessel. Water flows in, and the submarine sinks until she is running "awash," with the base of the conning-tower only just clear of the waves. She is now ready to dive. This she must do before getting within range of the cruisers out yonder. There are hundreds of keen eyes on the British warships, and even the conning-tower of a submarine a mile away will be seen. A wheel is moved, the boat tilts downward slightly at the bows, and in a few moments the water is swirling round the windows of the conning-tower. Diving has begun. Down, down she goes. Presently the wheel is moved again, and the boat returns to an even keel. The only part of her that now shows above the water is the periscope.

The commander glues his eyes to the mirror which gives him a view of the sea around. The images of the cruisers grow larger and larger; one of them, H.M.S. *Birmingham*, is now within range. He moves his boat so that the torpedo tube at her bow points directly towards the *Birmingham*. His hand hovers over the switch which will launch a torpedo on its death-dealing errand. Why risk missing to avoid the slight danger of discovery? Another five hundred yards, and then——

The fateful moment has come. His hand slightly trembles with excitement as he prepares to make the trifling movement which may send some hundreds of men to a watery grave, and a gallant ship, worth more than a million of money, to the bottom.

This picture gives an excellent view of a torpedo and its tube on board a destroyer. The tube, you will observe, can be trained like a gun, and thus a correct aim can be taken.

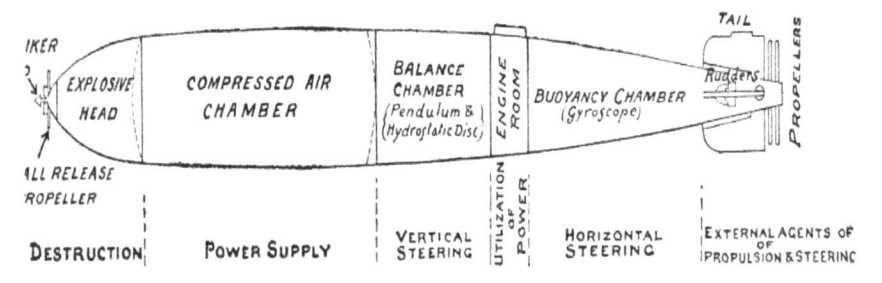

This diagram gives a section of a torpedo, which has been well described as a complete little warship. It has engines to drive it along; rudders to steer it; a special apparatus to make it return to the line of fire, if it should swerve; a supply of explosives to damage the enemy, and apparatus for firing the explosive at the right moment. A torpedo such as is used in our navy costs £1,000. Warships at anchor have steel nets around them as a protection against torpedoes. Some torpedoes, however, are fitted with a pair of powerful wire cutters, which enable them to pierce the net and strike the ship.

He presses the button; a flap opens in the tube in the bows; a valve admits compressed air into the rear end of it, and a shining torpedo leaps forward towards the quarry.

Crash! The image in the periscope has disappeared, and the submarine rocks slightly. The periscope has been sighted by a keen eye on the *Birmingham*, and a superb shot has carried it away. The submarine is now as blind as the giant after Ulysses had bored into his one eye. The biter has been bitten. It cannot remain under water, for a touch of the cruiser's steel bow will be the stroke of doom. If it comes up, a storm of shell will rage about it. The commander has a choice of perils. Desperately he decides to come up and endeavour to fire another torpedo.

The horizontal rudders are set in motion; compressed air is admitted to the ballast chambers, and some of the water is blown out. The conning-tower rises above the level of the water; but, before she can use her sting, all is over. The cruiser's quick-firing guns have been waiting, and the moment the deck appears a four-inch shell is discharged at it. The armour at the base of the conning-tower is cleft through as though it were a biscuit-box. Water rushes in, and a minute later the ill-fated craft, a marvel of ingenuity, lies on the bottom, twenty fathoms deep. There it will rust away long after the war in which it played such a brief part has passed into history.

Such is the story of how H.M.S. *Birmingham* sank the German submarine U 9. Some accounts tell us that the periscope was not shot away, but that when the torpedo from the submarine missed its mark, the cruiser made a rapid turn and drove straight at her, crumpling her to pieces by the terrible force of its weight and speed. This is the method which our cruisers usually adopt when attacked by submarines. They steam rapidly in a zigzag course, so as to disconcert those who are aiming the torpedo, and, at the first sign of the submarine's presence, charge down upon her and sink her.

A cruiser ramming a submarine.

CHAPTER XVIII.

INFANTRY AND ITS WORK.

Before I describe the German invasion of Belgium, I must explain certain military terms which will crop up again and again in the following pages. Unless you understand these terms, you cannot read war news intelligently.

An army, you know, is a body of armed men, trained and organized and disciplined for the work of war. Most of the fighting men in an army are either infantry, cavalry, or artillery. Let me tell you something about each of these "arms."

Infantry are foot-soldiers armed with rifles and bayonets. In time of peace you have seen them marching by in their scarlet and blue uniforms and smart spiked helmets. You have also seen the Highlanders, with their waving feather bonnets, short scarlet coats with yellow facings, white belts and gaiters, plaid stockings, and bare knees. In time of war all these fine uniforms are discarded, and the men are dressed in khaki.

Every foot-soldier belongs to a *regiment*, and is one of a *company* of that regiment. A company consists of 227 men of all ranks, and is commanded by a captain or major, with a captain as second in command. Every company is divided into four platoons under lieutenants, each of whom has a sergeant as second in command, and each platoon consists of four sections under junior sergeants, corporals, or lance-corporals.

In the British Army four companies form a *battalion*, which has been well called the household or family to which the soldier belongs. It consists, when at war strength, of 1,007 men, including what is called headquarters—that is, the battalion staff, the men of the machine-gun section, the signallers, pioneers, and the bandsmen who in time of war serve as stretcher-bearers. A battalion is commanded by a lieutenant-colonel, who is assisted by a major, an adjutant, a quartermaster, together with a number of sergeants, orderlies, and clerks. The adjutant is specially responsible for the book-keeping of the battalion, for issuing the orders, and for seeing that all military duties are properly performed. The quartermaster has charge of the stores, clothing, and the equipment of the men.

The strength of an infantry force is reckoned in battalions, not in regiments. Four battalions—that is, 4,000 men—form a *brigade* of infantry, which is commanded by a brigadier-general, who is assisted by a brigade-major and a staff-captain.

Foot-soldiers are now armed with what is called a magazine rifle. The short Lee-Enfield,[178] which our infantry carry, can fire a dozen aimed shots in a minute; and if the magazine is opened, the ten cartridges in it can be discharged in less than thirty seconds. With this rifle, which is sighted up to 2,800 yards, a man can hit a large object a mile and a half away, and if he is a good shot, can kill a man at half a mile. The cartridge—which contains bullet and powder in one case—is so light that a man can carry his one hundred and twenty cartridges without much discomfort. The powder used is smokeless, so that it is almost impossible to tell where the shots come from if the riflemen take *cover*—that is, if they conceal themselves behind bushes, rocks, or hedges. British soldiers are exceedingly good at taking cover, and they learnt the art from the Boers in South Africa. They are careful to notice the folds and waves of the ground, and to take advantage of everything which will hide them from the enemy. A skilful leader can march his company or platoon across country so that a man sitting still half a mile away from his route cannot catch as much as a glimpse of it.

Territorial Infantry marching along Fleet Street, London. Most of these men in private life are lawyers.

Photo, Record Press.

Before a man can fire accurately at a distant enemy he must know the range, and must sight his rifle accordingly. To show you how this range is found, let us suppose that a platoon sees a party of the enemy on a ridge in front of it. At one end of this ridge there is a little sand heap. "The lieutenant calls for three good shots from your section, of whom you are one. You go up and lie down, and your section commander tells you that you are to fire at the sand hill to get the range, which he thinks is 800 yards. You fire at 800 yards, and see no result; the next man fires at 750—no result. The third man fires at 700, and the sergeant, with a field-glass, sees a splash of dust on the sand heap. That settles the range."[179] When the troops occupy a position some time before the enemy is in sight, it is usual to mark distances. "Half a dozen men are told to cut sticks from the nearest trees, and to tie red rags on to each of them. Then they are to pace 600 yards in a straight line to the front, stepping yards as well as they can, and then to plant their sticks so that the line of red sticks may mark the 600 yards line from where their comrades are lying down."[179]

Each infantryman carries a short bayonet, about twelve inches long. When a charge is ordered, the bayonet is fixed on to the end of the rifle-barrel, and is used as a thrusting-sword. British soldiers have always been famous for their prowess with the bayonet. A bayonet charge usually occurs when an enemy has been beaten by gun fire, and his trenches are carried by a final rush.

Each battalion has with it two machine guns, manned by an officer, a sergeant, and sixteen men. Two wagons accompany this section to convey the guns and their ammunition.

A machine gun is nothing but a rifle barrel fixed into a machine so that it becomes self-firing. The barrel is surrounded by a large tube filled with water, to keep the barrel from getting too hot. The gun is so fixed on a tripod stand that it can be turned round in any direction. One man carries the gun, which weighs about sixty pounds, to the selected position, and the other carries the tripod on which it is fixed. On the march, both gun and tripod are carried in a wagon. Each gun is supplied with boxes containing 3,500 rounds, and 8,000 more rounds are kept in reserve.

On the next page you will see a picture of this gun at work. When it is fixed and sighted, a button is pressed, and the first shot is fired. The recoil of this shot empties and reloads the gun, and so the process goes on just as long as the button is pressed. Some three hundred shots can be fired in a minute very accurately, and the effect on a body of men advancing along a road or across a bridge is deadly in the extreme.

A concealed machine gun in action.   *Photo, Newspaper Illustrations Ltd.*

Besides their rifles and bayonets, each infantryman carries a light, short-handled shovel attached to his belt. This is for making trenches and rifle pits to afford protection against the enemy's bullets. In a very short time a battalion can "dig itself in," and, thus protected, fire on the enemy from shelter. A trench a hundred yards long, three feet deep, and two feet wide, can be dug in easy soil by forty men in about three hours. Every battalion is accompanied by mules or carts, carrying picks and additional shovels.

A trench made by infantry.

In the drawing the trench has been cut through vertically to show how it is made. "a" is the parapet piled up behind the hedge to protect the firer, who is shooting through a loophole ("d") made of bags of earth. "b" is the bank of earth thrown up behind the trench to protect the men from the "back blast" of shells, for when they burst, their effect is felt as severely behind them as in front. "c" is the bank of earth at the end of the trench to protect the men from enfilade fire—that is, from fire along the length of the trench. Frequently trenches are made in zigzags to avoid this danger.

A good infantryman must be able to shoot well and march well. If you are in good condition, you perhaps think nothing of a ten-mile walk. But suppose you are loaded up, as the soldier is, with rifle, bayonet, and knapsack, ammunition pouches, haversack, water-bottle, and entrenching tool, a total weight of about sixty-one pounds, you will find ten miles a long and very tiring distance. Our infantry usually march at about two and three-quarter miles an hour on a fourteen-mile march. The French are famous for what are called "forced marches"—that is, for marches more than twenty miles in one day—but British soldiers have done even better. In 1898, before the Battle of Atbara, some of our infantrymen covered 134 miles—mostly desert—in six and a half days, ninety-eight miles being covered in four successive days. The men were in fine condition, otherwise they could not have stood the strain. As it was, many of them arrived at their destination barefooted, the soles of their boots having come off owing to the rough nature of the country. This, of course, made the march all the more creditable.

In South Africa the 2nd Shropshire Light Infantry once marched forty-three miles in thirty-two hours. When pursuing De Wet in August 1900, the City Imperial Volunteers (C.I.V.) marched thirty miles in seventeen hours.

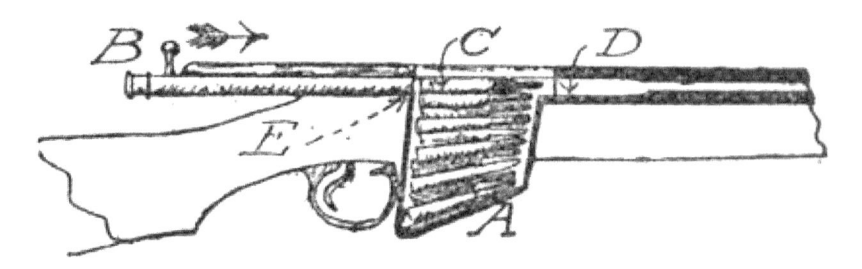

The Lee-Enfield Rifle.

A spring (A) at the bottom of the magazine pushes the cartridges up towards the top. By pushing forward the bolt (B) in the direction of the arrow, you shove the top cartridge (C) into the chamber (D). After you have fired, you pull back the bolt, and this pulls out the empty cartridge case. A small metal leaf can be pushed across the top of the magazine at E, so that you can load and fire the rifle without using the cartridges in the magazine. This leaf is called the "cut-off."

CHAPTER XIX.

CAVALRY AND ARTILLERY.

Cavalry are soldiers mounted on horses. One of the finest of our cavalry regiments is the 12th Lancers. In peace time the troopers of this regiment wear blue tunics with red fronts and cuffs, helmets with square-cut tops and red feathery plumes, and carry long, slender lances with red and white pennons. As they ride by, bolt upright on their splendid chargers, in all the glory of scarlet, blue, and gold, you cannot imagine a gayer and more gallant sight. None of this finery, however, is worn in war time; they are clad in the same kind of khaki as the infantry.

The fighting part of a cavalry regiment consists of three squadrons, each divided into four troops, with some additional officers and men. A troop consists of one officer and thirty-two men, and a squadron of 160 officers and men, so that a cavalry regiment numbers 480. At the head of the regiment is a lieutenant-colonel, and the "second in command" is a major, who takes the place of the colonel if he should be killed or put out of action. In every cavalry regiment there are also shoeing-smiths, saddlers, etc., as well as a doctor and a veterinary surgeon. Every cavalry regiment is accompanied by a machine-gun section. In the British Army three regiments form a cavalry brigade.

Each cavalryman is armed with a rifle and a sabre. In a Lancer regiment all the men carry lances as well; in a Dragoon regiment the front rank men alone are armed with these weapons. The rifle is carried with its butt in a leather case, and its barrel passes through a loop around the cavalryman's left arm. As you will see from the drawing on p. [194](#), he carries many other things as well. In time of peace a British cavalry regiment marches in double file, the officers riding on the flank of their respective troops or squadrons. On ordinary marches the horses "walk" at the rate of four miles an hour, and the "trot" of eight miles per hour is only resorted to when time presses, or when men and horses are becoming chilled. If for any reason the "gallop" becomes necessary, the men at once form fours, and dash along at the rate of fifteen miles an hour. In time of war a cavalry regiment usually operates at the "trot."

Troopers and their Equipment.

The trooper's uniform is the same as that of the infantryman. Until a few years ago he was armed with a carbine (3), which he carried in a leather bucket (4), attached to the right side of the saddle by straps.

He is now armed with the infantry rifle. This is not shown in the pictures, but is carried as the carbine was, with its butt in a leather case hanging by straps from the saddle near the man's left heel. Its barrel passes through a loop around his right arm, as the lance is carried. (See picture on the right.) 1 is the loop attaching lance to the arm; 2, the sabre; 3, the carbine; 4, the bucket; 5, the bandolier, carrying cartridges; 6, a pair of boots; 7, a cloak; 8, a saddlebag, holding knife, fork, spoon, brush, comb, towel, emergency ration, etc.; 9, a saddlebag, holding shirt, drawers, socks, currycomb, stable-brush, etc.; 10, breeches and puttees rolled in waterproof sheet; 11, hay net; 12, nosebag, holding corn; 13, picketing ropes; 14, haversack with man's food; 15, water-bottle; 16, two horse-shoes in leather case; 17, numnah (felt to save horse's back) and horse-blanket under the saddle; 18, halter; 19, halter-rope twisted up.

Cavalry used to be the most important of all "arms," and in the great historical wars cavalry charges usually carried the day. But with the coming of quick-firing rifles their importance has greatly lessened. In recent times they became the "eyes and ears" of the army, and nearly all the scouting was done by them. Though a good deal of scouting is now done by aeroplanes, cycles, and motor cars, it is still the duty of cavalry to precede the main body, and "feel" for the enemy. What is called a "cavalry screen" is pushed forward in the hope of drawing the enemy's fire, and thus showing his position. When cavalry are engaged in this work, they are said to conduct a *reconnaissance*. When our cavalry conduct a reconnaissance, they ride in scattered formation, so as to offer as small a target as possible to the enemy. Unfortunately, in dry weather the advance of such a force is often revealed to the enemy by the clouds of dust raised by the horses' hoofs.

Cavalry held up by Infantry.

This illustration shows a body of German horsemen attempting to attack infantry who have taken cover in a shallow trench. The Germans have had to charge across an open field, and the infantry, by rapid rifle fire, have shot down many of the men and their horses. Only a handful have been able to come within fifty yards of the trench, and these, as you see, have been thrown into confusion. Two of them are holding up the hand in token of surrender. From this drawing you will easily understand that "if infantry keep cool and collected, have plenty of ammunition, and can see the mounted men for some minutes before they arrive at close quarters, they can shoot down horses and troopers, and probably save themselves from being ridden over."

Generally speaking, cavalry secure the main body of the army from surprise. They also do good work by moving rapidly, and occupying positions in which they can hamper or delay the enemy. Sometimes they make raids far behind the enemy's army, and are able to blow up bridges, destroy railways, or capture stores of food and ammunition wagons. Cavalry are perhaps more useful than cyclists and men in motor cars, because they can travel across all kinds of country, while cycles and motor cars are chiefly confined to roads.

Sometimes cavalry are able to take the enemy's artillery unawares, or fall upon his infantry while it is in disorder. When this happens, their charge is very effective; guns are captured, and the infantry is dispersed. If, however, infantry keep cool and collected, have plenty of ammunition, and can see the mounted men for some minutes before they arrive at close quarters, they can shoot down horses and troopers, and probably save themselves from being ridden over. Cavalry has its best chance of success when it suddenly attacks infantry from a flank, and at the same time is secure from being taken in *flank* by the fire of other infantry or machine guns. When cavalry are called upon to charge, they do so in a line of two ranks, with the officers riding in front. Sometimes cavalrymen fight on foot, much as infantry do.

Now let us learn something of the guns and the men who work them. The gunner's weapon is simply a big rifle, very thick as compared with its length, and so heavy that it has to be hauled along by horses or motors. Guns meant for use in the field are mounted on a two-wheeled carriage. When the gun is in action the end of the trail or steel beam at its rear rests on the ground. On the march this trail is lifted up and hooked on to another two-wheeled carriage, called the limber. The four-wheeled carriage thus formed is drawn by six horses, driven by men riding on three of them. Along with every gun there are two carriages for transporting the shell and shrapnel which are fired from it.

Field guns are of various sorts and sizes, according to the work which they have to do. Our Royal Field Artillery is armed with a quick-firing gun, called an eighteen-pounder, because it throws a shot weighing eighteen pounds. This gun is made by winding strong ribbons of steel round a long steel tube. It can throw its charge for about three and a half miles, but it is most effective when the range is not more than about two and a quarter miles.

Most of the guns fire shells which are shaped like bullets, but are, of course, very much bigger. They consist of a hollow steel case, with rings of soft copper, some of which fit into the rifling or grooves of the gun. The shell, like the bullet from a rifle, is given a spinning motion by the grooving in the barrel, and this makes the shot travel point foremost.

Inside the shell there is a high explosive. When the shell reaches its target this substance explodes with such terrific force that it will smash a wall, a house, or an earthwork.

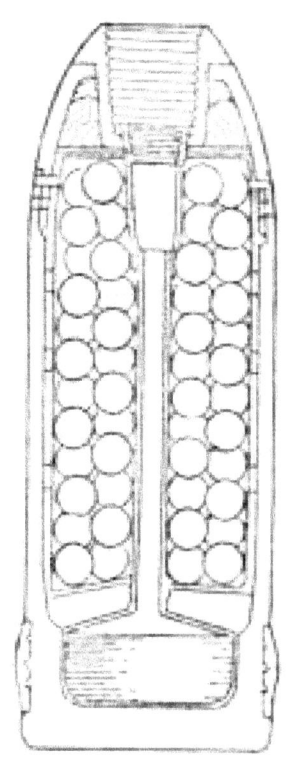

Shrapnel Shell. (Section.)

When the gunners are firing against troops they usually use shrapnel, which is so called from the name of its inventor, the English colonel Henry Shrapnel.[180] This also consists of a thin steel bullet-shaped case, which is divided into two parts. One part of it is filled with round bullets, and in the other part there is a charge of powder. Attached to this charge of powder is a fuse made of a slow-burning material which is lighted by the firing of the gun. The gunners "set" this fuse—that is, they make it of such a length that the burning part will reach the powder when the shell is some distance in front of its target. If a shot is aimed at troops which are two miles away, it will take about ten seconds to reach them. As the gunner wishes the shrapnel to burst about fifty yards before reaching the troops, he makes his fuse of such a length that it will explode the powder in a little less than ten seconds after the shell has left the gun.

Royal Field Artillery in Action. *Photo, Exclusive News Agency.*

Notice that the gun is hidden behind bushes. Sometimes the guns are covered with straw or branches of trees in order to hide them from observers in aeroplanes.

When the powder explodes, it blows out the bullets, which fly forward in a cone-shaped shower. A shrapnel shell contains 375 bullets, and when it has burst they travel fifty yards over a space about five yards wide and fifty yards long. As you may imagine, the bullets work great havoc on men and horses within this area. Sometimes the fuse does not explode the powder at the right time. In order that the shot may not be wasted, it is provided with a cap, which causes the shell to explode when it strikes the ground. A quick-firing gun, such as is used by the Royal Field Artillery, fires about six times a minute. When necessary it can fire much more rapidly than this. As many as twenty shots a minute have been fired from a British field gun.

You already know that the shells and cartridges are carried on wagons, each of which contains one hundred rounds. When a battery goes into action, each section has one of its wagons a few yards behind it. When all the shells and cartridges in that wagon are used, another wagon is brought up. When that is empty, the forty rounds carried in each gun limber are fired, and finally the two rounds in each gun carriage. After that, unless a fresh supply of ammunition is brought up, the gun is useless.

The 75 mm.[181] field gun used by the French is said to be the best in existence. It is a little over 8 feet 1 inch in length, fires a projectile weighing 15-2/3 pounds, and has a range of 7,110 yards. As each piece can fire twenty shots per minute, a perfect hail of shells can be kept up on an enemy's position.

It is a splendid sight to see a Royal Horse battery come into action. The teams advance at the gallop. At the signal "Halt! Section front," the gunners jump down from their seats on the gun carriages and limbers. Two of them lift the trail of the gun off the hook at the back of the limber, and two others man the wheels of the gun; the teams drive on with the limbers, the guns are spun round, and in three seconds are ready for firing.

Before the gun can do its work properly, the range—that is, the distance between the gun and the target—must be found. For this purpose trial shots are fired. The gunners guess the range, and then fire at a point some hundred yards less than the supposed distance. They watch for the puff of smoke which arises when the shell strikes the ground. If they see it in front of their target, they know that the range is short. Then another shell is fired one hundred yards beyond the supposed range. If this falls behind the target, they know that the range is too long. The next shot is fired at a distance midway between the short shot and the long shot, and thus the correct range is found. In order that the puffs of smoke may be distinctly seen, observers are sent forward to the right or left of the line of fire to watch where the shells fall. Sometimes they are provided with telescopic iron ladders, which they mount in order to have a better view. Field telephones are sometimes laid so that the observers can communicate with the batteries.

If an enemy has dug himself in and is firing from concealed trenches, aeroplanes are sent up to spy out the land. When the aviators discover a trench they drop down bits of tinsel, which glitter in the sunshine, or a bomb, which ignites when it strikes the ground, and sends up a cloud of smoke. The gunners then know where their target is. Sometimes the range is found by means of an instrument known as the range-finder. When firing begins the aviator watches the shots, and signals to the gunners until they are aiming correctly. The aeroplanes also discover the position of the enemy's artillery, so that it can be fired at. In order to deceive the airmen, the guns are covered with straw or boughs, so that they cannot be easily detected from above.

Another type of gun which is used in the field is called a *howitzer*. The great difference between the action of an ordinary gun and that of a howitzer is the difference between a boy throwing a stone at a mark which he can see and the same boy pitching a stone over a wall so that it will fall on something hidden from his view. The ordinary field gun has a long flat sweep of fire, and is therefore unable to shoot over hills, trees, or houses, or to drop shells on men lying close beside a bank or in a deep, narrow trench. Field guns can burst their shrapnel so that such men would not dare to look over the bank in front of their trenches and aim their rifles at the enemy, but they cannot actually hit the men in the trenches. In order to do this, the shots must be thrown high into the air, so that they will drop straight down on the trenches. Howitzers are used for this purpose. They are so made that the barrel can be tilted and the shots fired at a high angle.

Heavy German Howitzer for siege work.
(*Photo, Newspaper Illustrations.*)

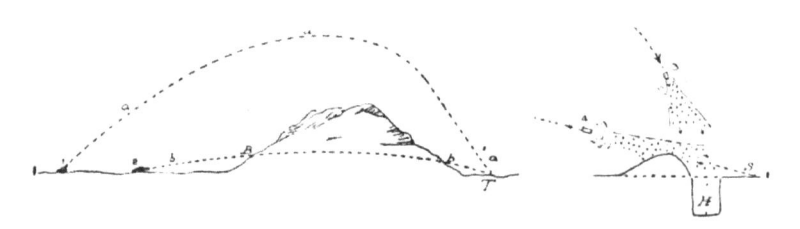

The left-hand picture shows the advantage possessed by a howitzer over a field gun when firing over a hill at some troops at T. I is the howitzer, and *a, a, a* is the track of its shell. 2 is the field gun, and *b, b* would be the path of its shell were it not stopped at B by the hill. The right-hand picture compares the effects on a trench of a shell from a howitzer and a shell from a field-gun. 3 is the howitzer's shrapnel shell bursting and pouring its bullets into the trench; but you will notice that the parapet of earth protects the occupants of the trench from the bullets of the field-gun's shrapnel shell, which is bursting at 4.
Both of these shells are fitted with "time fuses," which make them explode in the air as shown. If they were fitted with "percussion fuses," the howitzer shell would fall to the bottom of the trench, and

explode at H; while the field-gun shell would not burst until it hit the ground at S.

In both pictures the howitzer is firing at a range of 2¾ miles—that is, it is 2¾ miles from the target—and the field gun at a range of 2¼ miles.

You can easily understand that howitzers are very useful when troops are advancing on the enemy. They can be fired behind the advancing line, for the shots from them fly high over the men's heads. Ordinary guns cannot be used at such a time, for they must be in line with the infantry or in front of them. These guns are usually held in reserve until the enemy shows himself. Then they are brought forward, and open fire. The barrel of a howitzer has a wider bore than that of a field gun, and its shell is not so long. The 5-inch howitzer with which the Royal Garrison Artillery is armed is so heavy that eight horses are needed to haul it along good roads. When it is taken over broken country the team must at least be doubled. Six-inch howitzers are also used.

For battering down fortresses very heavy howitzers are brought up. The Germans have reserved as the surprise of this war a howitzer with a calibre of seventeen inches, which throws a huge weight of metal for a tremendous distance. The gun is so heavy that it is provided with caterpillar wheels, and is hauled by motor or by thirty-six or forty horses. It is fired by electricity, and it is said that the gunners stand four hundred yards behind it when it is discharged.

Armoured Train.

(Photo, Central News.)

Guns for firing high at aeroplanes are also used, and some of them are mounted on motor cars. On the railways naval guns are placed on armoured trains, which dash along the line and harass the enemy. Armoured motor cars are sometimes provided with machine guns, but these belong to the infantry, and not to the artillery.

Now let us see what part artillery plays in a modern battle. Its first object is to help the movements of its own infantry, and to harass the movements of the enemy's infantry. Guns are thus the handmaids of infantry. Almost every modern battle opens with what is called an artillery duel. The guns of the one side engage those of the other, so as to keep them busy, and prevent them from hampering the movements of the infantry when they are forming line of battle or are advancing.

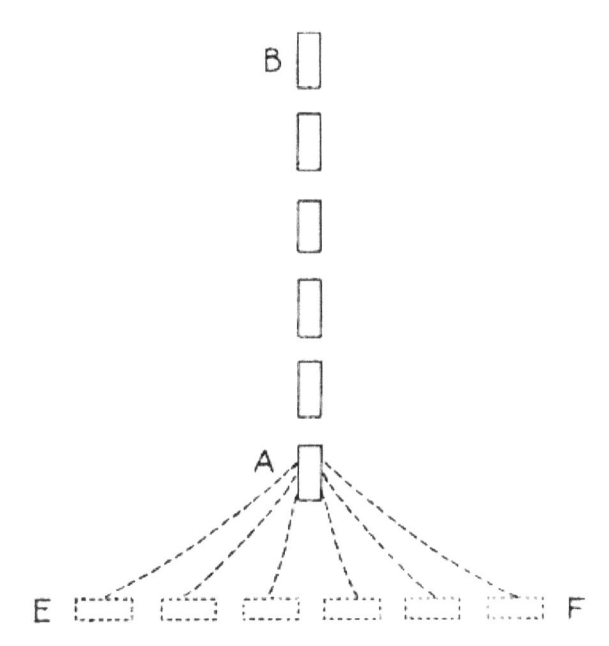

Columns marching along one road and deploying.

Infantry march to the battlefield in columns, one behind the other; but before they can attack they must *deploy*—that is, unfold, open out, and extend into a line so as to face the enemy with their full force. Suppose the six columns, from A to B, are marching along a road, and are required to attack. They must "deploy"—that is, march as shown in the figure to take up the positions indicated by the dotted blocks from E to F. I need not tell you that the deeper the columns are the longer they will take to deploy. A general, therefore, tries to choose a line of advance where there are many more or less parallel roads or railways leading in the desired direction. When his troops move in this way his deployment may be very rapid (see figure below). This is one reason why the Germans violated the neutrality of Belgium. They wished to have as wide a front as possible to advance their troops into France.

When the line E F begins to advance, its guns will bombard the position which it hopes to capture. They will also try to put out of action any guns firing on their troops, and will crush all attempts of the enemy's infantry to make a counter-attack. They thus prepare the way for an advance, and protect the advance while it is being made. If they are successful, their infantry will probably reach the goal in such condition that they can make a bayonet charge. When this time arrives the artillery cannot fire straight forward, because by so doing they will hit their own men. They therefore sweep the ground to the right and left in order to prevent the enemy from making flank attacks on the advancing force. When the position has been won the guns hurry up and begin the business all over again. Always remember that a battle is nothing but a great shooting match, in which both guns and rifles are used.

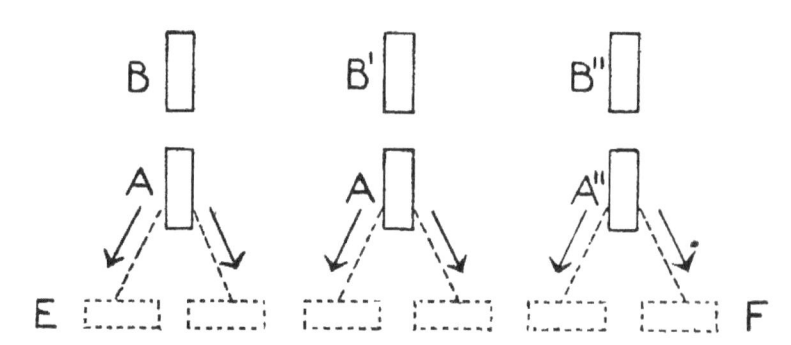

Columns marching along three parallel roads and deploying.

Guns work in groups or batteries of six guns each, and three batteries form a brigade. If you see artillery on the march, you will notice that the guns and their wagons always follow each other, and never go two abreast. In battle the artillery form a line of guns, with about nineteen yards between gun and gun. Three men work each gun, and they are protected by a steel shield. The horses and drivers take cover some distance in the rear of the guns, but within easy reach of them. Artillery officers always try to secure a position in which their guns are not easily seen, and yet have in front of them a large area of open country over which they can direct their fire.

In addition to riflemen, horsemen, and gunners, an army needs other services in order to make it an effective fighting machine. For example, it needs engineers to remove those obstacles in its path which prevent it from advancing quickly and easily. Engineers make roads and light railways, bridge rivers, or blow up bridges in order to delay the enemy. They also make fortifications and set up telegraphs and telephones, so that a general may know what is going on in all parts of his line, and transmit his orders as quickly as possible to the various commanders.

What is called a field company of Engineers is, roughly, of the same strength as an infantry company. It carries with it shovels for digging trenches, axes for cutting down trees, wire for making entanglements, sand-bags for protecting men firing from trenches, explosives, carpenters' and smiths' tools, water-supply stores, signalling apparatus, and the materials for making maps. All these things are carried in four-horsed carts and on the backs of pack animals. Six-horsed wagons are laden with the materials for building bridges, such as pontoons, trestles, planks, and so forth. An Engineer company can erect a bridge across a stream in a very short time, and take it down even more rapidly.

Engineers at work erecting a pontoon bridge over a river. *Photo, Newspaper Illustrations, Ltd.*

An army must be fed, or it cannot fight. This is what Napoleon meant when he said that an army marches on its stomach. The work of bringing food to an army or part of an army is entrusted to a very important branch of the service known as the Army Service Corps. Then there must be a Medical Corps, to look after the sick and wounded; a Flying Corps, for scouting purposes; and a Signalling Corps, to transmit messages from one part of the field to another. Signalling is done by "flag-wagging," by flashes of light sent from mirrors (heliographs[182]) or lamps, or by means of telegraphs, both wire and wireless, and by telephones. Our army is famous all over the world for its expertness in signalling. By means of relays of flag-waggers messages can be conveyed for fifty miles with great speed and certainty.

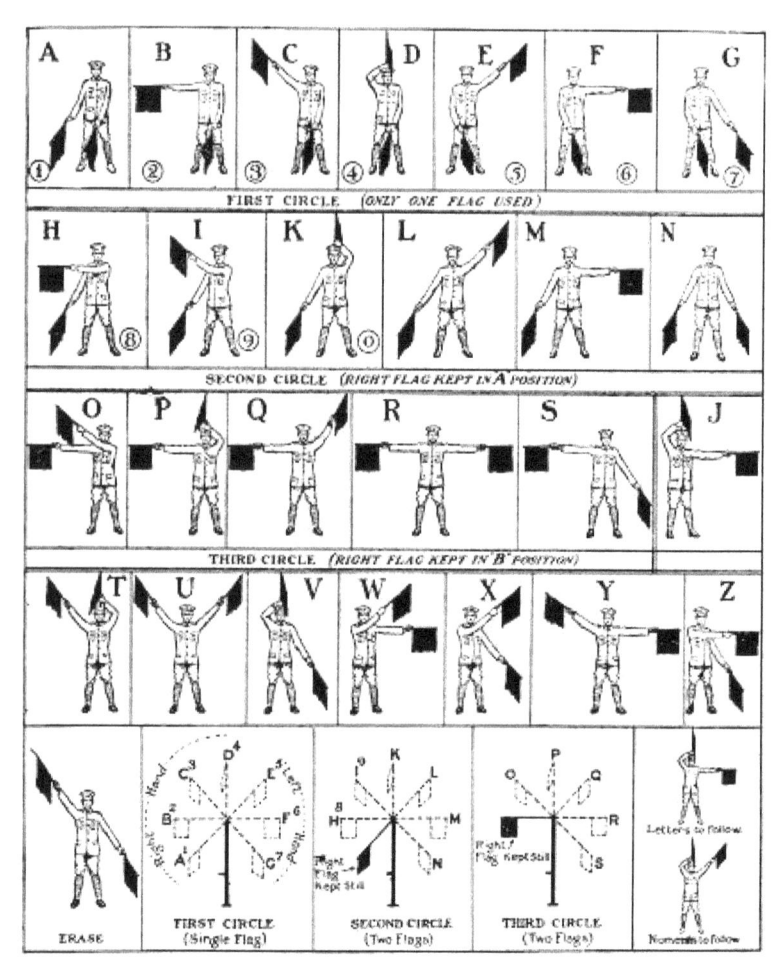

Signalling by means of two flags. Most signalling is now done by means of one flag.

On page 208 you will see a little picture which compares a man with an army. An army in the field is very like a man, as you will plainly see if you study the drawing.

First, let us look at the man's brain. By means of it he thinks, makes his plans, and orders all the movements of his body. What is called the *staff* of an army is the brain of the army. It plans how to outwit the enemy, thinks out ways and means, and controls the movements of all the troops.

Now consider the man's eyes and ears. With these he obtains information as to what is going on around him. Without them he is at the mercy of those who are better provided than he. The eyes and ears of the army are the *Flying*

Corps, the *motor cyclists*, and the *cavalry*. They discover the enemy's movements, and keep the staff well informed of his doings.

When a man is boxing, he usually leads off with a blow at the head from his left arm. We may call his left arm the *artillery*, for with its artillery an army strikes hard and far.

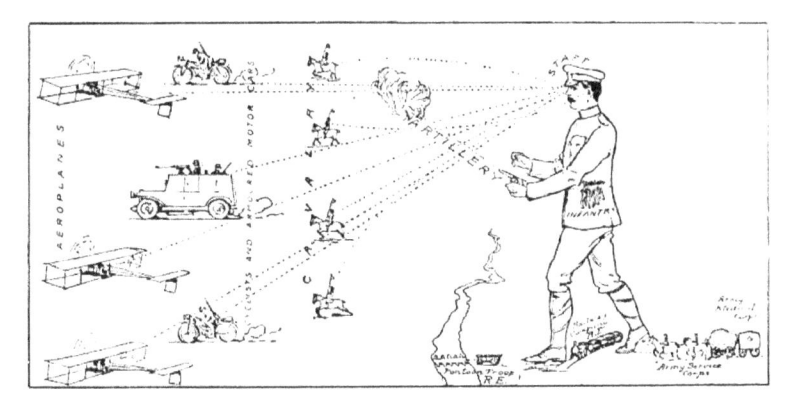

A comparison between a man and an army.

A man's feet enable his body to advance. We may call the *Engineers*, the *Army Service Corps*, and the *Royal Medical Corps* the feet of the army.

There now only remains the man's body, in which lies all his power. The body of an army is the mass of *Infantry* which comprises its chief force.

CHAPTER XX.

SOME MILITARY TERMS.

Before we proceed, we must clearly understand some terms which are used in war. In reading newspapers we frequently meet with the term army corps. A modern army is made up of a certain number of *army corps*, each of which is a complete army in itself. At the beginning of a campaign we may reckon an army corps to consist roughly of 40,000 men of all arms, under the command of a general.

An army corps is divided as a rule into two *divisions*, and each division is also a complete little army in itself.

Study this little table, and you will see the composition of a British division.

	Total Officers and Men.	No. of Horses.	No. of Guns, including Machine Guns.	No. of Vehicles, including those of the Artillery.
1 Headquarters	82	54	—	7
3 Infantry Brigades	12,165	741	24	309
1 Headquarters Divisional Artillery	22	20	—	2
3 Field Artillery Brigades	2,385	2,244	54	240
1 Field Artillery (Howitzer) Brigade	755	697	18	67
1 Heavy Battery and	198	144	4	19

Ammunition Column				
1 Divisional Ammunition Column	568	709	—	110
1 Headquarters Divisional Engineers	13	8	—	3
2 Field Companies of Engineers	434	152	—	102
1 Signal Company	162	80	—	53
1 Cavalry Squadron	159	167	—	9
1 Divisional Train	428	378	—	176
3 Field Ambulances	702	198	—	72
	18,073	5,592	100	1,169

Such a division on the march would cover from head to tail about 15¾ miles.

The supreme head of all the army corps which form an army is a commander-in-chief, or generalissimo, who is assisted by what is called the supreme general staff. The commander-in-chief and his staff are the brain and driving force of the army as a whole. It will interest you to learn how the commander-in-chief and his staff are linked up with every part of the army.

The commander-in-chief and his staff occupy what is called the general headquarters of the army, which is stationed in some town behind the area in which fighting is actually going on. Battles are now waged over so many miles that a commander-in-chief cannot possibly see for himself what is happening all along his line. He has to rely upon others, who bring him or send him information by telegraph, telephone, motor car, motor cycle, or aircraft. All day, and all night too, a constant stream of information as to the movements of the enemy, the position of his own troops, the progress of the fighting, and so forth, arrives at the headquarters of a commander-in-chief, and officers are set apart to receive this information and arrange it so that he may have a clear and full knowledge of all that is going on. Large maps are spread out on tables, and officers are constantly engaged in marking the movements of each side by means of flags or coloured chalks, so that at a glance the situation at any given moment may be seen. It is by the study of these marked maps that the commander and his staff decide what movements the army shall make to resist or attack the enemy.

This picture represents the headquarters of a French division in a village. Notice the cavalry and cyclist scouts and the men receiving messages by telephone. Notice also the officers writing orders and poring over maps.

Each army corps, division, and brigade has a similar headquarters, where the same kind of work is done and information is gathered up to be sent to the general headquarters, or the G.H.Q., as soldiers call it.

As the army moves backwards or forwards, general headquarters is moved from one place to another; but it is always far enough in the rear not to be disturbed by the guns of the enemy, and in such a position that it can easily be in touch with every part of the fighting line. It often happens that the commander wishes to be in closer touch with the operations that are going on, or perhaps he desires to meet his generals in order to consult with them, and to receive their reports in person. For this purpose he has report-centres, or what are called *postes de commandement*, nearer the front than general headquarters. Between the general headquarters and the headquarters of army corps officers constantly travel to and fro in motor cars. They carry messages to the various generals, and, if necessary, explain the commander's wishes to them more fully than could be done in writing.

In Trenches. *Photopress.*

These trenches have been occupied for a considerable time, and much has been done to make them habitable. Notice the parapet behind which the men stand to fire, and the dug-out in which they take refuge when the trench is heavily shelled.

Behind each army corps, and some way in front of general headquarters, but also sufficiently far from the turmoil of the fighting, are the army corps headquarters, which are exactly like general headquarters, though on a smaller scale. Here are stationed the corps commanders and their staffs. They, too, have *postes de commandement* nearer the front, and officers who go to and fro with messages and orders.

The headquarters of each *division* is pushed as far forward as possible without coming within range of the enemy's artillery. In the neighbourhood of divisional headquarters we first see signs that fighting is going on. The soldiers themselves we cannot see, because they are hidden away in villages, in woods, or in folds of the ground. But we shall probably see houses wrecked by the enemy's shells, and strings of wagons moving along the roads with food and ammunition for the fighting men.

Still nearer the fighting line are the *brigade* headquarters, which are usually within range of the enemy's guns. Four or five hundred yards farther on is the irregular line of trenches, occupied by the men engaged in firing on the enemy, or by the supports which are rushed up when the attack becomes too hot for the defenders. When the hostile forces have been facing each other in trenches for some time, the ground which they occupy is seamed with dug-outs, burrows, and holes of all sorts. The line of trenches is fringed with barbed wire, and is broken here and there by what are called "saps"—that is, by narrow trenches which are dug forward from the main trench towards the enemy's trenches.

Between the trenches of the hostile forces is a No Man's Land, strewn with the dead of both sides. When darkness falls, a patrol or a solitary "sniper" creeps out of his trench without a sound, and crawls along this dread space until he reaches some point from which he can, while concealed, examine the enemy's position, or fire with advantage on his foes. All that he can see in the light of the moon is a fringe of wire and long rows of low mounds marking the trenches occupied by the enemy.

Frequently in front of the firing line a secret position is found, which enables an officer or man to observe the enemy's movements. From these observation posts to the headquarters of the battalion, thence to those of the brigade, and onward to the divisional headquarters and the general headquarters, runs a long trail of telegraph wire, through which information is constantly being sent or orders are being transmitted. Away in front of the trenches this wire lies half hidden in the mud by the roadside; farther back it is looped from tree to tree or along the hedges. Still farther back it is carried on slender black-and-white poles, and finally it reaches the general headquarters on permanent posts.

These telegraph wires, you will observe, are just like the nerves which branch out from your brain to the uttermost parts of your body. Along them comes all the information which your brain can receive from outside. Your brain decides what action you will take, and messages flash along the nerves to the muscles which set the various parts of your body in motion. If you think of the commander and his staff as the brain of the army, and of the telegraph, telephone, motor car, motor cycle, and aircraft as the nerves of the army, you will have a good idea of how hundreds of thousands of men are moved and controlled by one master mind.

Another important term which you continually meet with is the word *communications*. Every army moves forward from what is called its base—that is, the place where its ammunition, food, and general supplies are stored. These stores must be continually brought up to the army as it needs them;

otherwise it would starve. There must, then, be a speedy and safe road or system of roads and railways between the army and its base. As the army advances this *line of communications* becomes longer and longer. It must be kept safe from the attacks of the enemy: for if a part of it between the *base* and the *army* were to be captured, the army would be cut off from its food and stores; and if it could not find a new line of communication, it would very soon be forced to surrender. Large numbers of soldiers are required to guard these lines of communications. You may think of them as the air-tube which supplies a diver with air. If by any means the air-tube should be cut or stopped up, the diver must immediately come to the surface, or perish.

Along the lines of communication there is a constant coming and going. Food, ammunition, general supplies, and new bodies of men are continually passing from the base to the front, and the wounded and the empty trains are continually being moved from the front to the base. When an army so spreads out that it has a wide front, it must have several parallel lines of communication, so as to keep itself supplied with the necessities of war.

So vastly important are these lines of communication that the opposing generals strive to cut them, and by so doing deprive their enemy of his supplies of food and ammunition.

Another important way in which a general seeks to overcome his enemy is by breaking through the line opposed to him in one or more places. If he succeeds in doing this, he has no longer a strong, united force opposed to him, but two or more fragments which he can overcome separately with his own united and unbroken force.

There are two ways of breaking an enemy's line. The first way is by holding the enemy all along his line, and suddenly bringing against one part of it a large, powerful force. If this force breaks through, it divides the opposing army, and can beat it in detail. Such an attack is known as a *frontal attack*. Napoleon tried it at Waterloo, but could not break through the "thin red line" of Wellington's heroes.

The other way of breaking the enemy's line is to *outflank* it, and then *envelop* or surround his forces. I have already used the word *flank* several times in these pages. It simply means the side or wing. If a man attacks you when you are sideways, you cannot well resist him. In order to do so you must turn your face towards him. So it is with an army. If it is attacked on its side or wing, it cannot properly resist until it forms a line facing the attacker. While it is doing this it runs the risk of being thrown into confusion, and perhaps destroyed.

Look at the diagram on p. 216. Let A-F be a British force, and *a-f* a German force equal in strength. While these forces are fighting front to front, suppose a new British force, G H I, should appear, and attack the flank *a*. It is clear that the soldiers at *a* can only defend themselves if they swing round to meet the attack of G H I. If they remain where they are, they will very soon have the foe behind them as well as in front of them, and they will then be between two fires, in which case they can hardly escape destruction.

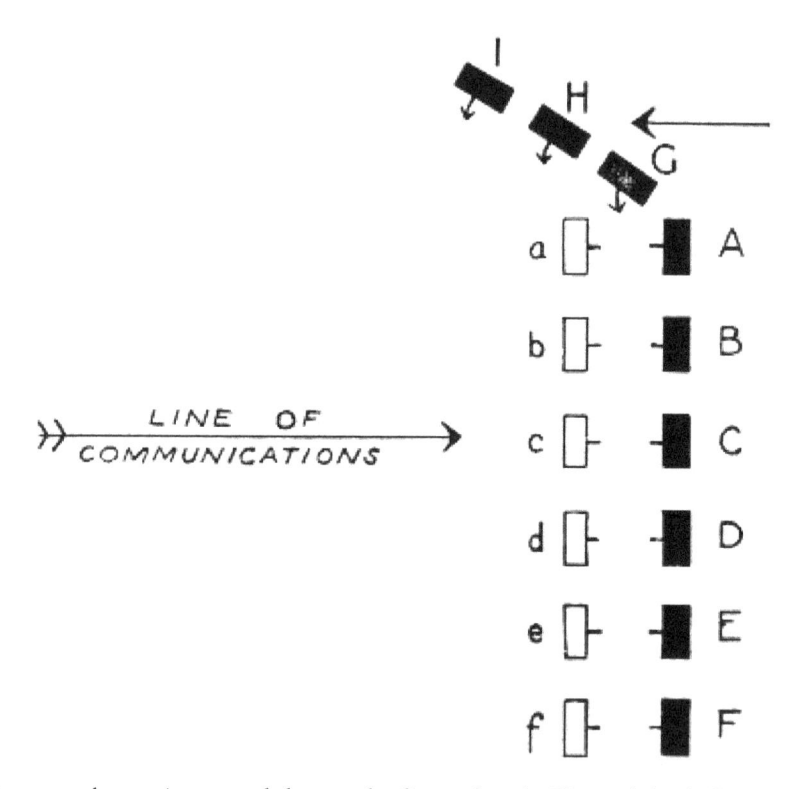

Suppose they swing round the two bodies *a*, *b*, as in Figure 1 (p. 217) to meet G H I, what happens? The German line is weakened. Instead of having six bodies to meet six bodies, they have now only four to oppose the six of the attacking force. Immediately E F will try to take *f* in flank, and soon the line will assume the position shown in Figure 2 (p. 217). You can easily see that the line of the enemy's communications is now in danger, and that if the movement continues the whole force will be surrounded. You will remember that the Germans managed to surround a large French army at Sedan and force it to surrender.[183] When a general finds himself being outflanked by a superior force, he is bound to retreat and straighten out his line again, if he is to save himself from disaster.

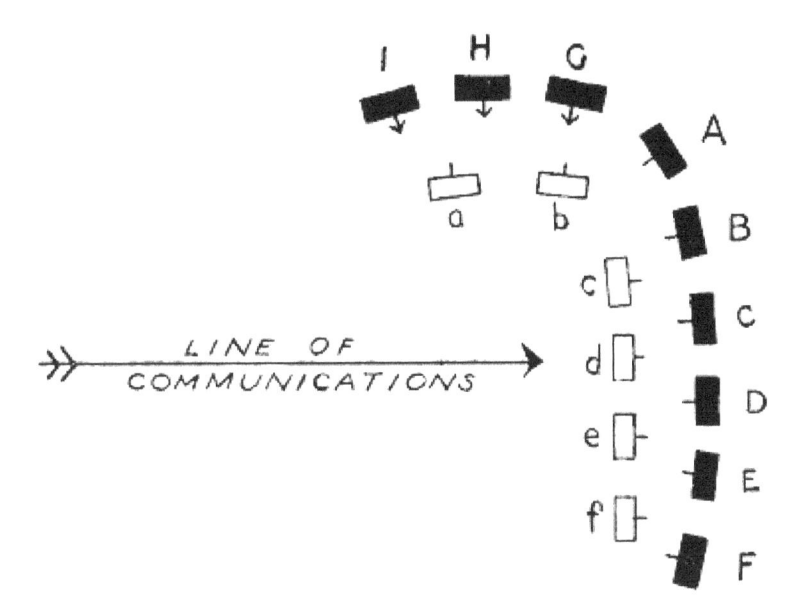

Fig. 1.

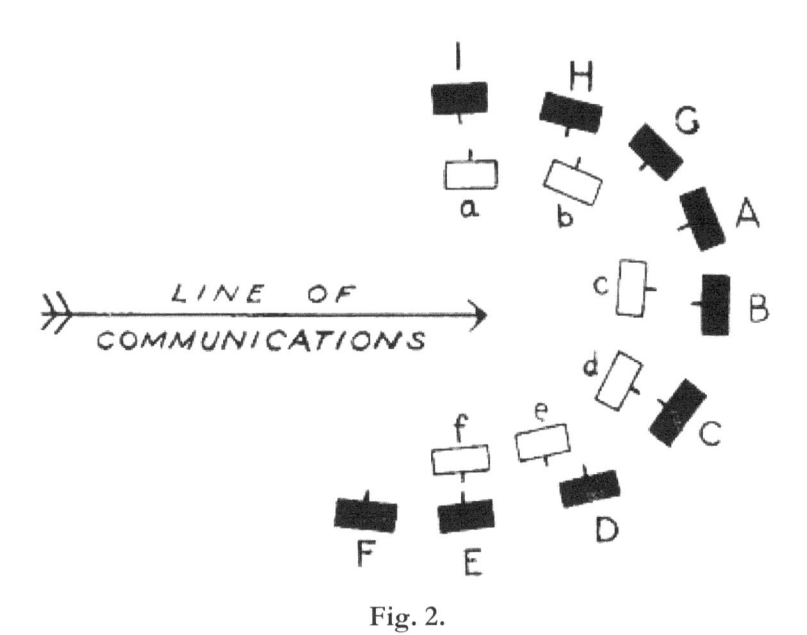

Fig. 2.

In reading war news you will often meet with the word *strategy*, which means the art of generalship, of moving and arranging great bodies of troops in order to put the enemy at a disadvantage, and so overcome him. I have given you some examples of strategy above.

Do you play draughts? When you do so, you and your opponent resemble the generals of two opposing armies. You think out every move of the game, and your object in making the move is to capture all your opponent's men, or to hem them in so that they cannot move without being taken. This is *strategy*, but the strategy of war is a far more puzzling business. In the game of draughts all the men are of the same value at the beginning, and you can only move them along certain fixed paths laid down by the rules. All the moves are open and above board, and if you and your opponent are equally skilful at the game, neither of you ought to be taken by surprise. The better strategist will win, or, if you are equally good, the game will end in a draw.

In the great game of war the opposing generals have to deal with men of flesh and blood, and not with wooden pieces. These men are bodies of infantry, cavalry, and artillery, which do different kinds of work on the battlefield, and move at different speeds. Before the general can make his first move—which may be the successful move or the fatal move—he must study the map of the country in which he is to operate, and must choose the line or lines of his advance, always taking care to have good and well-protected communications in his rear. Though he may fix on his plan of campaign beforehand, he must always be ready with another, to suit altered circumstances. Then he must calculate carefully the time which each "arm" will take to come into its required position, and in order to do this he must know the kinds of roads over which the men are to march, and the state they are in. And at the same time he must get all the information possible about the strength and movements of his enemy. He must form an idea of what the opposing general is aiming at, and must make arrangements to thwart him. He must make his moves as silently and secretly as possible, and whenever he can he must put his enemy on a false scent, so that he may fall upon him unawares. You can easily understand from this very imperfect account of a general's duty that he must be a man of great powers of mind and of much experience in war.

The commander-in-chief along with his staff settles the strategy, but the commanders of divisions, and battalions, and squadrons, and batteries must carry his plans into effect. The art of doing this is known as *tactics*. The way in which the battle line is formed at a particular place, the manner in which cavalry or artillery are used for a particular purpose, and generally the methods by which marches are conducted, camps are laid out, fortifications are made, and the actual fighting is done, come under the head of *tactics*. It has been well said that the art of strategy consists in getting two men to a place where only one man is ready to oppose them. The arrangements by which the two men would best attack the one man when they meet him, or by which the one man could resist the two, belong to the art of tactics.

CHAPTER XXI.

THE INVASION OF BELGIUM.

You already know that the Germans thought it a matter of life and death to get into France and strike a decisive blow as speedily as possible. For this reason they meant to make their way through Belgium. We know that they had long intended to take this route when they went to war with France. Along that part of their frontier which marches with Belgium they had built many railways, so that troops might be brought rapidly to the border. At all the stations, even those of small towns, long platforms, often five or six hundred yards long, and special sidings, had been made, so that men and guns could be rapidly detrained within a few miles of Belgian soil. Ever since the time of Frederick the Great, German soldiers have believed that the worst place to make war is their own country, and the best the enemy's.

On Sunday evening, 2nd August, the German Government sent a long message to the Belgian Government, declaring that the French were going to march through Belgium to attack Germany, and that it feared the Belgians would be unable to resist them. It had, therefore, decided to enter Belgium, so as to anticipate the attack of the enemy. This statement, as you know, was quite untrue. The French had never intended to do anything of the kind.

Then the message went on to say that the German Government would keenly regret if Belgium should consider the proposed invasion as an unfriendly act. If Belgium would agree to let the Germans pass through unopposed, they would promise neither to take away the independence of Belgium nor to deprive her of any of her territory, and would pledge themselves to leave the country as soon as peace was made. They would pay ready cash for any provisions that their troops might need, and would make good any damage that they might do. If, however, the Belgians should oppose the German soldiers in any way, especially by firing on them from the forts on the Meuse, or by destroying roads, railways, or tunnels, they would be compelled to consider Belgium an enemy, and when the country was conquered they would hold it as their own. The message ended by hoping that Belgium would do as Germany wished, and that the friendly relations which united the two neighbouring nations would become closer and more lasting. Belgium was given only twelve hours in which to reply—that is, until 7 a.m. the next day.

Can you imagine a more anxious twelve hours for the Belgian King and Government? Here was a little unoffending state of seven and a half millions of people, with a little army of about 263,000 men, threatened by a state of 67,000,000 of people, with the most powerful, the best organized, and the best prepared army the world has ever seen. The Belgians knew full well that, if they resisted, they could not hope to overcome the vast hordes that would be hurled against them. They knew that they would be at the mercy of a ruthless conqueror; that thousands of their people would be slain; that their fair fields would be trodden down, their industries destroyed, their homes rendered desolate, and perhaps the name of Belgium blotted out of the book of nations. Had they bowed the head and cried, "We are weak and you are terribly strong; pass on, we dare not resist you," no one could have blamed them. But to their eternal honour they did no such thing. The Belgian ministers met during the night, and about four in the morning returned the noble reply that they were ready to fight to the death to maintain their independence; that they were prepared to perish as a nation rather than sell their freedom. Never before has a nation made such a heroic choice. At one bound little Belgium rose to grandeur. She threw aside all thought of self, and prepared to suffer for the right. And she has already reaped her reward. All the nations of the world, outside Germany and Austria, have united to do her honour. She has written her name high on the scroll of history in letters of gold that can never fade.

"Wherever men are staunch and free,
There shall she keep her fearless state,
And, homeless, to great nations be
The home of all that makes them great."

In times of peace Belgium is much divided by political strife. In the face of the great danger which now threatened her, all parties united as one man and prepared for the terrible struggle. The head and front of the nation in this desperate endeavour was the "hero king," Albert, nephew of Leopold II. "A country that defends itself," he said, "cannot perish."

When he ascended the throne, in December 1909, he was almost a stranger to his people. They knew little more of him than that he was a tall man, a student, very intelligent, shy, and simple in manner and tastes, and that he had travelled widely, and had striven hard to make himself acquainted with the daily life of the Belgian people. One day the Press would tell of the Prince going down a coal-mine; another day of his driving a railway engine; again another day of his mountaineering exploits in the Tyrol.[184] His wife was a Bavarian princess, who had qualified as an oculist.

When he became king he soon won the favour, and indeed the admiration, of his people. So divided were the Flemings of the northern provinces and the Walloons of the southern provinces that it seemed likely they would set up separate governments. The king, however, acted as umpire and peacemaker, and by his wisdom and tact saved Belgium from this misfortune.

Then there was trouble with regard to Belgium's great African possession, the Congo Free State.[185] In this matter, too, King Albert was able to bring peace out of discord. So popular did he become that the Belgian Socialists said, "When Belgium becomes a republic, Albert will be its first president."

King George walking with King Albert in the main street of a Belgian town.

(*Photo, Newspaper Illustrations, Ltd.*)

He also threw himself whole-heartedly into the work of army reform. His father had clearly seen that, sooner or later, a war cloud would burst over Europe, and he had persuaded Parliament to agree to two important military measures. One was the building of forts along the Meuse; the other was the reform and increase of the army, which was then small in numbers and far from good in quality. At that time all men of military age were liable to serve in the army; but as only a certain number was needed, the men drew lots, and those on whom the lots fell were obliged to serve. But any man so chosen by lot could buy a substitute to take his place, and in this way the well-to-do men escaped service. King Leopold put an end to this system, and, just before his death, signed a law which made Belgian gentlemen and farmers serve their country in their own person. The army, which was soon to be at death grips with the Germans, was recruited partly under the old system and partly under the new. The new contingents, however, were not properly supplied with weapons and equipment, nor was the artillery well prepared for the terrible task which awaited it.

CHAPTER XXII.

HOW LIÉGE WON THE LEGION OF HONOUR.

On the next page you will see a map of Belgium. I want you to examine it carefully. You will notice that Belgium's real line of defence on the south and east is the river Meuse. After the war of 1870-71 the great military engineer, Brialmont,[186] was called upon to fortify the Meuse valley in such a way that an enemy advancing from the south or east might at least be delayed until other nations could come to the help of Belgium. He had already made Antwerp the chief citadel of the country.

In the neighbourhood of Liége the Meuse runs in a deep wide trench between masses of upland. On the north lies a tableland which extends for fifty miles to the neighbourhood of Louvain. On the east and south is the hill country of the Ardennes, a land of ridges and forests seamed by swiftly running streams, and sinking eastwards to the plains of the Rhine. The tableland to the north is flat, and is covered with fields of beetroot and cereals. An invader can cross it with ease. But the hill region to the east and south is too rough and broken for large armies to traverse without considerable difficulty. From the map you can readily see that the easy road from Germany into Belgium lies between the northern limit of the Ardennes and the Dutch frontier. Here stands Liége, and Brialmont naturally chose it as the site of a great fortress which should bar the way from Germany.

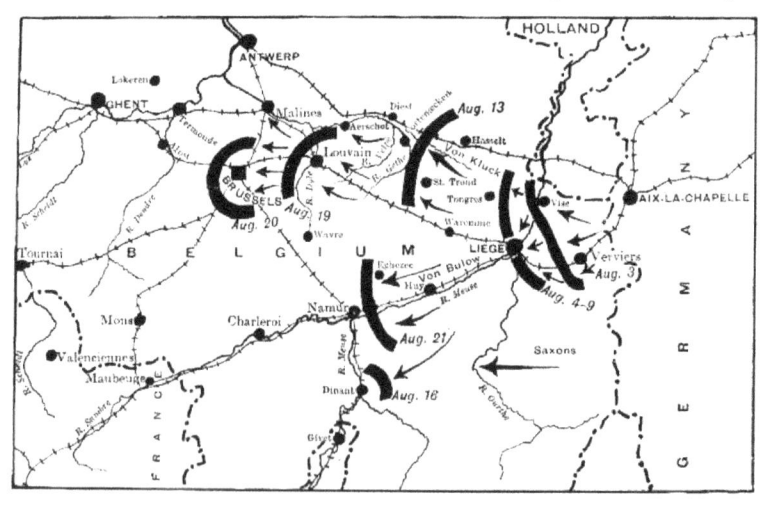

Map illustrating the War in Belgium (Aug. 9-20).

The sides of the wide valley in which the Meuse runs are sharply cut, and are clothed for the most part with scrub, oak, and beeches. Here we find the Black Country of Belgium, the chief coal-mining district of the country, where the smoke from many factory and colliery chimney-stacks darkens the sky. The chief centre of this Black Country is Liége, which stands in a strikingly picturesque situation on the lofty banks of the broad Meuse not far from its junction with the Ourthe. Most of the city stands on the left bank of the river, and here we find noble public buildings, stately churches, pretty parks, broad boulevards, and spacious streets. On the right bank is the industrial quarter, with many factories and the homes of the workers. There is an island in the river, by means of which several bridges unite the two portions of the city. Firearms are largely manufactured by the people in their own homes; and zinc foundries, engine shops, motor-cycle works, a gun factory, a cannon foundry, and flax-spinning mills give employment to thousands of other workmen. The inhabitants are Walloons, who have always been renowned for their independence and love of freedom.

Brialmont fortified Liége by building around it a series of twelve forts in a ring some ten miles across. From the little plan on page [236](#) you will see that these forts were at distances varying from 6,500 yards to 10,000 yards from the centre of the city. In the old days forts were strong castles, usually built on a high rock or hill; but when guns of great range and force came into use, engineers sank their forts into the earth as much as possible. To outward appearance a Liége fort seemed to be nothing but a low, grassy mound rising from a deep ditch. The mound was cased in with concrete and masonry, and its top was broken by a pit in which was fitted a "cupola," or gun-turret, which could be made to slide up and down by means of a piston. When the cupola was down, nothing was visible but the low mound; when it was up, the muzzles of the guns were seen sticking out of portholes. Inside this great molehill were the quarters for the garrison, the machinery for moving the guns and cupolas, the ammunition and supply stores, the electric-lighting arrangements, and the ventilating fans. The engineers and gunners entered and left the fort by means of a tunnel. You will see a diagram showing the structure of one of the most powerful of the Liége forts on page 229.

Brialmont meant the various forts which defended Liége to be joined to each other by means of trenches and gun-pits, so as to prevent the enemy from rushing in between them at night or in misty weather. Unfortunately these lines of trenches were never completed. Nevertheless the position was thought to be one of the strongest in Europe. Five years ago a German general reported that his army had no gun strong enough to destroy one of the Liége forts, and added that such a gun must be made. We shall soon see that his advice was taken.

Turn to the map on page 226, and find the position of Aix-la-Chapelle,[187] which the Germans call Aachen. It is an important military centre of Germany, and is on the great railway route from Berlin to Paris. Follow the railway, and you will see that it curves round by way of Verviers, and then runs along the valley of the Vesdre to Liége. As the crow flies, Aix-la-Chapelle is only twenty-five miles from Liége. About the same distance south of Aix-la-Chapelle is Malmedy,[188] the German Aldershot, where several army corps are always in training. About three years ago the Germans persuaded the Belgian Government to let them make a branch line connecting Malmedy with the Belgian railway system at the little town of Stavelot.[189]

On the morning of Tuesday, 4th August, German advance guards suddenly seized Stavelot and began to march upon Liége from the south-eastward. At the same time, troops from Aix-la-Chapelle crossed the frontier and occupied Verviers.[190] Picked soldiers in motor cars were also hurried across the plain towards Visé.[191] The invasion of Belgium had begun. Before the vast armies of Germany could advance, Liége must be captured. The eastern forts of the city commanded all the railways, and all the roads but one, and that was the road leading from Aix-la-Chapelle to Visé. The Germans expected little opposition from the Belgians, and believed that they had an easy task before them. There were no Belgian soldiers on the frontier to oppose them, and they advanced unmolested. They tried to make friends with the people in the towns and villages through which they passed; but many of the townsfolk and villagers at once fled by road and rail into Holland or towards Brussels.

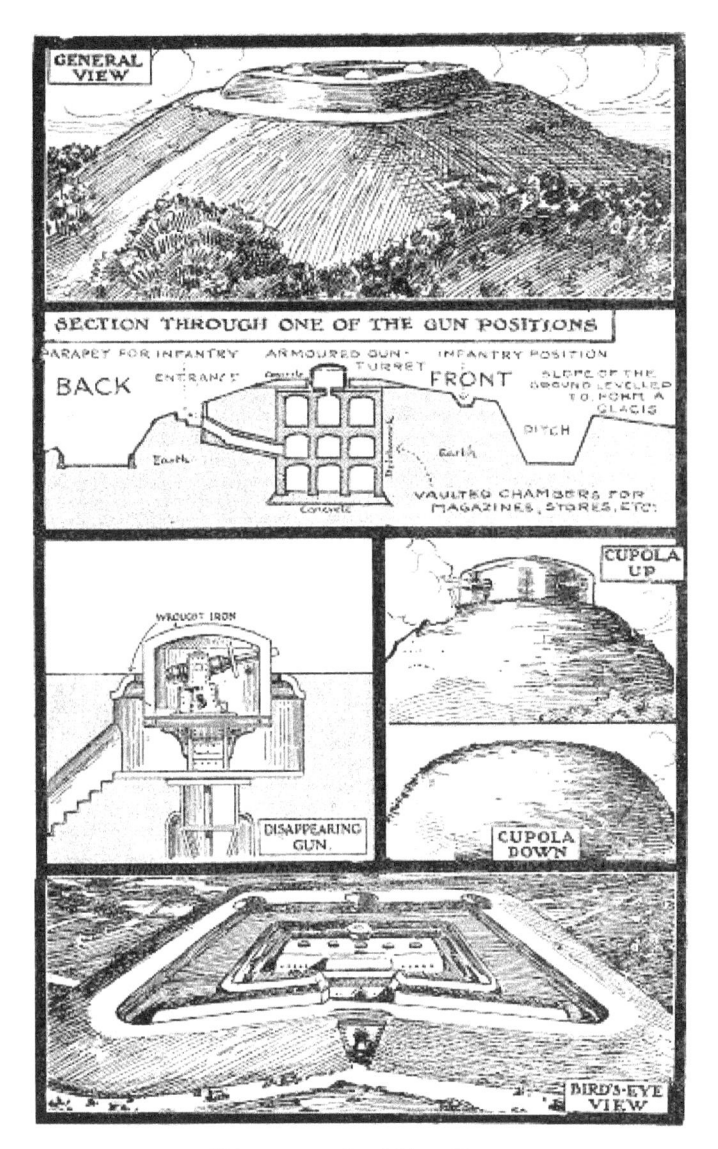

Diagram of a Liége Fort.

At this time the Belgian army was mobilizing along the line of the river Dyle,[192] to the east of Brussels. At midnight on the 4th of August the church bells were still ringing to call the soldiers to arms, and dogs were being collected to draw the machine guns. When news arrived that the Germans were marching on Liége a division and a brigade were hurried to the city; but, along with the Civic Guard of the town, they did not number more than 20,000 men. It had long been known that at least 50,000 men were needed to hold the forts and the intervals between them. It was a "scratch" force that attempted the task—infantry of the line, in their blue and white dress; cavalry in their peaked caps, green and yellow uniform, and flowing capes; and the Civic Guard,[193] in their high round hats and red facings. Already gangs of colliers and navvies were at work digging trenches and throwing up breastworks, and already houses, spinneys, and even churches in the line of fire from the guns of the forts were being levelled to the ground. Engineers were also at work blowing up bridges, viaducts, and tunnels in the Belgian Ardennes, so as to prevent the enemy from using the railways. By the afternoon of Wednesday, 5th August, the Belgians held in strength the line of the south-eastern forts, and cavalry covered the gap between the most northerly of these forts and the Dutch border. The army was under the command of General Leman,[194] an officer of Engineers, who had worked under Brialmont. He was a grave, silent man, more than sixty years of age, and was highly respected by his fellow-countrymen. Every Belgian in the trenches was a patriot, eager to defend his country, his wife, children, and home with his life.

Wednesday morning (5th August) dawned hot and rather dull. Soon the sound of firing was heard north of Liége. It came from the neighbourhood of the little town of Visé, where Belgian troops were holding the crossing of the Meuse. Watchers on the high ground above Liége saw black clouds of smoke drifting along the river. German guns were pounding the little town, and the shells had set fire to the houses. The Belgians, however, held the bank of the river and the houses near it with great bravery. They had blown up the bridges, and the enemy was forced to build others. In one place a number of Belgian troops lay concealed while a pontoon was being erected, and just as the work was completed they opened fire. The bridge was destroyed, and with it many of the engineers who were building it. After fierce fighting the Belgians were obliged to withdraw, and the Germans entered Visé.

General von Emmich, commanding the German Army in Belgium.

Every one expected that the main attack on Liége would come from this direction; but it began after dark next day on the southern side, along the wooded heights broken by the course of the little river Ourthe. About 11.30 p.m. shells came screaming through the darkness, and burst over the southern forts. The German guns were some three miles away, and they were firing in the blackness of the night at targets which they could not see. Nevertheless, by means of large-scale maps, they were able to aim their guns with great accuracy, and shell after shell exploded on the ramparts of the forts. Their heavy siege pieces had not yet come up, and they were using their field guns. The shells fired from them were filled with some high explosive which gave forth a bright greenish light as they burst. The guns of the forts replied to the German fire; but they probably did little damage, as the enemy's guns were carefully concealed. For nearly three hours the bombardment continued.

Towards three in the morning of 6th August a rattle of infantry fire was heard in the woods on both sides of the river Ourthe. The Germans were advancing to attack the trenches between Fort Boncelles and Fort Embourg. Parties of Belgians were sent forward to check them, but were driven back, and just as dawn was breaking the Germans bore down on the trenches in dense masses, shoulder to shoulder, believing that they could carry them by sheer force of numbers. Upon these closely-knit ranks the Belgians poured volley after volley, cutting wide lanes through them until the dead were heaped high before the trenches. "It was death in haystacks," said a Belgian soldier, who played his part in the fight.

Again and again, like sheep driven to the slaughter, the Germans advanced, while the Belgian rifles cracked and the guns of the forts thundered. Again and again they were driven back, and more than once, when the Germans were but fifty yards away and the whites of their eyes could be seen, the Belgians left their trenches and swept the foe before them at the point of the bayonet. At the sight of the gleaming steel many of the Kaiser's men turned and ran or held up their hands and surrendered. At eight in the morning they withdrew, and the wearied Belgians cheered and cheered again, for they had won a victory.

Meanwhile, however, the fort of Fléron[195] had been silenced. A shell had burst on the turret, and had smashed the machinery of the cupola. A furious bombardment was also kept up on Fort Chaudfontaine,[196] at the point where the railway line from Aix-la-Chapelle passes through a tunnel. The German artillery fire reduced the fort to a heap of ruins, but it never surrendered. Its heroic commander blocked the tunnel by causing railway engines to collide within it, and then, in order that the German flag should never fly over even the broken remains of his fort, he set fire to his ammunition magazine, and thus completed its destruction. The fall of Chaudfontaine opened up the railway to the invaders.

Long ago Julius Cæsar wrote, "Bravest of all peoples are the Belgæ." One who knows the Belgian soldier well says: "Greater even than my admiration of his careless courage is my liking for the man. For all his manhood, he has much of the child in him; he is such a chatterbox, and so full of laughter; and never are his laugh and his chaff so quick as when he has the sternest work in hand. Unshaven, mud-bespattered, hungry, so tired that he can hardly walk or lift his rifle to his shoulder, he will bear himself with a gallant gaiety which I think is quite his own, and altogether fascinating." No doubt in the eyes of the Germans the Belgian soldiers, almost untrained, clothed in a quaint jumble of curious uniforms, slovenly in appearance, and without any of the smartness of the drill-ground, appeared absurd; but they were patriots, every man of them, fighting freely, and indeed gladly, for all that they held dear.

During the fighting which I have just described, a lad of nineteen actually managed to capture a German general single-handed. When the general surrendered, his captor found that he was carrying a satchel containing not only papers but six thousand pounds in notes and gold. The young Belgian handed over the money to the Red Cross Society, to aid it in its splendid work of tending the wounded. He kept for himself, however, the satchel and the general's silver helmet.

While the forts were being bombarded, an examination was going on at the university. Most of the candidates finished their papers, and then trooped from the hall to the battlefield, where many of them lay dead a few hours later.

During that day and the next the Germans tried to "rush" the forts by hurling dense masses of men against them. Let me tell you the story of one of these attacks, from the lips of a Belgian officer.

"As line after line of the German infantry advanced we simply mowed them down. It was terribly easy, monsieur, and I turned to a brother officer of mine more than once and said, 'Voilà![197] they are coming on again, in a dense, close formation. They must be mad!' They made no attempt at deploying, but came on, line after line, almost shoulder to shoulder, until, as we shot them down, the fallen were heaped one on top of the other in an awful barricade of dead and wounded men that threatened to mask our guns and cause us trouble. I thought of Napoleon's saying, if he said it, 'It is magnificent, but it is not war.' No, it was slaughter—just slaughter!...

"But, would you believe it, this wall of dead and dying actually enabled these wonderful Germans to creep closer, and actually charge up the glacis! They got no farther than half-way, for our Maxims and rifles swept them back. Of course, we had our own losses, but they were slight compared with the carnage inflicted upon our enemies."

On Thursday, 6th August, most of the forts were still holding out; but the Germans had brought up two more army corps from the south and southeast, and it was now clear that the garrison of Liége was too small in numbers to hold the forts and the intervals between them. At nightfall, though the forts remained intact, bodies of German troops pushed through the spaces between the two forts which look south-east towards the German frontier. On the morning of the 7th it was discovered that a considerable force of Germans had got within the ring of forts, and was in the town of Liége itself. Nevertheless, until the forts were silenced the roads and railways which they commanded could not be used, and the German advance was, therefore, held up.

General von Emmich,[198] who was in command of the German forces, now brought up 8.4-inch howitzers, and probably one or two still heavier mortars, and began a furious cannonade of the forts. These guns fired shells which burst with such terrible power that they crashed through twelve feet of concrete, and crushed the sides of the forts as though they were sand castles on the seashore. They howled through the air, exploded with a terrific thunderclap, and then gigantic clouds of dust and smoke arose above the trembling ground. Nothing could resist them; the forts of Liége were doomed as soon as the Germans brought up their siege guns.

Yet, terrible as the cannonade was, the garrisons of the forts stuck to their guns with marvellous courage. Here is a passage from the diary of an officer who served in one of the forts during that awful time:—

"*At 8 p.m.*—Two German officers asking us in French to surrender. This is about what they said: 'You've been able to judge of the formidable power of our guns; you have been struck by 278 shells; but we have still bigger and more powerful guns, and they will destroy you in a moment. Surrender!' Reply of our officers was, 'Our honour forbids us to surrender; will resist to the end.' Our men all cheered."

Think of it—"Our men all cheered." Though the great shells were smashing the forts to pieces and grinding them to powder, though the solid concrete was crumbling into dust, and the place was strewn with dead and dying, their honour forbade them to surrender, and when their officer told the enemy so, the doomed men cheered. Never was greater courage shown.

Bringing Provisions to Forts.

Photo, Central News.

By the evening of the 6th General Leman had decided that his troops could make no further resistance, and that they would be shut up in Liége unless they were got away at once. He therefore ordered them to fall back from the city towards the Dyle, and so hurried was their retreat that they had only time to blow up one of the twelve Meuse bridges, and were obliged to leave an ambulance train and some twenty engines in the railway station. But the army had done its work. It had made a great and gallant stand; it had proved that the Germans were not invincible, and had won priceless time for the Allies. A time-table found on a German showed that they proposed to be in Brussels on 3rd August, and in Lille on 5th August. Already they were three days behind time. Not only had the gallant little Belgian army upset the German time-table, but it had inflicted such loss on the enemy that on the evening of

Friday, 7th August, General von Emmich asked for a truce of twenty-four hours in which to bury his dead. This was refused.

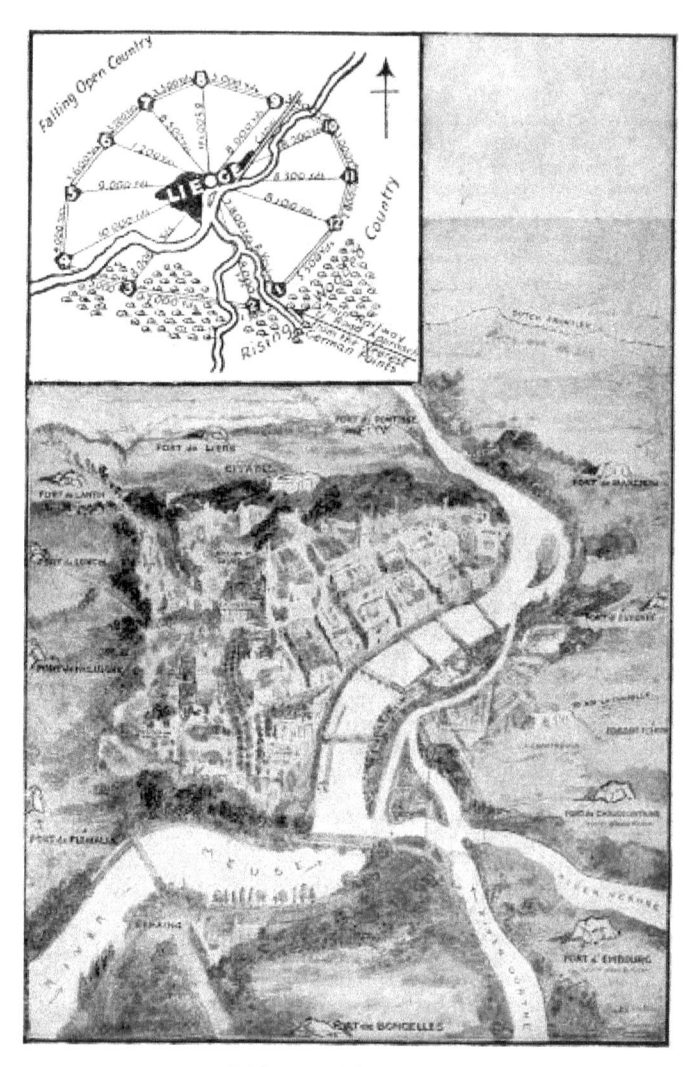

Liége and its Forts.

Note that the forts are not shown in their proper positions, but only indicate their direction with reference to the city.
(*By permission of the Illustrated London News.*)

The city of Liége was now in the hands of the Germans. The cannonade had done but little harm to the buildings of the city; the inhabitants had taken to their cellars, and but few of them had been killed. When the German infantry marched in, the Burgomaster and the Bishop arranged terms with them. They behaved themselves well, and paid for all supplies. The people of Liége were surprised to see how young the German troops were, and how spick and span they looked in their new greenish-gray uniforms. They were housed in barracks, schools, convents, and other public buildings, and good order was kept.

Now that Liége was in their hands, vast quantities of stores were poured into the city, and brigade after brigade came flocking in from North Germany. The hill roads of the Ardennes were choked with troops and convoys; the railways which the Belgians had destroyed were repaired, and over these, and over the undamaged lines from Luxemburg, came an almost endless stream of men, guns, and supplies.

Meanwhile the Germans were able to attack all the forts on the right bank of the river from the rear. These soon fell; but those on the west of the city still held out. The most powerful of them was Fort Loncin, situated on the great main road to Brussels. On 11th August the bombardment of this fort began. A German officer with signal flags advanced up to about two hundred yards from it, and directed the fire of the big guns. During the whole night, at intervals of ten minutes, the Germans threw their shells into the fort, causing great damage. The outer works were destroyed, and the armour plating of the windows was crushed. All the outer works were so filled with the fumes from the shells that the men were driven into the fort. Soon the suffocating smoke found its way inside, and almost choked the men working the guns.

Fort Loncin after Bombardment. *Photo, Alfieri Picture Service.*

On the morning of the 15th the end came. A large number of heavy German guns were trained on the fort, and they literally smothered it with explosive shells. The vault occupied by General Leman and his staff suffered terrific blows which made the whole place tremble. The ventilating apparatus was destroyed, and the room was filled with deadly fumes and dust. During an interval in the firing the general left the fort to view the awful destruction around him. When the bombardment began again he started to return to the vault, but had hardly moved a few paces when a strong and powerful rush of air threw him to the ground. He rose and tried to go, but was kept back by a flood of poisonous fumes which nearly suffocated him. Then he tried to save the garrison, but fell down in a swoon, and was discovered by the enemy pinned to the ground by fallen beams. When he recovered he found himself in the hands of the Germans, who gave him water, and carried him from the ruins which he had so nobly defended.

At the moment when he was stricken down the fort was blown up, and the Germans scrambled over the broken masses of concrete. Suddenly from one of the galleries which the explosion had not wrecked came the sound of shots. The Germans stopped in their advance. By the light of their torches they saw, massed at the end of the corridor, all that was left of the garrison. Black with powder, their faces streaked with blood, their clothes in ribbons, their hands grasping their shattered rifles, stood twenty-five men, all prepared to sell their lives dearly. Touched by the sight of such splendid heroism, the Germans made no attempt to attack. Instead of firing, they flung aside their weapons, and ran to the aid of the brave Belgians, who were already half choked by the poisonous gases set free by the explosion. Of the 500 men who formed the garrison of Fort Loncin, 350 were dead and more than 100 severely wounded.

Meanwhile General Leman had been carried in an ambulance to the headquarters of General von Emmich. He had sworn not to be taken alive, and he had only been captured while unconscious. Sadly he handed his sword to the general, who, with a courteous bow and generous words of congratulation, immediately returned it to him, as a tribute to the glorious courage which he had displayed.

To spare the fallen, to show mercy and kindness to the conquered, is the duty and pride of every soldier worthy of the name. In the following pages we shall read of many black and shameful deeds done by the Germans; but let us here honour them for their treatment of General Leman and the gallant twenty-five who fought with him to the end.

General Leman was carried prisoner into Germany; but before he left Belgium he was allowed to send the following touching letter to King Albert:—

"Your Majesty will learn with sorrow that Fort Loncin was blown up yesterday at 5.20 p.m., and that the greater part of the garrison is buried under the ruins.

"That I did not lose my life in the catastrophe is owing to the fact that my duty called me from the stronghold. Whilst I was being suffocated by gas after the explosion a German captain gave me drink. I was made prisoner and taken to Liége.

"For the honour of our armies I have refused to surrender the fortress and the forts. May your Majesty deign to forgive me. In Germany, where I am going, my thoughts will be, as they have always been, with Belgium and her king. I would willingly have given my life the better to serve them, but death has not been granted me.

"Lieutenant-General LEMAN."

General Leman, the heroic defender of Liége.

Photo, Alfieri Picture Service.

All the world applauded the heroism of the Belgians in this first great encounter with the vastly superior forces of the enemy, and President Poincaré bestowed upon the city which had held out so nobly the highest honour which the French can bestow upon a civilian—the Legion of Honour.[199]

Belgian Cavalry.

(*Photo, Underwood and Underwood.*)

CHAPTER XXIII.

THE RAID INTO ALSACE.

Perhaps you wonder, as the Belgians did, what the French and the British were doing while the Germans were battering down the forts of Liége. You will probably ask why they did not rush at once to the help of the gallant Belgians, and fight the Germans on their own frontier. The answer is that neither France nor Britain was prepared for war. Both were hoping against hope that Russia and Austria would come to some peaceful arrangement. The fact that neither we nor the French were prepared shows clearly that we had no desire for war. The fact that within twenty-four hours after the declaration of war the Germans had three army corps in front of Liége shows equally clearly that they had long determined to fight.

All that the Belgians could do was to hold up the German advance for a short time. As the terrible hours slipped by, the people grew very anxious, and on every lip were the questions, "Où sont les Anglais?" "Où sont les Français?" A solitary motor car appeared, decorated with the Union Jack, and as it passed through the towns and villages the people cheered it to the echo. "The British are coming!" they cried. "Hurrah! hurrah!" Alas! both the French and the British were too far away to help the gallant Belgians struggling in the forts at Liége.

While the French were mobilizing as rapidly as possible they sent a brigade, with some cavalry and artillery, into Upper Alsace. I need not tell you what their object was. You will remember that ever since 1871 most Frenchmen have longed for the day when Alsace should again belong to France. The Alsatians have been harshly treated by the Germans. The German soldiers stationed in their towns have always been bitter against them because of their French sympathies.

In the year 1913, at the little Alsatian town of Zabern, a German lieutenant is said to have offered a reward to any of his men who stabbed a "Wacke," the German nickname for a native of Alsace. Disturbances arose, and in the course of them the lieutenant drew his sword and cut a lame cobbler over the head. The people of the town were very angry at this treatment, but when they protested their chief men were seized and imprisoned. An appeal was made to the Prussian Parliament. The War Minister supported the soldiers, but the Parliament stood up stoutly for the people of Zabern, and a military court sentenced the lieutenant to forty-three days' imprisonment. A higher court, however, did away with this sentence, and also found that no blame attached to the colonel of the regiment. While the trials were taking place the Crown Prince sent a telegram to the colonel praising him for what he had done. Thus, you see, the Germans had overthrown the rule of law in Alsace, and in place of it had set up the rule of the sword. Knowing all this, the French thought that the Alsatians would welcome their former fellow-countrymen with open arms, and would rise as one man against their oppressors. The appearance of French soldiers in Alsace would be a sign to them that the day of deliverance had arrived.

We must not think of this advance into Alsace as part of a well-thought-out plan by the French commander-in-chief. The forces employed in the work were far too weak to hold Alsace, even if they had been able to conquer it. From the point of view of strategy it was a mistake.

Look at the map on page 98, and find, to the south of the Vosges Mountains, the great French fortress of Belfort. From this place you will see a little plain across which an army can move easily to the Upper Rhine. While the Germans were advancing on Liége, French airmen flew across the plain and discovered that only a few of the enemy's troops were on the left bank of the Rhine. The French thereupon determined to occupy the country up to the left bank of the river. On the evening of Friday, 7th August, the day on which von Emmich asked General Leman for a truce so that he might bury his dead, a French brigade marched out of Belfort and crossed the frontier. Just before sunset it reached the little town of Altkirch, about a dozen miles inside German territory, and there found small bodies of Germans lining the trenches and awaiting an attack. The French infantry advanced with great spirit, carried the trenches, and by bayonet charges put the Germans to flight. Cavalry at once followed up the retreating enemy, and worked great havoc on them.

Then the French entered Altkirch, bearing before them the tricolour. The townsfolk rushed out of their houses to welcome them, and when they saw the flag under which they had lived and prospered forty-four years ago, they raised cheer after cheer. Already some of the villagers on the frontier had torn up the poles which marked the border-line between France and Germany.

In less than an hour the French were on the outskirts of Mulhouse, the largest and most important manufacturing town of Alsace, nine miles to the north of Altkirch. The people of Mulhouse have always been deeply attached to France. When the town became German in 1871, large numbers of them left their homes and settled in France and Algeria, in order that they might not be severed from the country which they loved so well. Mulhouse was occupied with but little resistance next day, and that evening General Joffre sent out the following message to the people:—

"Children of Alsace,—After forty-four years of sorrowful waiting, French soldiers once more tread the soil of your noble country. They are the pioneers in the great work of revenge. For them, what emotions it calls forth, and what pride!

"To complete the work, they have made the sacrifice of their lives. The French nation as one man urges them on, and in the folds of their flag are inscribed the magic words, 'Right and Liberty.' Long live Alsace! Long live France!

"General-in-chief of the French Armies,

"JOFFRE."

The news that the French army had entered Alsace was received in Paris with pride and delight. Men were thrilled with the thought that the lost provinces were on the eve of being restored to them. The Alsatians living in Paris, led by Alsatian women in Alsatian costume, and carrying palm branches, went in procession to the Place de Concorde. Ladders were placed against the monument, and an Alsatian climbed up and wound a broad tricolour sash around the statue. The crowd below cried, "Away with the crape!" and in an instant all the signs of mourning that had been on the statue since 1871 were torn away. After hearing a patriotic speech, the crowd sang the Marseillaise, and marched away cheering.

On Sunday morning, August 9th, came bitter disappointment. Large bodies of Germans, very nearly a whole army corps, were seen closing in upon the town from the north and east. The French were too few to hold them back, and were obliged to retire. "To retreat," said the French report, "was the wisest course."

When the French retreated the Germans lost no time in taking vengeance on the Alsatians. One of the deeds which they did was so terribly cruel that you will hardly be able to believe it. Yet the story was told in one of the German newspapers, and the writer actually gloried in the dastardly crime that he there set forth. It seems that a German column was passing along a wooded defile when it met a French boy scout, who was seized, and asked where the French troops were. He refused to say. At this moment a French battery opened fire from a wood only fifty yards away. The Germans managed to get into cover, and took the boy with them. When they asked him if he knew that the French were in the wood, he did not deny it. They told him that they were going to shoot him, but he showed no fear. He walked with firm steps to a telegraph post, stood against it, and with the green vineyard behind him, smiled as they shot him dead.

The Brave Boy Scout.

"He walked with firm steps to a telegraph post, stood against it, and with the green vineyard behind him, smiled as they shot him dead."

The German who told the story said that "it was a pity to see such wasted courage." The boy's courage was not wasted. It has inspired many a French boy and girl, as I am sure it will inspire you, to be just as fearless as he was, and to prefer death to the betrayal of one's countrymen.

Now let me tell you an incident of quite another character. During one of the fights the Germans retired, leaving behind them a young wounded officer. The French soldiers picked him up and treated him with that kindness which the Allies always show to those who fall into their hands. The young man, however, was dying, and nothing could save his life. His last words were, "Thank you, gentlemen. I have done my duty. I have served my country as you are serving yours."

This young man was the son of a former German ambassador in London, and up to a short time before the outbreak of war was a Rhodes scholar[200] at Oxford.

So the raid into Alsace ended. The French had gained nothing, but they had not fought in vain. They now knew that Alsace was not strongly held by the Germans, and they had proved that their artillery was far better than that of the enemy. They had shown, too, that the French infantry was just as gallant and dashing as it had been in the brave days of old, and they had encouraged the Alsatians to expect that the yoke of the tyrants would soon be broken.

On the day that the French retired from Mulhouse, General Joffre decided that the raid should be followed by an invasion. The forces brought together for this purpose were commanded by General Pau, an old soldier who had fought in the war of 1870-71. Like Nelson, he had lost an arm. He was considered one of the best of French commanders.

The French advanced to the north of their former route, and carried all before them. On 19th August they again attacked Mulhouse. There was a good deal of fierce fighting, but the Germans were driven out of the town, and no fewer than twenty-four of their guns were captured. On 20th August Mulhouse was in the hands of the French once more.

Then they marched south to Altkirch, and the Germans, who were afraid of being cut off from the bridges of the Rhine, retreated before them. The French seized the heads of the bridges on the left bank of the river, and then began to move northward along the plain towards the fortress of Colmar, which protects the main crossing of the Rhine. All the time more and more French troops were swarming across the passes of the Vosges, and were threatening to cut off the Germans from Strassburg. Things were looking extremely well for the French. It seemed that before long they would be in front of Strassburg and Metz.

All this time, however, the Germans were bringing up an overwhelming number of troops, and on 20th August they began their counter-attack. It was at once successful; the French were driven back, and the Germans claimed to have captured 10,000 prisoners and fifty guns. On the Belgian border, as we shall learn in the following pages, the Germans were also winning victories, and France needed all her troops to defend her own soil. By the 25th of August the French had left Alsace. The invasion was over. It had failed.

The Fight at Mulhouse on August 9, 1914, during the French Raid into Alsace.

Uhlans on the March.
Photo, Newspaper Illustrations, Ltd.

CHAPTER XXIV.

THE GERMANS IN BELGIUM.

Now we must return to Belgium, and see what was happening there. The heroic manner in which Fort Loncin had held out had delayed the Germans for a whole week. Until the last of the forts fell they had no command of the railways, and therefore could not push forward great masses of men across the plains to the north of the Meuse. But they could push forward cavalry with emergency rations,[201] and bid them take food wherever they could find it. Some artillery, a few machine guns, and infantry accompanied them.

The object of sending forward this cavalry screen was to prepare the way for the slower advance of infantry when Liége should be in German hands. The cavalry advanced westwards to Tongres,[202] which was occupied on Sunday, 9th August. Though this little town was within hearing of the guns of Liége, the appearance of the enemy came as a great surprise to the inhabitants. They were streaming out of their churches when there was a sudden cry, "The Germans are coming!" and almost immediately a squadron of the 35th Uhlans[203] trotted into the main street. They told the people that they had come from Danzig,[204] at the other end of Germany. Riding up to the town hall, they ordered the mayor to give up his money chest, and to pull down the flag floating above the building. He refused to strike his flag, so the Germans pulled it down for him. They seized the town's money and all that they could find in the post office; then they ordered food, for which they paid, and the troops camped in the market-place. Later on a cavalry division made the town its headquarters.

The behaviour of these men was good. The Germans did not yet believe that the Belgians were going to hold out. They thought that when the last of the Liége forts fell, the Belgians would consider that they had done enough to protest against the invasion of their country, and that they would then permit the Germans to pass through unmolested. They were soon to be undeceived.

Westwards from Tongres the German cavalry, in small detached bodies, spread over the country, and soon came in touch with detachments of the Belgian army. It was not the business of these bands of horsemen to fight battles but to skirmish, so that when they met Belgian riflemen they usually withdrew. Now and then one of them would miss his way, and would be captured in a starving condition. Rumours began to spread that the Germans were without food. A Belgian scout said, "One does not want a rifle to catch these Germans. They will surrender if you hold out a piece of bread."

On Wednesday, the 12th, German cavalry had pushed forward to a line extending from Hasselt, through St. Trond, to Huy, a town on the Meuse, about sixteen miles south-west of Liége. Huy is a picturesque old town, with a citadel standing on a rock high above the river, but it has long ceased to be a fortress. At the foot of the citadel-rock close by the river is a fine old church, and in the neighbourhood is a monastery, in which Peter the Hermit, the preacher of the First Crusade,[205] lies buried. The German cavalry were at first beaten back at Huy by the Civic Guard, but they afterwards seized the town and held the bridge. The capture of the town gave the Germans possession of an important railway connecting Luxemburg with the Belgian plain.

On the same day the Belgians won a real victory over the invaders. Look at the map on page 226, and find the town of Diest, which stands about twelve or thirteen miles to the north-west of Hasselt. A few miles east of Diest is the village of Haelen, at the junction of the two rivers Gethe and Velpe. News reached the Belgian headquarters at Louvain that a strong force of German cavalry was trying to pass between Hasselt and Haelen, in order to turn the flank of the Belgian army, which, you will remember, was lying along the river Dyle. The Belgians determined to meet the Germans at Haelen. They hurriedly threw up barricades, dug trenches, placed guns in position, and waited for the appearance of the enemy.

About eleven o'clock in the morning the Germans drew near to the Belgian position. They were allowed to come quite close before the Belgian guns began to speak. At once the Germans unlimbered, and an artillery duel began. The Belgians had previously found their ranges, and they were able to burst their shrapnel amongst the German cavalry with great effect. The fighting grew very fierce, and both sides showed great courage. The Belgian Lancers forded the Gethe and tried to charge the Uhlans, but were foiled by the broken ground. In turn, the German cavalry charged down on the Belgian barricades, but were met by a withering fire from rifles and concealed machine guns that swept large numbers of them down. Again and again they tried to break through the barricades, but every time they were repulsed, and about six in the evening they withdrew, having lost three-fifths of their fighting strength.

The Huns marching through a Belgian village.

Photo, Record Press.

There was great joy amongst the Belgians when the battle was over. The whole nation felt proud of the success of its little army. You must remember that few of the men who so bravely met the Germans were regular soldiers. Most of them were reservists called hurriedly from the factory, the shop, and the field to the work of war. All these men showed the highest courage. Their hearts beat high because they were fighting in a holy war; they were defending their native land against a greedy and grasping foe.

Many notable deeds of bravery were done that day. A farrier sergeant at the head of eight men charged a whole squadron of Uhlans, who scattered in all directions and fled, leaving many dead and wounded. He and his brave comrades were able to return to Haelen in safety, leading with them a dozen German horses as the spoils of victory.

During the afternoon a lieutenant, who was told off to defend Diest, was asked to send reinforcements to a neighbouring village which was threatened with attack. He had no men to spare, so he called together the Fire Brigade, and picking from them as many soldiers as he needed, sent them forward to the village, where they pumped lead on the Germans as skilfully as they had pumped water on burning houses in days of peace.

Numerous other small fights took place, and in all of them the Belgians fought like heroes. One such skirmish took place at Eghezee, a village about ten miles north of Namur. A party of 350 Uhlans and about sixty cyclists rode into this place, and put up in it for the night. Early in the morning a Belgian airman flew over the cornfield where they had encamped their horses. He was fired at, and thus the position of the Germans was revealed. Hearing the rattle of rifle fire, a number of Belgian scouts rode towards the place, and took the Germans completely by surprise. Most of them were sitting quietly in cafés when the alarm was sounded. Instantly they took to their heels, leaving horses, rifles, machine guns, and three motor cars behind them.

Seeing their comrades decamp, the few Germans who were guarding the horses set them loose, and a bugler who was with the men who were running away sounded a call. The horses trotted towards the sound of the bugle, and just as the Belgian scouts, who were only thirty in number, came into view, the Uhlans flung themselves on their horses and began to gallop off. About five hundred yards away there was a trench in a field of beetroot, and to this the Belgians dashed. They opened fire on the Uhlans, and shot down many of them.

By this time the Germans knew that the Belgians would fight to the last for their hearths and homes. Their pretended friendship now turned to bitter hate, and they went from village to village killing and looting. Goaded to frenzy by their terrible treatment, the Civic Guards and the peasants lay in wait for the Germans, and killed them whenever they could. About four miles north of Liége is the village of Herstal, the Belgian Woolwich, in which there is a great national factory for the manufacture of small arms. Most of the men engaged in this factory were with the army, so the women and children made up their minds to defend the factory. They armed themselves with revolvers and other weapons, and several times beat back the attacks of the Uhlans. When their ammunition was all gone they kept the Germans out by pouring boiling water on them from the windows. For two days they kept their flag flying. At last the Germans burst in and took a terrible vengeance on the women and children who had defied them so long.

With the fall of Fort Loncin the great German advance into Belgium began. Wave after wave of troops rolled over the frontier and surged across the open country towards Brussels. King Albert knew that his little army would be wiped out if it attempted to fight this vast array. His only hope was that the French would come to his assistance; but, as you know, they were not ready to take the field.

On the 14th of August the Belgians withdrew from the river Gethe, where, as you will recollect, they had beaten the advance guard of the Germans. They now strove manfully to stem the torrent of the invaders near the town of Aerschot, a few miles north of Louvain. All their efforts, however, were in vain.

Belgians defending a Barricade.   *Photo, Sport and General.*

CHAPTER XXV.

DEEDS OF SHAME AND HORROR.

I could fill a whole book with the stories which have been told of the dreadful cruelty shown by the Germans to the Belgians as the days went by and they discovered that they could not advance as rapidly as they had hoped to do. In order to delay the Germans the Belgians not only fought bravely, but wrecked their railways and bridges and blew up their roads. All this angered the Germans, for it was a matter of life and death to them to strike a blow at France as quickly as possible. We are told of babies slaughtered, of old men hanged and burnt alive, of mothers with little children hanging to their skirts shot down, and young women and girls tortured in the most horrible manner. Perhaps all these terrible stories are not true; but no one can deny the gross cruelty of the Germans in Belgium.

In the year 1900, when the Emperor William sent his troops to China, he addressed them in the following words: "Whoever falls into your hands is a forfeit to you, just as a thousand years ago the Huns under King Attila[206] made a name for themselves in tradition and story." What sort of man was this Attila whom the Kaiser thus set up as his model? He was a ruthless, obstinate savage, who never felt the "dint of pity." Wherever he passed he left his mark in wasted lands, blazing cities, ruined homesteads, and heaps of slain. He was called the "Scourge of God," and at the very mention of his name men trembled. The modern Huns, urged on by their pitiless War Lord, have beaten even the shameful record of Attila.

The Germans try to excuse themselves by declaring that the townsfolk brought this harsh punishment on themselves. According to the laws which civilized nations observe in war, civilians are only free from violence if they remain quiet and peaceful. What are called "lawful combatants" are men under the command of an officer, wearing some fixed badge or uniform, carrying arms openly, and fighting according to the rules and customs of warfare. All others who attack the enemy are unlawful combatants, and are liable to be put to death if they are caught.

Now there is no doubt that some Belgian civilians, maddened by the destruction of their homes, did actually fire on the enemy; but this is no excuse for the awful vengeance which the Germans took upon men, women, and children who were innocent of any such offence. Even in war it cannot be right to punish innocent and guilty alike, nor is it lawful to burn down whole cities because some of the inhabitants have offended. We know, however, from the War Book which the Germans issued to their officers, that they were encouraged to be pitiless, and to do all sorts of deeds of "frightfulness." According to this book, any deed may be done, however black or shameful, if it helps to defeat the enemy.

You now begin to see what the victory of Germany would mean. Not only would the conquered lands lose their independence and be treated as provinces of Germany, but there would be a return to the days of savagery in warfare. Men would thereafter fight like wild beasts in the jungle. A soldier would no longer be a knight but a fiend. We should bid farewell to that noble ideal which Tennyson set before the warrior in his "Idylls of the King":—[207]

"To break the heathen, and uphold the Christ,
To ride abroad redressing human wrongs,
To speak no slander, no, nor listen to it,
To honour his own word as if his God's."

I must now tell you how the Germans behaved in some of the Belgian cities. You already know that even in the Middle Ages Belgium was a rich and flourishing land. The wealthy merchants of Flanders built themselves stately houses, and filled them with costly and beautiful things. They also gave their money freely to build glorious churches, quaint belfries, and noble town halls. Artists were encouraged to paint pictures for their adornment, and craftsmen vied with each other in beautifying them with lovely designs in wood and metal. Before the war there was hardly a village in the whole land which could not show some beautiful building or some priceless work of art.

Germans in the Church at Aerschot.

(From the painting by E. Matania. By permission of *The Sphere*.)

Let me tell you what happened at Aerschot when the Germans marched into the town. The men broke into the houses, stole everything of value, and destroyed the furniture. In the cellars they found stores of wine, and large numbers of them were soon mad with drink. They stabled their horses in the beautiful church, broke down the carved woodwork, and showed the utmost contempt for the sacred place. While the German commander was standing on the balcony of the mayor's house he was shot dead, it is said, by the mayor's fourteen-year-old son, though probably it was the act of a drunken German soldier firing his rifle in sport. At once one hundred and fifty of the men of the town were seized, and in their presence the mayor, his son, and brother were shot. Then the males of the town were forced to run towards the river while the Germans fired at them. More than forty of these poor fellows were killed.

There is an old monkish rhyme which tells us that Brussels rejoices in noble men, Antwerp in money, Ghent in halters, Bruges in pretty girls, Louvain in learned men, and Malines in fools. The monks were not very complimentary to Ghent and Malines, but you will notice that they gave praise to the other cities. I will now tell you the fate of the city that was famed for learned men—Louvain. You will find it on the map, by the side of the river Dyle, about eighteen miles east of Brussels.

If you had visited Louvain in July 1914, you would probably have called it a dull town, and said that its inhabitants were either priests or students or landladies. But if you had been interested in history, you would have found Louvain anything but dull. Its university, which is one of the oldest and most famous in the world, has been called the Oxford of Belgium. It was founded in the days when Chaucer was writing his "Canterbury Tales," and amongst its students were many who have made a great mark in history. For hundreds of years English scholars flocked to it, and amongst them was our own Sir Thomas More,[208] who wrote an account of his visit. You perhaps know that his greatest work is "Utopia,"[209] a fanciful picture of a land in which everybody had a chance of being healthy, happy, wise, and good. More tells us at the beginning of his book that his friend Peter Gillies, who lived at Louvain, introduced him to a sunburnt sailor with a black beard, and that this man gave him that account of Utopia which he set down in his book. When the book was written More had it printed at Louvain, for the city was famous for its printers and booksellers. Some people think that More built his house at Chelsea on the model of a friend's house in the old city.

Another famous scholar who was very fond of visiting Louvain was Erasmus.[210] You can read his very interesting story in Charles Reade's novel "The Cloister and the Hearth." Erasmus loved Louvain, and was charmed with its delicious skies and its studious quiet. Indeed, scholars in all ages have loved the city. One of them wrote: "Hail, our Athens, the Athens of Belgium! O faithful, fruitful seat of the arts, shedding far and wide thy light and thy name!" Every year up to the time of the war thousands of people from all parts of the world used to visit this "Athens of Belgium."

Since 1432 the university has been housed in a handsome hall which was first built as a warehouse for the Clothmakers' Guild. Its library, which was founded in 1724, was one of the most valuable in Belgium. It contained 150,000 volumes, in addition to many priceless manuscripts.

There are several other beautiful buildings in Louvain. There is the town hall, the finest building of its kind in Belgium; and the Church of St. Peter, which was finished in the early part of the sixteenth century, and stands on the site of a much earlier church. Before the war St. Peter's was full of art treasures, the wood-carving and the metal work being specially fine. The carved rood screen and the cross were said to be without equal in Europe, and a bronze font was specially prized because it was the work of Quentin Matsys,[211] who was born in Louvain, and began life as a blacksmith. As a young man he fell in love with an artist's daughter, and asked her hand in marriage. Her father, however, refused it, and said she should only marry an artist. Quentin loved the girl very much, so he threw down his hammer and took up the paint-brush. Soon he was a better painter than his future father-in-law, and the marriage took place. In the cathedral at Antwerp there is a tablet to his memory, setting forth that it was love that taught the smith to paint.

The Town Hall of Louvain.

Photo, Newspaper Illustrations, Ltd.

The Germans have always told us that they are great lovers of art and learning, and they constantly boast of their culture. You would have thought that when they entered this glorious old city of Louvain they would have done everything in their power to preserve it from harm. What they actually did was to burn down a large part of it, and in a few hours reduce several of its glorious old buildings to charred and blackened ruins. Mr. Asquith, our Prime Minister, described their work at Louvain as "the greatest crime against civilization and culture since the Thirty Years' War."[212]

You know that the Germans have laid the blame for some of their crimes on the townsfolk, whom they accuse of firing on them. They had no such excuse in the case of Louvain, for *all the arms had been handed in by the people some days before the Germans arrived.* The mayor had posted placards warning the people that if they attacked the enemy in any way they would bring down vengeance upon themselves and their city.

When the Germans in overwhelming force had beaten back the Belgians who were trying to defend Louvain, and had placed their guns in position to bombard it, they sent an officer to the mayor offering to spare the place if the townsfolk would find food and lodgings for their soldiers. They promised that if this was done the soldiers would not molest the townsfolk, and that those of them who were not billeted in private houses would pay cash for all the goods which they needed. To this the mayor agreed, and the Germans marched in. Soon, however, they broke all their promises. The German soldiers rushed into private houses and took what they fancied, without any payment but worthless paper. They broke open the cellars and drank the wine in them as though it were beer. Their officers ordered the city treasurer to give them 100,000 francs, and grumbled greatly when he could only find part of the money. Meanwhile, though the city was full of drunken Germans, the people remained very quiet and orderly.

On Tuesday evening, 25th August, the foul deed was done. That day the Belgians had made an attack on a body of Germans outside the town, and had driven them helter-skelter into it. The drunken Germans in Louvain thought that the fugitives were Belgians, and began firing on them. This was a bad mistake, which would be certain to bring down blame on the officer in command. In order to cover up the mistake, he pretended that the townsfolk had attacked his soldiers, and proceeded to punish them for a crime which they had not committed. A number of the male inhabitants were shot, and then he ordered his men to burn the city down.

An eye-witness, who was threatened with death, tells us the terrible story. "At six o'clock," he says, "when everything was ready for dinner, alarm signals sounded, and the soldiers rushed into the streets; shots whistled through the air; cries and groans arose on all sides; but we did not dare leave our houses, and took refuge in the cellars, where we stayed through long and fearful hours.

"At break of day I crawled from the cellar to the street door, and saw nothing but a raging sea of fire. At nine o'clock there was a lull in the shooting, and we resolved to make a dash for the station. Leaving our home and all our goods except what we could carry, and taking all the money we had, we rushed out. No pen can describe what we saw on our way to the station.

Everything was burning; the streets were covered with bodies, shot dead and half burnt...

"The station was crowded with people, and I was just trying to show an officer my papers when the soldiers separated me from my wife and children. All protests were useless, and a lot of us were marched off to a big shed in the goods yard, from which we could see the finest buildings in the city burning fiercely.

"Shortly afterwards German soldiers drove before them 300 men and lads to the corner of a street, where they were shot. The sight filled us with horror. The Burgomaster,[213] two magistrates, the rector of the university, and all police officials had been shot already.

"With our hands bound behind our backs we were then marched off by the soldiers, still without having seen our wives and children. We were taken out of the town to a neighbouring hill, from which we had a full view of the burning town. St. Peter's was in flames, and the guns were firing shot after shot into the unhappy place."

Louvain was not burned down by accident. The soldiers worked on a plan. They began in the heart of the city and set the place on fire house by house and street by street. For thirty-six hours or more they continued to fire the houses. A student of Oxford, who was in the town on 29th August, tells us that "burning houses were every moment falling into the roads; shooting was still going on. The dead and dying, burnt and burning, lay on all sides. Over some of them the Germans had placed sacks. I saw the bodies of half a dozen women and children. In one street I saw two little children walking hand in hand over the bodies of dead men. I have no words to describe these things.

The Destruction of Louvain.

Photo, Newspaper Illustrations, Ltd.

"The town hall was standing on Friday morning last, and, as we plainly saw, every effort was being made to save it from the flames. We were told by German officers that it was not to be destroyed. I have no doubt that it is still standing. The German officers dashing about the streets in fine motor cars made a wonderful sight. They were well dressed, shaven, and contented looking; they might have been attending a fashionable race-meeting. The soldiers were looting everywhere; champagne, wines, boots, cigars—everything was being carried off."

Until the Germans are driven out of the city we shall not know the full extent of the ruin which they have wrought. The Church of St. Peter has been terribly damaged, but not, perhaps, beyond repair; but the buildings of the university have been almost wiped out. The great library has been given to the flames. I think you can imagine the anguish of a professor who watched the burning from his garden, and saw the charred leaves of priceless manuscripts floating past him. About the time that the English were winning England a Saracen chief named 'Amr burned the great library at Alexandria, and the world has never forgotten his infamous deed. What will it say of the burning of the Louvain library, more than twelve and a half centuries later, by men of a race which boasts of its culture?

Let me tell you something of the heroism of a famous citizen of Louvain—Dr. Noyons, head of the medical school of the university. When the Germans marched in he was in charge of the hospital, which was filled to overflowing with wounded, both Germans and Belgians. The Red Cross flag flew above the building, and according to all the rules of civilized warfare the hospital should have been spared. Nevertheless the Germans set it on fire. While some of his helpers were trying to put out the flames, the doctor and his wife calmly went on attending to the wounded. Next morning the hospital staff was ordered to leave the town, as it was to be bombarded; but Dr. Noyons and his wife decided to disobey the order and remain. They could not bear the thought of leaving their poor wounded to perish, so they and their assistants carried them into the cellars of the hospital, and for two days ministered to them underground. When, however, all danger of bombardment was past they brought the men up to their wards again, and continued to attend them as before.

Now we must turn to the story of Malines, the city which, according to the old monkish rhyme, rejoices in fools. I have spent some time in this city, and have seen something of its people, and I can assure you that they are very far from being fools. Malines is renowned through Belgium for its love of education and for the large number of its citizens who are eager to make life better and happier for toiling men and women. Before the war, the heart and centre of the town was the Grand'-Place. On the right as you enter it stood a sixteenth-century Cloth Hall; to the left was the town hall; behind it the huge tower of the cathedral. All round were quaint gabled houses. During the day the Grand'-Place was almost deserted, but at night, when the lights began to glow in the little cafés, the people gathered at the tables outside them in little family groups to drink "Bock" and listen to the band. I remember wandering through the old-world streets, peeping into little narrow byways, stopping to examine painted shrines at the street corners, crossing the Dyle with its many bridges, and admiring the quaint riverside houses and the gaudy, broad-beamed barges that lay at the quays. Everywhere I saw the little milk-carts drawn by dogs. One Sunday afternoon the school children gathered in the Grand'-Place for a festival. I shall never forget the heartiness with which they sang the Belgian National Anthem, while the townsfolk, bareheaded, swelled the strain:—

"Again, O Belgium, still our Mother,
We pledge thee in blood and in song;
Surely to thee and to no other
Our swords, our hearts, our lives belong!
While thy deeds live in history's pages,
Deathless thy fame shall ever be;
And the cry still ring through the ages:
'For King and Law and Liberty.'"

On that bright September day the Malinoise had no thought of war and bloodshed. They could not possibly foresee that, before many months had passed, Belgians would be called upon to give their swords and hearts to their Mother, and that in their heroic strife they would add such a glorious page to their history that thenceforward throughout the ages they would win deathless fame.

Before the war, the glory of Malines was its cathedral. Its huge tower, which soared above the city, was 318 feet high, and was intended to be the highest tower in Christendom, but was never finished. No one could be within the bounds of the city for more than a few minutes without hearing the wonderful chimes that floated out from this tower. The dials of its clock were 44 feet in diameter, and the carillon was famous all over the world. Every Monday evening in summer it performed a programme of music, and every quarter of an hour, day and night, it played a tune. Robert Browning, in his poem "How they brought the Good News from Aix to Ghent," refers to the bells of Malines Cathedral in the following line:—

"And from Mecheln church steeple we heard the half-chime."

Mechlin is the Flemish name of Malines. All the girls who read this book have heard of Mechlin lace, which was formerly made in the city. Now its chief manufactures are woollen goods and "Gobelin"[214] tapestry.

The cathedral was built with money collected from pilgrims who flocked to the city in the fourteenth and fifteenth centuries. Within it were more treasures than in any other Belgian cathedral, except in the most famous church of Brussels and in the cathedral at Antwerp. The pulpit was a miracle of wood-carving, and the altar-piece was a picture of the Crucifixion, by Van Dyck,[215] who was a pupil of the great Rubens,[216] and court painter to Charles I. of England, by whom he was knighted. The stained-glass windows were of wonderful richness. There were three or four other churches in

Malines of great interest and beauty, and several public buildings with historic memories.

Malines Cathedral before the Bombardment.

Now I must tell you how the Germans treated this interesting old city. Four separate times they bombarded it; yet there does not appear to be any good reason why they should have turned their guns upon it at all. It was not fortified, and it offered no resistance. The first bombardment was on 27th August, when the town hall was battered down, and the roof, walls, and stained glass of the cathedral suffered greatly. The people deserted the city, and when the guns were silent it was as quiet as the grave. A second time it was bombarded, and still more damage was done. Happily the Malinoise had removed some of their treasures, including Van Dyck's altar-piece, to the safety of bomb-proof cellars.

On 2nd September the third bombardment took place. Over a hundred shells were burst over the place: great gaping holes were blown through the tower of the cathedral, and its superb gateway was battered into a heap of ruins. The bells of the carillon were knocked to pieces, and never again will the ancient chimes of Malines be heard.

Though the Germans had worked such havoc on the unoffending town, they could not forbear to assault it a fourth time. On 26th September Belgian troops attacked a German detachment not far from the city and drove it back in disorder. In revenge for this reverse, the Germans next morning shelled the place again. It was on a Sunday morning that the deadly rain began to fall. Many of the people had returned to the city, and were leaving the ruined cathedral after Mass, when a shell fell amongst them and killed some of them. Shortly afterwards another shell exploded in a café, and wounded some of the people who had taken refuge in it. The railway station, the barracks, several public buildings, factories, and many private houses were utterly destroyed, either by the guns or by the fires which afterwards broke out.

On page 272 you will see a picture of the little town of Termonde as it appeared when the Germans had wreaked their vengeance upon it. A Scottish member of Parliament, who visited it a few weeks after the bombardment, tells us that he went through street after street and square after square, and found every house entirely destroyed with all its contents. In the early days of August it was a beautiful little town of 16,000 inhabitants; now it was utterly destroyed and completely deserted, save for a blind old woman and her daughter who groped amongst the ruins.

When we look at this sad picture we can realize in some degree the sufferings of the poor Belgians. Their houses have been destroyed, their cherished belongings have been given to the flames; tens of thousands of their bravest and best have been slain, in some cases with the foulest cruelty, and hundreds of thousands of those who survive are homeless and ruined. All over the land ancient monuments of art and learning are in shapeless ruin. The love and labour and pride of centuries have been swept away, and a prosperous land has been reduced to beggary. And what have the Belgians done to deserve this hideous treatment? They have dared to defend their own country; they have dared to stand in the way of a ruthless nation that had sworn not to trespass on their soil; they have refused to sell that which was dearer to them than life itself—the independence of their land; and for this they have suffered martyrdom. Let us never forget that the Belgians have fought and suffered for us. Had they given the Germans free passage through their country, or had they feebly resisted them, a great and sudden swoop would have been made upon France at the very moment when she was unprepared to meet it. Not only might France have gone down, and the work of the Allies in overcoming the enemy been made doubly difficult, but the Germans might have established themselves on the north coast of France, from which they could have seriously threatened our shores. By her splendid courage and staunchness Belgium has saved Europe, and the civilization of the world is her debtor.

"They gave their homes for the Huns to tread, Their homes for the Huns to burn; For our very lives they gave their dead, *And what shall we give in turn?*"

Termonde. *Photo, Central News.*

CHAPTER XXVI.

THE RALLY OF THE BRITISH EMPIRE.

What was the British Empire doing while the Germans were overrunning Belgium? At home, the War Office[217] was working night and day to equip and dispatch an army for service in France. The Territorials were stationed at all the points which needed defence, and the recruiting offices were very busy. On all the hoardings appeared placards calling upon men between the ages of nineteen and thirty-eight to serve their king and country. Every day fine, stalwart recruits, full of energy and zeal, flocked to the colours. Large camps were formed in the south of England, and the work of training the new armies was carried on with the utmost speed.

But what of Britain overseas? The Germans had been taught to believe that the British Empire was only a very loose collection of states, with no bond of union between them and the mother country. It was a jerry-built empire, so they thought, and they were assured that when the time of stress came it would tumble to pieces like a house of cards. Canada, they said, was drifting towards the United States, and would one day be part of that country; Australia had long wished to "cut the painter;" South Africa was yearning to throw off the yoke; India was a powder magazine which would explode with a spark; Egypt was only waiting for a chance of rising in revolt. The moment a great trial of strength came there would be an end of the British Empire. Such was the belief of the Germans. What really happened you shall now hear.

Men of the New Army drilling in Hyde Park, London.   *Photo, Central News.*

One of our poets speaks of the peoples of the Dominions as

"Children of Britain's island-breed,
To whom the Mother in her need
Perchance may one day call."

That day had arrived. The Mother in her need had called, and with one heart and one voice her sons across the seas replied, "Lo! we come."

When war began to threaten, the Dominions lost no time in sending offers of help and words of cheer to the Home Government. Britons beyond the seas rallied gloriously to the old flag. In Canada men of all parties at once forgot their differences and stood shoulder to shoulder, just as they were doing in Great Britain and Ireland. On the day that Germany declared war on Russia (1st August), Sir Robert Borden, the Prime Minister of the Dominion of Canada, held a Cabinet Council, at which arrangements were made for guarding all the points of danger, and for calling up the Militia, which correspond to the Territorials of the British Isles. In time of peace these number about 44,500 men. Within a few hours fifteen regiments had volunteered for active service, and thousands of men were begging to be allowed to serve. Never before had such enthusiasm been seen in the Canadian cities. The Duke of Connaught, the Governor-General of the Dominion, spoke the simple truth when he said, "Canada stands united, from the Pacific to the Atlantic, in her determination to uphold the honour and traditions of our Empire." On Tuesday, 3rd August, news arrived that Britain had declared war on Germany. The crowds which had gathered about the newspaper offices stood silent for a moment, and then turned to go. The time for shouting had gone by; the hour of work and sacrifice had arrived.

In a few days, more than 100,000 men had offered themselves. Old members of Strathcona's[218] Horse, and the Royal Canadians, who had fought so gallantly in South Africa, pressed forward eagerly to re-enlist. From all parts of the Dominion they came—French Canadians from Lower Canada; farmers, and artisans, and clerks from Ontario; the hardest riders and the best shots of the prairies; the miners, trappers, and pioneers of the west and north. Every province sent its quota of men. Two hundred frontiersmen from Moosejaw,[219] finding that they could not be enlisted as cavalry, took the road to Ottawa at their own expense, and having purchased their outfits, declared that, if they were not accepted for service, they would hire a cattle ship and sail for Europe "on their own." It is pleasant to note that 60,000 citizens of the United States offered to enlist in the Canadian army.

Nor were the Redskins behindhand. Many applied for enlistment, and a few were allowed to join. Some of the tribes sent money to the war funds, and the Blood Indians of Alberta passed the following resolution: "The first citizens of Canada, the old allies of warring French and British, the Redskins, the devoted wards of Victoria the Good and of her grandson, King George, are no whit behind the Sikhs of India, the men from South Africa, or the British Regulars in testifying to their loyalty to the Crown or to the unity of the British Empire." Two chiefs sent £200 from their tribal funds, and hoped that Great Britain would ever remain the guardian of the weak. Other tribes also sent money and proffers of help.

Rich citizens opened their cheque-books freely to fit out the regiments. One Montreal[220] millionaire offered to provide all the money for raising, equipping, and supporting Princess Patricia's Light Infantry, or "Princess Pat's," as they are known in Canada. A Calgary[221] cattle-dealer offered fifty thousand dollars to equip a legion of frontiersmen, and the various provinces vied with each other in sending money and provisions for the use of the British forces. The Canadian Government offered a million bags of flour, Ontario 250,000 bags, and Manitoba 50,000 bags. Alberta and Prince Edward Island sent oats, Nova Scotia coal, Quebec cheese, New Brunswick potatoes, British Columbia tinned salmon, and Saskatchewan horses. In addition, Canada offered her two cruisers, the *Niobe* and the *Rainbow*, for general service, and her two submarines for duty on the Pacific coast.

Views in Quebec.

1. Dufferin Terrace. 2. The Citadel and Château Frontenac. 3. Plains of Abraham, and Wolfe Monument. 4. Sous-le-Cap Street. 5. Montmorency Falls. 6. Church of Notre-Dame des Victoires. 7. Parliament Buildings. 8. French Cathedral.

The women of Canada subscribed for naval hospitals, and the Canadian Red Cross Society sent a fully-equipped field hospital and £10,000 in money. When Canadians learned that the Belgians were in distress, they opened their purses most generously. Everybody did his or her "little bit." A newsboy of Toronto[222] gave a street car ticket worth a few cents; it was afterwards sold

- 226 -

for a thousand dollars. The citizens of Berlin,[223] Ontario, sent the following cable message to Lord Kitchener:—

"Berlin, Ontario, a city of 15,000 population, of which 12,000 are Germans or of German descent, purposes raising £15,000 or more for the National (Canadian) Patriotic Fund. The German people want to see militarism[224] in Germany smashed for good, and the people set free to shape a greater and better Germany. We feel confident that England has appointed the right men in Mr. Churchill[225] and Lord Kitchener to boss the job."

At first the Canadians intended to raise a force of 22,000 men to be sent overseas, and another 10,000 men to guard the Dominion; but so many men wished to go to the front that the strength of the first force sent to Britain was largely increased. The men were fitted out with the best of everything. Their clothes and weapons were as good as money could buy, and their horses were especially fine. Motor transport and an ammunition train were provided, and more than a hundred fully qualified nurses went with the troops. Wealthy men provided the regiments with machine guns; they had their own aviators, doctors, and chaplains. By the end of September the force was ready to be transported overseas. It numbered 31,250 men, with 7,500 horses, and everything necessary for taking the field. The force was assembled at the Valcartier[226] Camp, near Quebec.[227]

The departure of the troops from Valcartier at the end of September was a sight never to be forgotten. At various times in the day trumpets sounded, the battalions packed their kits, and long lines of khaki-clad men marched along the road to Quebec amidst crowds of cheering Canadians. The bands struck up "It's a Long Way to Tipperary," and the troops trudged off in the highest possible spirits.

The greater part of the artillery marched late in the afternoon and at night. Rain fell heavily, and they arrived in Quebec soaked and mud-spattered, but as full of enthusiasm as ever. The guns, ammunition wagons, transports, and horses filed along narrow roads flanked by autumn-tinted trees and fringed by quaint French-Canadian villages. At one point, we are told, the white-haired old curé[228] of a French village stood for nearly half an hour up to his knees in the wet grass of his orchard, plucking apples from the trees, and throwing them to the men as they swung along. They cheered him, and a French-Canadian battery which passed sang the Marseillaise.

Never since the days of Wolfe[229] had Quebec witnessed such martial scenes as when the troops tramped through the steep streets of the old city to embark on board the thirty-two transports which were to convey them to the mother country. Everywhere one heard cheering and the music of bands and bagpipes. Wives and sweethearts bade farewell to their dear ones, and then crept away from the noisy throng to weep in solitude or to return to their homes, where the long, anxious hours of waiting were to be passed until the war should end and the heroes return. Alas! many of them were destined never to return, but to find a last resting-place in the clay of France and Flanders.

At last came the day when all the troops were on board ready to depart. Dufferin Terrace, overlooking the harbour, was black with thousands of men and women waving handkerchiefs, and ever and anon breaking into loud cheers, as the transports steamed slowly one by one down the river and past Point Levis.[230] The cheers did not cease until the last of the big vessels, carrying the pride of Canada's soldiery, disappeared from view between the Isle of Orleans[231] and the mainland.

Guarded by grim warships, the transports crossed the ocean, and on the morning of October 15th arrived in Plymouth Sound. It was very fitting that the gallant sons of Canada should tread English soil in the port from which their sires in the brave days of old had gone forth to discover new homes for British people in the great continent of the West. Those of them who knew anything of British history must have felt their hearts swell as they gazed at the grassy slopes of Plymouth Hoe. The list of great seamen who trod that greensward before sailing to the New World is in itself a page of romance— Sir Richard Grenville[232] for Virginia, Sir Humphrey Gilbert[233] for Newfoundland, Sir Martin Frobisher[234] for the North-West Passage, and, above and beyond all, Sir Francis Drake[235] for the circumnavigation of the world.

In the days following their arrival the Canadians were landed, and marched through the streets to the railway station, *en route* for Salisbury Plain, where their training was to be completed. As they passed along the Plymouth streets between the lines of townsfolk all sorts of gifts were pressed upon them. "We were snowed under with good things," said one of the men.

While the first contingent was hard at work in the mud of Salisbury Plain, a second and a third contingent were being raised in Canada. As soon as it was announced that more men were needed, a far larger number of recruits flocked to the standard than could be accepted. Within a little more than four months after the outbreak of war Canada had raised over 90,000 men for the service of king and country.

Transports arriving at Plymouth. *Photo, Central News.*

The island of Newfoundland stands outside the Dominion of Canada; so she made a special effort of her own, for she was just as eager to come to the help of the mother country as any other of our overseas possessions. The coasts of Newfoundland, as you know, are inhabited by fishermen—fine, hardy fellows, who are at home in stormy seas, and can turn their hands to almost anything. In the old days the Newfoundlander was the backbone of our navy, and a branch of the Royal Naval Reserve has long been established in the island. On the outbreak of war Newfoundland offered to increase her naval reserves up to 3,000 men, and to provide and equip 500 soldiers for active service overseas.

In this rally of the Empire Australia played her part right manfully. The Prime Minister of the Commonwealth spoke for all when he said: "We must sit tight now and see the thing through at whatever difficulty and whatever cost. We must be steadfast in our determination. Our resources are great, and British spirit is not dead. We owe it to those who have gone before to preserve the great fabric of British freedom and hand it on to our children. Our duty is quite clear. Remember, we are Britons." Mr. Andrew Fisher, who became Premier a little later, spoke in the same strain. "Australia," said he, "will support Great Britain with her last man and her last shilling."

Australia and New Zealand were in a better position to send assistance to the mother country than any other members of our overseas empire. Australia possesses a navy of her own, consisting of one battle cruiser, three light cruisers, three destroyers, and two submarines, and these she at once placed at the disposal of the Admiralty. Every able-bodied male in Australia and

New Zealand is obliged to serve as a cadet from twelve to eighteen years of age, and in the Citizen Defence Corps during manhood. When war broke out Australia had 85,000 cadets under training, and 50,000 men in the Citizen Defence Corps, the latter being fully armed and equipped. One of our generals, who inspected the Australian artillery some time ago, was much struck with the smartness and skill of the men. "I would not be afraid," he said, "to take them into action against European troops to-morrow."

The Commonwealth at once asked for 20,000 volunteers, and immediately twice as many men as were needed rushed to enlist. They were such fine fellows that it was difficult to decide which of them to accept and which to reject. The Queensland Bushmen offered to provide a regiment, and were prepared to supply their own horses, while the yachtsmen of Australia were ready to join the Royal Naval Reserve. Even the German settlers stood by their fellow-Australians in this crisis, and declared that they were prepared, if the necessity arose, to sacrifice their property and their lives for the welfare of the British Empire. Instead of "cutting the painter," Australia doubled it, and made it more secure than ever.

Canadian Troops on Salisbury Plain.

Photos, Alfieri and Central News.
The King reviews Canadian troops on Salisbury Plain (top). Three cheers for his Majesty the King! (middle). The armoured motor cars of the Canadians (bottom).

Gifts of money and produce were most generously made to the Belgians, to the Red Cross Society, and in aid of other war funds. The sheep farmers of New South Wales gave 40,000 carcasses of mutton, 1,500 sheep, 1,000,000 cartridges, 20 tons of dried fruit, and 1,500 horses up to the end of September, and in November added another 7,600 carcasses of mutton. From all parts of Australia came flour, wine, bacon, beef, condensed milk, butter, arrowroot, biscuits, sheep, fruit, and clothing.

Australians for the Front. *Photo, Central News.*

Before long 20,000 men, together with a Light Horse Brigade of 6,000 men, were ready to embark. Meanwhile many thousands of other men were being trained, and it was decided to send 2,000 of them regularly to Great Britain to repair the wastage of war.

The troops departed in silence and secrecy. There was a squadron of German warships in the Pacific Ocean, and had the commanders of these vessels known when and by what route the transports were to set sail, you may be sure that they would have tried to sink them. When the vessels arrived off the Cocos-Keeling Islands[236] in the Indian Ocean, Japanese warships warned them that the Germans were near at hand, and that part of their route had been strewn with mines.

Perhaps you are surprised to learn that Japanese warships were then policing the Pacific Ocean for Britain. In the year 1905 we came to an agreement with the Japanese that if any Power made an unprovoked attack upon us or upon them both countries would join their forces to fight the enemy. On 15th August Japan gave notice to Germany that if she did not clear out of Kiao-chau[237] war would be declared. Germany refused, and on 23rd August war was declared. At once Kiao-chau was attacked, and the ships of the fine Japanese fleet took over the work of patrolling the Pacific Ocean. In the next volume we shall learn how Japan played her part in the war.

One of the Australian soldiers tells us that the Japanese warned them that German cruisers were about, in the evening, and that orders were at once given to the men to put on life-belts and fall in at their messes. At eight o'clock they were all lined up on deck; the ship's lights were put out, and in the pitch-black darkness they waited for the enemy's attack. All were bare to the waist, and had their trousers rolled up to their knees. Thus they stood for a full hour, without a word being spoken except by the officers. Suddenly they heard the boom of a gun some distance astern, and soon afterwards saw the dark form of a cruiser dash across their bows and disappear in the darkness. It was the famous German cruiser *Emden*, of which we shall hear in our next volume. She was in too great a hurry to stop and attack the transport, for the biggest and fastest vessel of the Australian Navy, H.M.S. *Sydney*, was chasing her. The danger had passed away, and the rest of the voyage was uneventful.

Australians near the Pyramids. *Photo, Record Press.*

This picture shows Sir George Reid, High Commissioner of Australia, visiting the camp of the Australian contingent in Egypt. In the course of a speech he said, "The Pyramids have been silent witnesses of many strange events, but never before have looked upon such a splendid array of troops."

When the transports arrived in the Suez Canal the men learned that they were not to proceed to the front, but were to disembark and help to protect Egypt. This was, of course, a disappointment to them; but they were somewhat consoled when they learned that they might see active service very soon, for the Turks had joined the Germans, and were talking of attacking Egypt.

You know that New Zealand has also her cadets and her Citizen Defence Corps, and was, therefore, able to send trained men overseas without delay. Long before volunteers were asked for, men were besieging the Minister of Defence with offers of service. By eleven o'clock on the morning of 6th August, a thousand volunteers had handed in their names in the city of Auckland[238] alone. Gifts of money and produce, horses, and motor cars were at once forthcoming, and a few weeks later New Zealand presented the mother country with an aeroplane.

Less than three weeks after the declaration of war, a cable message was sent to the War Office in London, saying that New Zealand had 8,000 men ready to go to any part of the world at a moment's notice. These troops consisted of mounted rifles, field artillery, and infantry, and along with them were 500 Maoris,[239] who were most eager to fight for Britain. Two hundred of them were sent to Egypt to be trained, and it was thought that they would prove admirable scouts. Amongst the white volunteers were five members of the famous "All Black" football team which played so well in Great Britain a few years ago, and three Rhodes scholars. All the men were splendid specimens of young manhood. Their voyage was without incident, and they were landed in Egypt to join the Australians and British Territorials in the defence of that country.

British South Africa found herself, on the outbreak of war, with German forces on her frontiers. In the German colony of South-West Africa there was a large and well-equipped German army, and in German East Africa there were other forces. Further, there were some Boers who had not yet become resigned to British rule, and it was thought—as afterwards proved to be the case—that they had been bribed by the Germans, and would seize the opportunity to rise in rebellion. South Africa could not, therefore, send forces to help the mother country; but, under the command of General Botha,[240] who himself had been a leader of the Boers[241] in the late war, she undertook to guard herself and attack the Germans on her borders without the help of soldiers from Great Britain or from any of the Dominions. We shall see in the next volume how she carried out this duty. Meanwhile she sent many gifts of money and produce to Great Britain.

There was no part of the British Empire, however small, which did not, to the best of its ability, help the mother country in her hour of need. From the Barbadoes came £20,000; from the Falkland Islands, £1 per head of the population, as well as £750 for the Prince of Wales's Fund.[242] St. Kitts and

Nevis, in the West Indies, sent £5,000 to the same fund; Mauritius, British Guiana, and Jamaica sent large gifts of sugar; Southern Rhodesia sent maize, and Hong Kong a large donation to the Prince of Wales's Fund. Take a map of the world and search out one by one the overseas possessions of Great Britain. You cannot find a single place under the Union Jack that did not rally to the Empire as soon as the call to arms was sounded. No wonder the King was deeply touched by these tenders of loyal service, and no wonder that he thanked his overseas subjects in a noble message. The hearts of all Britons in the mother country were deeply stirred to feelings of joy and pride when they knew that the men of the Dominions were

"Welded, each and all
Into one Imperial whole,
One with Britain, heart and soul—
One life, one flag, one fleet, one throne!
Britons, hold your own!"

CHAPTER XXVII.

HOW INDIA ANSWERED THE CALL.

"Sons of Shannon, Tamar, Trent,
Men of the Lothians, men of Kent,
Essex, Wessex, shore and shire,
Mates of the net, the mine, the fire,
Lads of desk and wheel and loom,
Noble and trader, squire and groom,
Come where the bugles of Britain play,
Over the hills and far away!
"Southern Cross and Polar Star—
Here are the Britons bred afar;
Serry,[243] O serry them. See, they ride
Under the flag of Britannia's pride;
Shoulder to shoulder, down the track,
Where, to the unretreating Jack,
The victor bugles of Britain play,
Over the hills and far away!"

In Chapter XXVI. you learned how Britons all over the world answered the call to arms. The verses which you have just read might almost have been written to describe the great rally. But the greatest surprise of all was the response of India. It is a vast land, equal in area to the whole of Europe outside Russia, and containing nearly one in five of all people that on earth do dwell. These people consist of many races and many religions, and large numbers of them are ruled by their own princes. During recent years many educated Indians have asked for a larger share in the government of their own country, and this has been granted to them in some measure. Nevertheless, there are still many of them who are not satisfied with our rule, and the Germans, as you know, hoped and expected that when Great Britain was in straits these dissatisfied persons would rise and throw off the British yoke.

Types of our Indian Soldiers: Sikhs are seen above, and Cavalry below. *Photo, Central News.*

Even in this country some people feared that there would be trouble in India; but their fears were soon set at rest, for in the course of a few hours India showed clearly that Britain's quarrel was her quarrel, and that she was as loyal to the Empire and as eager to help it in the hour of trial and stress as any of the Dominions. It is remarkable to note that several of those who had been most bitter against British rule at once ceased their work of stirring up the people, and called upon them to rally in Britain's cause. Thus India, instead of being a weakness to the Empire, proved a tower of strength; instead of a danger, she became a staunch bulwark.

In times of peace we maintain in India 70,000 British troops and a native army of about 160,000 men, recruited from many castes and races. Chief amongst these are the Sikhs, a fierce warrior caste, whose home is in the Punjab.[244] Long and bitter strife was necessary to overcome them; but when they were finally conquered they threw in their lot with the British, and ever since have proved themselves faithful and skilful allies. Our native army also contains fine fighting men from the lofty mountainous country on the northwest frontier of India, and from the rugged tableland of Beluchistan. Perhaps the best known of all our native Indian troops are the Gurkhas, little, tireless mountaineers of Nepal,[245] famous for their marching and shooting. I remember seeing some thousands of these fine little soldiers in Burma. They were clad in dark green, and armed with a murderous-looking knife, known as the kukri, in place of the bayonet. They marched on to the parade ground, behind the bagpipes, to the strains of the "Cock o' the North."

The Indian army is highly trained, and is under the command of British officers, who know and respect their men, and are trusted and esteemed by them. It has seen much fighting, not only against rebellious Indian tribes, but in Afghanistan, Uganda, the Sudan, Egypt, Persia, and China. It was in China, in the year 1900, that Indian soldiers made the acquaintance of the Germans, with whom we were then engaged in fighting the Boxers.[246] German officers and men during that expedition looked down upon our Indian troops with contempt, and talked of them as "coolies" and "niggers." As you know, they belong to the oldest and proudest races on earth, and their British officers always show them the highest possible respect. You can easily understand how deeply they were offended by this treatment. They have long memories, and when they were told that they were to fight in Europe against those who had insulted them in China, they were not only proud and glad to stand shoulder to shoulder with their British comrades, but eager to pay off old scores.

Gurkha Soldiers and Officer.

Photo, Underwood and Underwood.

Some of the Indian princes are allowed to maintain bodies of Imperial Service troops, which they equip and train at their own expense. These troops number in all some 22,000. As soon as the princes knew that Britain had need of soldiers, they gladly offered their troops to fight for their King-Emperor. The Maharajah of Mysore[247] gave £330,000 to fit out a force, and other princes sent large sums of money and thousands of horses, while little hill states in the Punjab and Baluchistan[248] offered camels and drivers. The Maharajah of Rewa[249] instantly asked, "*What orders has my King for me?*" and forthwith placed his troops, treasury, and even his private jewels at the disposal of his Majesty. Nor were the smaller chiefs behindhand. All were eager to help, even beyond the measure of their ability. Even the Dalai Lama[250] of Tibet, whose country was invaded by British troops as recently as 1904, offered soldiers, and ordered the priests throughout the length and breadth of the land to pray for the success of British arms and for the souls of the fallen. From private persons came money gifts, and from Indian societies blessings on the campaign. Almost every Indian prince desired to fight for us, and the Agha Khan,[251] the spiritual leader of 60,000,000 Mohammedans, offered to take his place as a private in the ranks. Many of the princes were accepted for service, and amongst them was Sir Pertab Singh,[252] who long ago swore that he would not die in his bed. Though seventy years of age, he was as eager as a boy to ride forth to the last and greatest of his wars. In this muster-roll of princes every great name in India was represented. Chiefs whose line of descent went back to the days of Alexander the Great, and whose forefathers had fought many a good fight against us in the days when we were winning India, were now assembled in battle array to do and die for Britain and her King.

I am sure that you have read with feelings of great pride and thankfulness this brief account of how the Empire rallied as one man in the day of trial. What an effect this splendid response must have had upon the Germans! They had sent their agents with bribes and lying tales into every part of the Empire where they thought men were discontented with British rule, and they hoped that when war broke out we should be so troubled with risings in many lands that we should be quite unable to fight them on the continent of Europe. A bitter disappointment awaited them. Except in South Africa, where there was a small rebellion which was easily put down without a single soldier being sent from Great Britain, the Empire proved as firm as a rock and as staunch as steel. Our Allies, the French and the Russians, were much struck by this wonderful unity. It proved to them, as it has proved to all the world, that, though we may have made mistakes in the government of our Empire, the races under the Union Jack know that we have honestly tried to do our duty by them, and have made their welfare our first and foremost consideration. So in this great and fateful struggle they stand by us, one in heart and mind, and we are knitted closer to them, and they to us, by their splendid loyalty in this hour of danger.

The Germans call the British army "a multicoloured travelling circus." One of their writers has said that the British have got together the peoples of the earth to fight them, and have shipped to France a variegated white, black, brown, yellow, and red medley of races. What else did they expect when they challenged an Empire that has possessions in every continent on the face of the globe? We have every right to be proud that men of such diverse races, creeds, and colours have united so gladly and freely against the common foe. In an earlier chapter of this book I told you how the states of Germany were welded together into an empire after they had fought side by side in the war against France. As Lord Rosebery tells us, "blood shed in common is the cement of nations." Now that miners of the Yukon, trappers of Athabasca, backwoodsmen of British Columbia, cowboys of Alberta, stalwart sons of Manitoba, Ontario, Quebec, New Brunswick, Nova Scotia, and Newfoundland, stockmen and sheep farmers of Australia and New Zealand, Boers of South Africa, and men of a thousand towns and villages in the old country, stand shoulder to shoulder with Sikhs of the Punjab, tribesmen of the Khyber, Gurkhas of Nepal, Egyptians of the Nile, and Maoris of the Southern Seas, may we not hope that hereafter a new and stronger bond will unite all the scattered states of the British Empire? The war of 1870-71 made the German Empire; the great war in which we are engaged bids fair to make the British Empire.

CHAPTER XXVIII.

THE GERMAN ADVANCE ON BRUSSELS.

Now we must return to Belgium, and follow the progress of the German forces in that country. There were two armies in Belgium—the one under General von Buelow,[253] and the other under General Alexander von Kluck.[253] We shall hear much of the latter general in the next volume of this work. If you were to examine his portrait, you would say that he is a man of sullen fierceness and great doggedness. This is by no means his first war: he fought against Austria in 1866, and was wounded at Metz in 1870. You already know that most of the officers holding high command in the German army are of noble birth. Von Kluck is an exception: he was only ennobled after he became a colonel.

The two German armies in Belgium were only part of the vast force intended for the invasion of France. This force consisted of six main armies, which, on 7th August, were stationed as follows:—The Sixth Army was assembled in and around Strassburg; the Fifth Army, under the Bavarian Crown Prince, lay just south of Metz; the Fourth Army, under the Crown Prince of Germany, was on the border of Luxemburg; the Third Army was in the Moselle valley, facing the Ardennes; the Second Army was south of Aix-la-Chapelle; and the First Army was in and around that city.

Indian Troops camping in a London Park. *Photo, Topical Press.*

We shall not know for many years to come what was the exact manner in which the Germans meant to move these armies into France. Some say they intended to mass nearly all of them on a wide front in Belgium, north and west of the Meuse, and then march them south into France. It is more likely, however, that they meant to use Metz as a pivot and swing the first five armies in a great circling movement to the west, like a gate upon its hinges; while the Sixth Army defended Alsace, and checked any advance of the French through the Vosges. Lay your pencil on the map with the point on Metz. Hold the point in your fingers, and sweep round the rest of the pencil to your left, and you will see exactly what I mean. It is said that the Germans had about two millions of men in the armies which were to make this movement. Of course, many of them would be required to mask[254] the fortresses and guard the lines of communication. Probably the actual German fighting line consisted of something between one million and one million and a half men. The Emperor, as War Lord, was in supreme command; but the real conduct of the campaign was in the hands of Count Helmuth von Moltke, the Chief of the General Staff. His uncle had brought France to its knees in 1870-71; he was to shatter the forces of France and Britain in 1914.

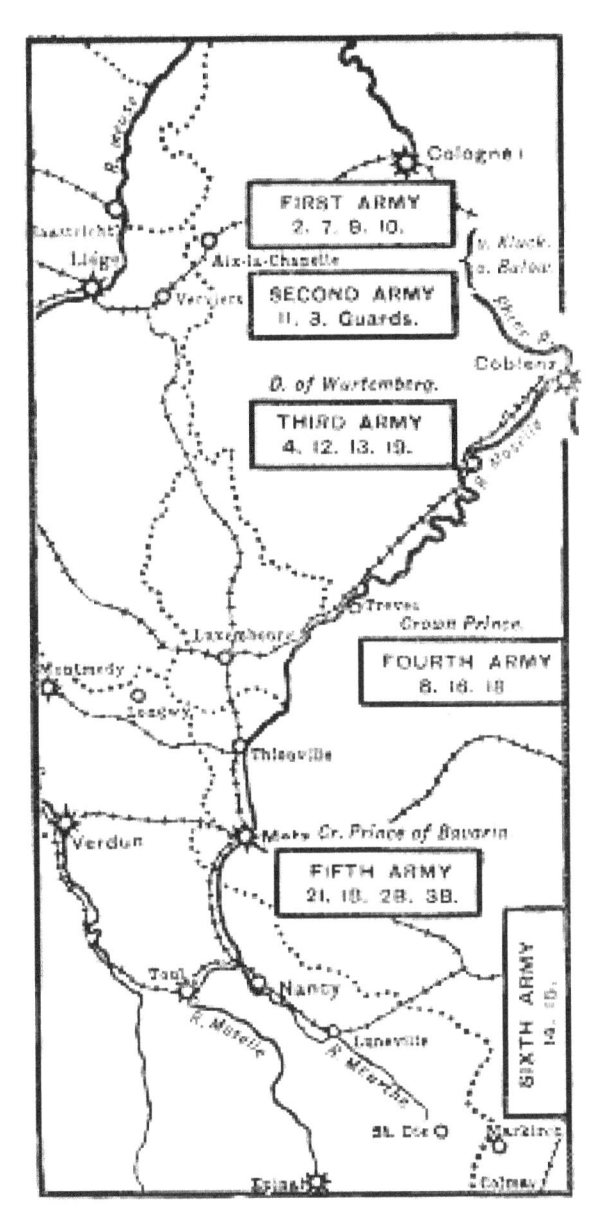

Map showing how the German Armies were stationed on the Western Frontier.

Now let us turn our attention to the First and Second Armies, which, as you know, were actually in Belgium when I broke off my story to tell you how the British Empire girded up its loins for the fray. Von Kluck's army (the First Army), which was to form the extreme right of the German line, had crossed the Dyle on 19th August, and von Buelow's army (the Second Army) was rapidly advancing towards the strong fortress of Namur, which stands at the point where the Meuse and the Sambre unite. The Belgian army at this time stood in danger of being enveloped; so it withdrew, much reduced in numbers, but still unbroken and undefeated, to the shelter of the Antwerp forts, leaving the capital, Brussels, open to the enemy. The Belgian Government had already left the city, and its headquarters were now in Antwerp.

Brussels, as you know, stands on the river Senne, and is one of the finest cities in Europe. It has noble buildings—churches, libraries, museums, picture-galleries—and broad boulevards, with a carriage drive down the middle, and a riding track on either side, shaded by rows of trees. Some of these boulevards have been made on the site of the old walls, which were pulled down many years ago. At one end of a pretty but not large park stands the king's palace, and at the other end are the Houses of Parliament. Much of Brussels is modern, but the Grand' Place belongs to the Middle Ages. On one side of it stands the town hall, which was built in the fifteenth century, and is a glorious old building, with a high steep roof, pierced by many little windows, and a front dotted with statues. Above its lofty and graceful spire is a gilded figure of the Archangel Michael, which serves as a wind-vane.

The other sides of the square are enclosed by quaint gabled houses, which formerly belonged to the Merchant Guilds. Some of them have gilded mouldings, and one of them is shaped like the stern of a ship. In the paved middle of the square a flower market is held, and here you may see the women of Brabant[255] in their white caps and large gold earrings. The largest and finest of all the modern buildings is the Palace of Justice, in which the law courts sit. It is said to have cost £2,000,000. As it stands on a little hill, and is so big and tall, it can be seen from every part of the city. The people of Brussels are perhaps the gayest and most lively in all Europe. Nowhere do you find men and women so fond of jokes and fun, and so eager for amusement. They call their city "Little Paris."

Brussels is very well known to British people, not only because the city is frequently visited by our tourists, but because some of our great writers have described it in their books. Laurence Sterne,[256] the Irish novelist, tells us much about Flanders in his "Tristram Shandy." The finest character in the book is Captain Shandy, or Uncle Toby, as he was more commonly called. This delightful old soldier was wounded at Namur,[257] and spent his peaceful old age in following Marlborough's campaigns[258] with the help of maps, books, and models. On his bowling-green he made trenches, saps, barricades, and redoubts, just as Marlborough was then doing; and he and his servant,

Corporal Trim, fought many great battles on the greensward before his house.

William Makepeace Thackeray,[259] in his "Vanity Fair," gives us a wonderful picture of Brussels in the year 1815, when the great battle of Waterloo was fought; and in his "Esmond" there is an exquisite account of the hero's visit to his mother's grave in a convent cemetery of the city. Charlotte Brontë,[260] in what is perhaps her best story, "Villette," describes her own experiences as a girl in Brussels very fully and vividly—so much so that many British readers cannot think of the city without thinking of "Villette." Here is her picture of Brussels on a festal night: "Villette is one blaze, one broad illumination; the whole world seems abroad; moonlight and heaven are banished; the town by her own flambeaux[261] beholds her own splendour—gay dresses, grand equipages, fine horses, and gallant riders throng the bright streets. I see even scores of masks.[262] It is a strange scene, stranger than dreams...Safe I passed down the avenues; safe I mixed with the crowd where it was deepest. To be still was not in my power, nor quietly to observe. I drank the elastic night air—the swell of sound, the dubious light, now flashing, now fading."

On Monday, 17th August, the people of Brussels knew for certain that the Germans were approaching the city. Crowds of refugees came pouring in from the villages and towns which the enemy had destroyed, and the condition of these poor folks would have melted a heart of stone. Mothers, weary and footsore, carried or dragged by the hand little children, weeping with weariness and hunger. Old men struggled along with bundles on their backs, or in wheelbarrows, or even in perambulators, containing all the little store of worldly goods which they had been able to save from the wreck of their homes. There were many widows and many fatherless in the sad throng, and they had terrible tales of sorrow and suffering to tell. Peasant women sent a shudder through the townsfolk by relating how their sons or husbands had been hanged for resisting the Uhlans. Young boys told how the priest, the doctor, and the schoolmaster of their villages had been shot, and the rest of the men carried off as prisoners of war. Still, in spite of all these alarms, the people of Brussels kept their heads. The Government put up notices warning them not to resist the German troops, and ordering them to stay in their houses with closed doors and windows, so that the enemy might have no excuse for shooting them down.

Belgian Civic Guards

All Belgian towns have what is known as a Civic Guard, composed of men who prepare themselves to defend their homes in case of attack. If you had seen these men on parade you would probably have smiled. Many of them were stout, elderly shopkeepers or workmen, and they wore on their heads a hard bowler hat, sometimes decorated with a bunch of dark green glossy feathers at the side. But in spite of their unsoldierlike appearance, they were brave fellows, all ready to lay down their lives in defence of hearth and home. While the Germans were approaching Brussels, the Civic Guard drilled daily in the park, dug trenches in the outskirts and even in the streets, and set up barricades of wire all along the roads by which the enemy could enter the city. The townsfolk constantly heard the dull roar of explosions as bridges and roadways were blown up to check the German advance. In the suburbs the people gladly gave the contents of their houses to form barricades. "Hundreds of people," we are told, "sacrificed all their household furniture in the common cause. Beds, pianos, carts, boxes, baskets of earth—one child I saw filling up a basket from the gutter—are all piled up."

Soon, however, it was clear that Brussels could not be defended. Even if all the Civic Guards fell, they could not hope to beat off the German army that was hourly drawing nearer and nearer. The only result would be that the city would suffer the fate of Louvain—all its grand buildings would be battered down, and Brussels would be no more.

At once there was a great exodus from the city. Motors, carts, carriages, and all kinds of conveyance were pressed into service, and were filled with people all bent on reaching the coast. Most of the vehicles were plastered with huge red crosses cut out of wall paper or old petticoats. Thousands of the poor people who had no means of escape went aimlessly to and fro in the streets, weeping and wailing. Every train was packed with people, and the roads leading to Holland were black with men, women, and children tramping onwards towards safety.

M. Adolphe Max, Burgomaster of Brussels.

The greater part of the townsfolk, however, remained, and went about their work as of yore, hoping against hope that the British or French would soon arrive. On Thursday, 19th August, the brave Mayor, M. Adolphe Max, posted a notice telling the people that, despite the heroic efforts of the Belgian troops, it was to be feared that the enemy would occupy Brussels. He advised the people to be calm, and avoid all panic, and he promised them that as long as he was alive he would try to protect their rights and dignity. "Citizens," he said, "whatever may befall, listen to your burgomaster. He will not betray you. Long live a free and independent Belgium! Long live Brussels!"

M. Max was as good as his word. By his fearless dealing with the Germans he won a renown which will last long after Belgium is free again. Whoever in future days writes the history of the war in this little heroic country will give M. Max a place beside King Albert and General Leman.

German Soldiers parading the Streets of Brussels. *Photo, Sport and General.*

CHAPTER XXIX.

HOW THE GERMANS ENTERED BRUSSELS.

One Thursday morning, attired in his scarf of office, M. Max drove out in a motor car, along with several other city officers, to meet the German general, and to arrange terms of surrender. He was received with that lack of politeness for which the German officer is notorious. After roughly ordering him to remove his scarf, the German general asked him if he was ready to surrender the city. If not, it would be shelled. M. Max replied that he had no choice in the matter; and was then informed that he and the other city officers would be held responsible for the good behaviour of the people, and that if they offended they would suffer. It was then arranged that the Germans were to march in next day, and that they were to be housed and fed at the expense of the city. When the burgomaster returned to Brussels, the Civic Guard, to their great disappointment, were ordered to give up their arms.

The German General Staff meant to make the entry into Brussels a matter of great pomp and display, so as to impress the citizens. They therefore arranged that an army corps which had not yet been engaged in fighting should be marched through the streets. The men were halted outside the town and given time to furbish themselves up for the occasion. The people of Brussels were not to be allowed to see the Germans against whom their fellow-countrymen had fought so bravely. There were to be no thinned ranks, no scarred, wounded, or war-weary soldiers in their streets, but an army as fresh and spick and span as though it were parading before the Kaiser at Potsdam.

Germans in Grand'-Place, Brussels. *Photo, Central News.*

The news that Brussels was in German hands had been flashed to every corner of the Fatherland, and had been received with loud rejoicings. Surely some of the more sober-minded Germans, even in that hour of rapture, must have remembered the remark of Napoleon, "The capture of an undefended city is no glory."

Try to realize the feelings of the people of Brussels as they gathered in the streets on that black day to see a ruthless and faithless enemy take possession of their beautiful and beloved capital. "Belgians," said an old soldier, with tears in his eyes, "can never forget this." They suffered then what their forefathers had suffered on the eve of Waterloo:—

"While thronged the citizens with terror dumb,
Or whispering with white lips,
'The foe!—they come, they come!'"

At two o'clock in the afternoon of 20th August the distant sound of guns announced the coming of the foe. Imagine the surprise of the people when the news flitted from mouth to mouth that their own M. Max was riding at the head of the German army. He had insisted on taking this place, because he was, as he reminded his captors, the first citizen of Brussels. On the wan, strained faces of the townsfolk there was the ghost of a smile when they saw him appear. Their quick-witted burgomaster was receiving the Germans not as a captive but as a host! It was a good joke, and the people could appreciate it, even on such a sad occasion.

Now the sound of bands was heard, and the advance guards of the Germans entered the city. By the side of M. Max rode a Prussian general—"a swarthy, black-moustached, ill-natured brute, dressed in khaki gray," as a bystander described him. I am sure that if he had been an angel of light the people of Brussels would have found fault with him at such a time. On came the waves of men, singing "Die Wacht am Rhein."[263]

"The wind-tost banners proudly fly;
While runs the river, sounds the cry,—
'We all will guard with heart and hand
The German Rhine for German land.'
Dear Fatherland, untroubled be,
Thy Rhine Watch stand true, firm, and free."

Anon they broke into the strains of "Deutschland über Alles,"[264] the first verse of which I translate roughly as follows. It is sung to the air of the Austrian National Anthem, composed by Joseph Haydn, the greatest of Austrian musicians, in the year 1797.

"First in all the world, my Germany,
First and foremost shalt thou be.
When thy sons in soul united
Grasp the shining sword for thee,
From the Maas, yea to the Mernel,[265]
From the Adige[266] to the sea,
First in all the world, my Germany,
First and foremost shalt thou be."

The Brunswick,[267] Death's Head, and Zieten[268] Hussars led the way; then came the infantry, followed by artillery with siege howitzers, and a hundred motor cars armed with quick-firing guns. As the men moved into the main streets they broke into that stiff-legged parade step which has been the triumphal march of the German army since the days of Frederick the Great.

The townsfolk in deep dismay watched the Germans filing into the Grand'-Place, and many of them muttered under their breath, "They will never come back again; the Allies will do for them." It is said that the German officers behaved very rudely to the people, and laughed scornfully in their faces, as though they wished to goad them into acts which would excuse an attack upon the city. The people, however, restrained themselves, and there was no bloodshed or destruction.

The city was placarded with notices threatening stern punishment to all those who opposed the troops, and a fine of £8,000,000 was levied on the place.

Food and lodging were provided for the troops, and when the Staff arrived they made the town hall their headquarters. M. Max was ordered to furnish three hundred beds for them. "I will provide three hundred and one beds," said he, "for, of course, *I* shall sleep there too."

When he was ordered to hand over a hundred of the chief men of the city as hostages[269] for the good behaviour of the people, the brave burgomaster refused to do anything of the sort. "I will be your hostage," he said, "and I will provide you with no others." On every occasion he was more than a match for the German officers. When one of the generals tried to browbeat him, and laid a revolver on the table to show him what his fate would be if he did not do as he was told, the burgomaster calmly picked up a pen and laid it beside the weapon. Even the slow, heavy Germans saw the meaning of this action. "The pen is mightier than the sword." Mr. Max meant them to understand that though they might kill him, writers in the future would tell the story of their shameful deeds, and brand their name with infamy for ever.

The Germans could do nothing with this brave, gay Belgian, who stood up so sturdily for the rights of his people; so at last they removed him from his office, and sent him to a German fortress in what they called "honourable custody." You may be sure that the townsfolk grieved greatly when their burgomaster was thus removed, and the Germans soon discovered that they were far more difficult to handle than when they had been under the care and guidance of the good M. Max.

The Germans occupied Brussels in force for a single day only. A garrison was left to hold the city, and the march through Belgium was continued. Meanwhile huge bodies of men, under the command of von Buelow, were passing unnoticed along the north bank of the Meuse towards Namur. At the same time two other armies were marching through the leafy Ardennes, where the overhanging foliage hid them from the eyes of the Belgian airmen. The great line was slowly but surely deploying for the long-delayed march into France.

With the occupation of Brussels by the Germans the first stage of the war comes to an end.

CHAPTER XXX.

HOW THE BRITISH ARMY WAS CARRIED OVERSEAS.

On the morning of 18th August, when the fate of Brussels was hanging in the balance, our newspapers contained a brief paragraph which was read by Britons all over the world with great satisfaction—our army had been landed on French soil without the loss of a single man. It was a great feat, and we were rightly proud of it. To many of us the news came as a great surprise. We British are not good at keeping secrets; but on this occasion, like Brer Rabbit, we lay low and said "nuffin." Thousands of people knew what was going on, but they did not talk about it, and in the newspapers there was scarcely a hint of what was happening. For once we kept a secret; and we were rewarded, for our transports crossed the narrow seas without the slightest attempt on the part of the enemy to molest them.

But for our navy this feat could never have been performed. A naval writer once said: "I consider that I have command of the sea when I am able to tell my Government that they can move an expedition to any point without fear of interference from an enemy's fleet." This is exactly what Admiral Jellicoe was able to tell his Government. He had "bottled up" the German navy in its ports, and the Channel and the Strait of Dover were as safe as ever they had been. From the first we had the great advantage of the command of the sea.

Let me tell you how our army of about 110,000 men, with guns, horses, and stores, was carried in safety to France. You know that the army was mobilized on 3rd August, and in a day or two most of the regiments were ready to depart with everything necessary for the grim work of war. Outside the barracks, in the early mornings, wives and mothers might have been seen bidding farewell to their husbands or sons; but there were few other signs that a great movement of troops was in progress. The Government had taken over the railways, and as soon as each unit was ready it was hurried off by train towards the south coast. Never were the railways so busy as at that time, and never did they work more smoothly; yet all was done with the utmost secrecy. Even the drivers of the engines were not told beforehand the name of the place to which they were bound. You can form some idea of the great strain upon the railways when I tell you that the London and South-Western dispatched three hundred and fifty trains each of thirty-five cars to Southampton in forty-five hours. During the first three weeks of the war seventy-three such trains arrived at the quays every fourteen hours. Every ten minutes, day and night, they steamed in, all up to time. We ought not to forget the splendid part which our railwaymen played at this time.

The men stationed in the Irish camp at Curragh sailed from Dublin; the men in the camp on Salisbury Plain boarded the transports at Avonmouth; while those at Aldershot found ships awaiting them at Southampton. Other bodies of men were embarked at Plymouth, Newhaven, Folkestone, Dover, and London. The busiest port of all was Southampton, which was entirely handed over to the army. On the outskirts of the town a rest camp had been formed, and in it the men who had travelled long distances were allowed some time to recover. Many of the trains were run directly to the quayside; in other cases the soldiers marched through the streets. Night and day for more than a week the streets of Southampton echoed to the tramp of khaki-clad men, the rattle of baggage-wagons, and the rumbling of guns.

All sorts of passenger ships were pressed into service—the Holyhead-North Wall steamers, the Fishguard boats, the Channel packets, vessels plying between Harwich and the Hook of Holland, Antwerp, and Hamburg, and many others. One Atlantic liner carried three thousand men on a single trip. When the soldiers were on board, the transports steamed off, and not even the captains knew the port to which they were to sail until they were ten miles out at sea. Then they opened sealed envelopes, and for the first time knew their destination. Think of the foresight and arrangement needed to engage all these ships and send them to their proper stations at the right time and in the right order without confusion and delay.

But this was not all. Arrangements had to be made for the troops to be landed at the various French ports, and to be encamped until they could be carried by rail to the front. Some of our officers were sent across to France before the troops arrived to prepare for their coming; and French officers came to England to arrange matters on this side. Everything was done according to a carefully-thought-out plan, and it worked as smoothly as a well-oiled machine. Long before the troops landed, enormous quantities of stores had been shipped to the French ports, so that depôts for the supply of the army might be established.

Our troops were landed on the Continent at the French ports of Havre, Dieppe, Boulogne, Calais, and Dunkirk. All day long, and all night too, streams of transports crossed and recrossed the Channel. The weather was perfect, and the men were packed on board the ships like Bank Holiday trippers. They suffered no discomfort, for the passage did not in any case occupy more than about fifteen hours. Many of the men were surprised to find that no armed vessels accompanied them as an escort. British warships, however, were keeping their Watch on the Brine, though the soldiers could not see them. A squadron of cruisers patrolled the narrow seas between the North Foreland and the French coast, and thus closed the North Sea entrance to the Channel. Aeroplanes and a naval airship hovered above the same waters, keeping a bright lookout for enemy craft. It is said that the crew of one seaplane engaged in this work did a most daring deed in mid-air. Something went wrong with the propeller, and it had to be changed. The pilot thought he would be obliged to descend for the purpose, but two of the crew offered to do the work in the air. They climbed out on to the bracket carrying the propeller, and actually changed the blade while soaring two thousand feet above the sea!

A daring feat in mid-air.

(*From the picture by Cyrus Cuneo.*)

On former occasions, when our soldiers have been sent abroad to fight for their country, we have gathered in crowds to give them a hearty "send off." They have departed to the noise of ringing cheers, the blare of bands, the waving of banners, the flutter of handkerchiefs. But those were days when we did not fear the secret menace of mines, submarines, and aeroplanes. On this occasion there were no public farewells. The men, however, were not allowed to depart without a fervent "God speed" from him who speaks in the name of us all. Before embarking, each soldier was presented with two printed messages—one from the King, the other from Lord Kitchener.

Here is the King's message. You will notice how quietly confident it is, and how full of dignity. It is just the message which we should expect a British king to send to British soldiers.

"You are leaving home to fight for the safety and honour of my Empire. Belgium, which country we are pledged to defend, has been attacked, and France is about to be invaded by the same powerful foe. I have implicit confidence in you, my soldiers. Duty is your watchword, and I know your duty will be nobly done. I shall follow your every movement with deepest interest, and mark with eager satisfaction your daily progress. Indeed, your welfare will never be absent from my thoughts. I pray God to bless you and guard you, and bring you back victorious.

"GEORGE, R. et I."[270]

The men also received a little printed letter of counsel and guidance from Lord Kitchener. It has been rightly called the noblest message ever sent to fighting men. Read the following three paragraphs very carefully, and try to remember them. Never before has so fine an ideal been set before the British soldier.

"Remember that the honour of the British Empire depends on your individual conduct, and you can do your country no better service than in showing yourself in France and Belgium in the true character of a British soldier.

"Be invariably courteous, considerate, and kind. Always look upon looting as a disgraceful act. You are sure to meet with a welcome, and to be trusted; your conduct must justify that welcome and that trust.

"Do your duty bravely. Fear God. Honour the King.

"KITCHENER, Field-Marshal."

More of our soldiers were landed at Boulogne than at any other French port. Boulogne has a special interest for us: it was the port at which Napoleon made his preparations, between June 1803 and September 1805, for the invasion of England. He marched a hundred thousand men—a very large army in those days—to Boulogne, and every road by which his soldiers passed bore the sign-post, "To England." A huge flotilla of flat-bottomed boats was collected, and the men were exercised in embarking and disembarking within sight of the white cliffs of Dover. "The Channel," said

Napoleon, "is but a ditch, and anyone can cross it who has but the courage to try." You know that he never tried to cross it. He could not win that command of the narrow seas on which the success of his invasion depended. His fleet lured Nelson to the West Indies, and then sailed rapidly back; but it was met off Ferrol, and was so crippled that Napoleon was forced to give up his project in disgust. He broke up the camp at Boulogne, and marched his army against the Austrians and Russians instead.

Many of our soldiers at Boulogne rested almost in the shadow of a tall column, 172 feet high, which stands about two miles from the port on the road to Calais. It was erected in 1804 to commemorate the invasion which never came off, and was left unfinished until 1841. On the summit is a statue of the emperor. Our men must also have been much interested in the crumbling forts which were built by Napoleon to protect his flat-bottomed boats from attack.

A friend who was in Boulogne when the transports were expected, tells me that weather-beaten sailors watched the sea eagerly for days on end, and at last, when they saw the hulls of our ships on the horizon, broke into loud cries: "Les Anglais arrivent!"[271] At once the townsfolk flocked to the quays, and as our men marched down the gangways they received them like old friends. They were full of admiration for the fine, trim, well-set-up Britons who had come to their help, and they loudly praised their arms, clothing, horses, and guns. They flocked around them, shaking them by the hand and patting them on the shoulder. "So milord Kitchener has sent you," they said. "He is indeed a fine fellow, a tough customer."

Many of the soldiers were marched straight from the boat to the train, which they boarded in their usual business-like fashion. "Those English," said an admiring townsman, "take their departure as if they were going for a walk. They are indeed brave soldiers." You can imagine the bustle and excitement on the quays and in the streets of the town as infantry, cavalry, artillery, Army Service corps, and nurses came ashore, and the delight of the people as they saw aeroplanes hovering overhead like huge dragon flies.

Some of our soldiers were sent to a rest camp on the low hills outside the town, and before long they won the hearts of the townsfolk by their cheery good humour and excellent behaviour. All sorts of presents were exchanged; little French tricolours, bonbons, flowers, and cigarettes were pressed upon them, in return for which our men parted with their buttons and badges. "They are English gentlemen—that's what they are," said French men and women alike. Many of the French soldiers in the town could speak English well, and with these our men struck up a close comradeship at once. "Hallo!" said one "Tommy" to a French corporal, "does your mother know you're out?" To which came the quick reply in perfect English, "Well, she ought to, for there are six of us out."

Those early days in France were delightful to our men. The weather was perfect, their surroundings were novel, they had little to do, and they were surrounded by hosts of friends. "This isn't like war," said one of them; "it's just a bit of a holiday, with nothing to pay." All our soldiers were provided with a sheet of paper containing the French words and phrases which they were likely to need. As you may imagine, the attempts of some of the Tommies to speak French with this slender equipment were amusing in the extreme.

And now, while our army is being rapidly carried by train to the front, where it is to form the extreme left of the Allied battle-line, let us learn something of its commander-in-chief, Field-Marshal Sir John French.[272] The general public knew little of him before the war, but he has always been most popular in all branches of the service. In 1866 he joined the navy as a cadet, and served as a midshipman for four years; but he gave up the sea in his twenty-second year, and obtained a commission in the 8th Hussars, because he wished to see active service, and there seemed little likelihood of naval warfare for a long time to come. He soon showed himself a keen cavalry officer, but he had to wait many years for the chance to draw his sword against an enemy. When General Gordon[273] was shut up in Khartum, Major French, as he was then, commanded the single cavalry squadron in the little army which was sent—alas! too late—to save him. Though the expedition was a failure, several desperate battles were fought, and Major French came home with a very good record. In 1885 he was promoted lieutenant-colonel, and later on was sent to India, where he made a great name as a leader of cavalry.

When he joined the army most officers believed that the work of cavalry was to wait until the guns had shaken the enemy's infantry, and then to charge down upon it in a solid mass, and put it to flight. French did not think that this was the chief part which cavalry had to play in modern warfare. He believed that it ought to be the "eyes and ears" of the army, and that it should devote itself largely to scouting and to "feeling for the enemy." He trained his regiment on these lines, and though there were some of the "old school" who opposed him, he found a warm friend and supporter in the Duke of Connaught.

British soldiers making friends with the people of Boulogne.

By permission of the Illustrated London News.

It was during the South African War that General French was able to put his principles into practice, and by so doing he showed how valuable they were. He only just escaped being shut up in Ladysmith;[274] he left it by the last train to take charge of the cavalry division which relieved Kimberley,[275] stopped the retreat of Cronje at Paardeburg,[276] and entered Pretoria.[277] His striking success in South Africa marked him out as the greatest of our cavalry leaders. Naturally we should expect him to be fond of horses. The charger which carried him through the South African War wore a medal round its neck, with a record of its services. When this charger died Sir john was much grieved, and he buried it under a memorial stone at Aldershot.

Sir John French.

Those who know General French well tell us that he has real genius. When he has a problem to solve he seems more like a dreamer than a man of action. Suddenly, however, when he has fully grasped the situation, he springs to his feet, having fully made up his mind what he is going to do and how he is going to do it. He sketches out his plan in the fewest possible words, and frequently astonishes his staff by the daring and novelty of his plans. "Deeds, not words," is his motto, and he fully deserves his nickname, "Silent French." He loves his profession, and no general has ever been so ready to pay such generous tributes to those of his officers and men who deserve them. Amongst the rank and file he is known as "Johnny," and all of them know that their welfare is his chief concern. A chaplain at the front tells us that "no matter how hard he has worked during the day, he always tries to spend a little time in a field hospital at night with the wounded."

Our French allies were delighted that Sir John French had been made commander-in-chief of the British army which was to fight side by side with them. Most of the leading French officers knew him well, and admired him greatly. They were specially pleased that his name was French, and they said that he must be a Frenchman by descent. When they discovered that he had Irish blood in his veins they found a new reason for giving him a hearty welcome. Many Irish soldiers, as you know, have fought bravely and died nobly for France. Before setting out for the front, he paid a flying visit to Paris, and was greeted with loud cheers by the Parisians who lined the streets in his honour.

And now, while millions of men are grasping their rifles, ready for the first clash of arms in this gigantic struggle which will decide the fate of Europe, the first volume of this book comes to an end. The greatest story of the world has yet to be told—a story of strife on a scale far beyond the experiences of mankind, of combats so vast and long enduring that the battles of history seem in comparison but puny skirmishes, of slaughter that has horrified the watching world, and of heroisms that have thrilled it with pride.

"Troops to our Britain true
Faring to Flanders,
God be with all of you
And your commanders.
"Fending a little friend,
Weak but unshaken—
Quick! there's no time to spend,
Or the fort's taken.
"He hath his all at stake;
More can have no man.
Quick, ere the barrier break,
On to the foeman.
"Troops to this Britain true,
And your commanders,
God be with all of you
Fighting in Flanders."

END OF VOLUME I.

FOOTNOTES:

[1] *Mes-sē´na*, town of Sicily on the Strait of Messina, which lies between the island of Sicily and the toe of Italy.

[2] The Great Powers are the leading nations of the world. They are rich in men and money, and keep up large armies or navies, or both. Great Britain, the United States of America, Germany, France, Russia, Austria-Hungary, Italy, and, since 1905, Japan, are the Great Powers.

[3] A letter sent by one government to another, referring to some matter which is in dispute between them.

[4] *Ar-ma-ged´on*.

[5] People of partly Finnish and partly Turkish descent, now the ruling people in Hungary. There are nearly ten million people speaking the Magyar language.

[6] Descended from the people who live in the north-east of Asia Minor.

[7] *Bel-grād´*.

[8] *Bos´nia*.

[9] *Her-tse-go-vē´na*.

[10] Means the Ox Ford.

[11] *Dar-da-nelz´*.

[12] *Tre-es´tā*.

[13] *Sal-on-ē´ka*.

[14] *E-jē´an*.

[15] *Ra-goo´za*.

[16] *Mos´tar*.

[17] *Al-ba'nia*, a country on the coast of the Adriatic Sea to the south and west of Servia.

[18] *Sa-ra-yā´vo*.

[19] We speak of Servia and Servians, but it is more correct to say Serbia and Serbs.

[20] *Kos´so-vo*, battlefield to the west of Pristina. (See map on p. 8.)

[21] *Ve-en´na*, called by the Austrians and Germans *Wien*.

[22] *Shar-le-mān'* (Charles the Great), became king of the Franks in 768, and reigned for forty-six years.

[23] *Ish'l.*

[24] *Bo-he'mi-a*, a kingdom in the north-west of the Austrian Empire fenced in by lofty mountains.

[25] *Ag-a-mem'non.*

[26] *Kī'ser*, a German form of Cæsar, the name given to the Roman emperors.

[27] Former duchy of Germany, consisting of what is now Würtemberg Baden, and South-west Bavaria.

[28] City of Bavaria, 90 miles north by west of Mūn'ich, the capital.

[29] Title given to certain princes of Germany because they had the right to *elect* the Emperor.

[30] Chief town of the province of Brandenburg, 16 miles west of Berlin. It contains a royal palace, and is practically the German Windsor.

[31] Born 1795, died 1881. A great writer of history and philosophy. His *History of Frederick the Great* was begun in 1852, and occupied him for thirteen years, during which he paid two visits to Germany.

[32] *Mä-rī'a Ter-e'sa*, Queen of Hungary and German Empress; reigned from 1741 to 1780. She was the mother of Marie Antoinette (*ong-twa-net*), wife of Louis XVI. of France.

[33] *Sil-es'i-a*, since 1742 a province of Prussia in the extreme south-east, between Poland and Bohemia. Most of it is in the basin of the Oder. It is very rich in iron, coal, and metals, and is an important manufacturing region.

[34] Now a province of Prussia, stretching from the Netherlands east to the Elbe, and from the North Sea south to Westphalia and Hesse Nassau. It contains the following German ports—Emden, Harburg, Papenburg, and Wilhelmshaven. The town of Hanover, which still contains the favourite residence of George I. and George II., is 112 miles by rail south of Hamburg.

[35] *Krā'kō*, the old capital of Poland; stands on the left bank of the Vistula, in the Austrian crown land of Galicia.

[36] *Ga-lish'i-a*, crown land of Austria, on the north side of the Carpathians. Its north-west frontier is formed by the Vistula, and the eastern parts are drained by the Dniester, Pruth, and Sereth. The country is rich in petroleum, from which the spirit is made by which motors are propelled. As motors are now so largely used in war, the possession of Galicia is a great advantage to Austria and Germany.

[37] *Sō'bē-es'kē*, John III. of Poland; reigned from 1674 to 1696.

[38] A form of government in which the head of the state is not a king, but a citizen elected by the people for a number of years.

[39] *Mar-sā-yāz'*.

[40] *Roo-zhā' d'lēl'* (1760-1836).

[41] Capital of Alsace-Lorraine, on a small tributary of the Rhine. It became German in 1871.

[42] *Mar-selz'*, chief city of South France, on the Gulf of Lions, one of the two great ports (the other is Genoa) on the Mediterranean Sea.

[43] Native of Corsica (*Kōr'si-ka*), large French island, 110 miles south of the coast of France. The chief town is Ajaccio, in which Napoleon's birthplace is still shown.

[44] *Too-lon'*. French naval port, 42 miles east of Marseilles.

[45] German town on the left bank of the Saale, 14 miles E.S.E. of Weimar.

[46] *Ne'men*, river rising in the Russian government of Minsk, and flowing to the Baltic Sea in East Prussia.

[47] *Boo-lō'ny*, town on the English Channel, connected with Folkestone by a daily cross-Channel service.

[48] Old capital of Russia, on the Moskva, a tributary of the Oka, 390 miles south-east of Petrograd. Its huge citadel is called the Kremlin.

[49] People living in the south and east of Russia who give military service to the Czar in return for the lands on which they live. They are very fierce and warlike, and are the best light cavalry in the Russian army.

[50] *Byer-ye-zē'na*, tributary of the Dnieper, in the Minsk government of Russia.

[51] *Met'ter-nich*, chief minister of Austria from 1809 to 1848.

[52] *Blüch'er*, field-marshal of Prussia; a very warlike, upright, and loyal man, but no great general. He hated Napoleon.

[53] Village, Prussia, 12 miles south of Berlin.

[54] Capital of the kingdom of Saxony, on the Elbe; a great centre of art and learning. It has given its name to a kind of porcelain.

[55] Small island (area 86 square miles) off west coast of Italy.

[56] *Kā-tr'brā'*, village, 19 miles south-east of Brussels. It stands at cross-roads, whence its name (four arms).

[57] *Lĕ'ny*, village, 25 miles south-east of Brussels.

[58] Village in Belgium, 11 miles south of Brussels.

[59] Island of the South Atlantic Ocean; area, 47 square miles. Napoleon was kept prisoner at Longwood.

[60] *Zoi'der*, means south.

[61] Cape of south-west Spain, at the entrance of the Strait of Gibraltar, memorable for Nelson's victory over the combined fleets of France and Spain (Oct. 21, 1805).

[62] German word meaning alliance or league.

[63] *Sax'ony*, kingdom of South Germany, north of Bohemia. It is divided into two halves by the river Elbe.

[64] *Vür'tem-berg*, kingdom of the German Empire, to the west of Bavaria. It is drained for the most part by the river Neckar (tributary of the Rhine) and its tributaries.

[65] *Ba-vä'ria*, kingdom of the German Empire, to the west and south-west of Bohemia. It still has its own king, and is the most independent part of the German Empire.

[66] An assembly for making laws.

[67] *Frank'fort*, a city of Prussia, in the province of Hesse-Nassau, on the river Main, 22 miles above its junction with the Rhine. The German Diet met here from 1816 to 1866.

[68] Succeeded to the throne on the death of his father in 1840. He was born in 1795, and died in 1861.

[69] The famous hero in Swiss legend who refused to reverence the ducal hat of Austria, set up in 1307 at Altorf, and shot the apple off his son's head. He afterwards led the successful revolt against Austria.

[70] Prussian statesman, born at Nassau in 1757; died in 1831.

[71] Born 1803, died 1879. In 1859 he was appointed Prussian Minister of War.

[72] *Molt'ka*, born 1800, died 1891.

[73] In Continental countries the "great general staff" consists of a body of officers, who form the thinking and directing head of the army.

[74] These duchies now form one Prussian province between the North Sea and the Baltic Sea. Through the province runs the Kaiser Wilhelm or Kiel

Canal, which enables ships to pass from the North Sea to the Baltic Sea without rounding Denmark.

[75] The great battle which marked the downfall of Prussia (see page 61).

[76] French order of merit founded by Napoleon in 1802. The emblem of the order is a five-rayed star of white enamel edged with gold, bearing on one side the image of the republic, with the inscription, *République Française*, and on the other side two flags, with the motto, *Honneur et Patrie*. It is crowned by a wreath of oak and laurel, and is hung from a red ribbon.

[77] *Bo-hē´mi-a*, a kingdom in the north-west of the Austrian Empire. It is almost square in shape, and is shut in by lofty mountains. It is mainly drained by the Moldau, a tributary of the Elbe.

[78] *Sā´do-wa*, village in Bohemia, 8 miles north-west of Königgrätz (on the Elbe).

[79] *Ker´nig-gräts*, town of Bohemia, on the Elbe, 65 miles east of Prague, the capital.

[80] Son of the Emperor William I., born at Potsdam in 1831, and on the death of his father in 1888 became the Emperor Frederick III.

[81] *Kēl*, seaport of Prussia, on a bay in the Baltic, near the Baltic end of the great Kaiser Wilhelm Canal, and 70 miles by rail north of Hamburg. It is the chief naval station of the German Empire.

[82] *Con´cord*, peace and goodwill.

[83] *Shans-e-lees-ay*, the Elysian fields; amongst the Greeks the abode of the blessed after death.

[84] *Mad´lenn*, in honour of Mary Magdalene.

[85] *Tweel´ree*.

[86] *Ghee-nyol.*

[87] *Gil´o-tēn*, the beheading instrument, so called from its inventor, Joseph Ignace *Guillotin* (1738-1814).

[88] *Lē´ong*, city of France, at the confluence of the Saône and the Rhone; the great centre of French silk manufacture.

[89] Fortified town of France, near the Belgian frontier, 66 miles south-east of Calais. It is noted for the manufacture of linen, cotton, velvet, and woollen goods.

[90] *Roo-ong´*, chief cotton port of France, on the Seine, 87 miles by rail north-west of Paris.

[91] *Bor-do´*, port of France, on the Gironde, 60 miles from the sea; the great wine-exporting port.

[92] River of Germany, tributary of the Rhine, which it enters at Mainz.

[93] (1808-73). Son of Louis Napoleon, brother of Napoleon I. He was elected President of the French Republic in 1848, and on December 2, 1852, after he had overthrown the Government by armed force, was proclaimed emperor as Napoleon III.

[94] *Krī´me-a*, peninsula of Southern Russia, in which the British, French, and Turks fought the Russians (1854-6).

[95] Watering-place of Hesse-Nassau, Prussia, 11 miles by rail east of Coblenz (at the confluence of the Rhine and its tributary the Moselle).

[96] Called the mitrailleuse (*me-trah-yuse*).

[97] Fortified town of Lorraine, on the Moselle.

[98] Body of troops kept in hand to be called up when needed.

[99] That branch of the army which handles the big guns.

[100] Horse soldiers armed with sabres, carbines, and sometimes lances.

[101] *Brüzh*, 63 miles north-west of Brussels, 8 miles inland from the North Sea, with which it is connected by two canals. From the 12th to the 16th century Bruges was the largest business city of Northern Europe. It is now a quiet, quaint old city, with many ancient and interesting buildings.

[102] Sound the *g* hard; 32 miles north-west of Brussels, on the rivers Scheldt and Lys (*leese*). It is divided by canals into some forty islands, and has over two hundred bridges. Though it is now a manufacturing place, it preserves its ancient appearance, and is a most interesting city.

[103] *Ep´r´*, 32 miles by rail south-south-west of Bruges. Its Cloth Hall and St. Martin's Church date from the thirteenth century.

[104] *Skelt*, rises in department Aisne, France, and enters the North Sea by two main channels formed by islands, the outermost of which is Walcheren. Length, 250 miles, 210 of which are navigable.

[105] Rises in the French department of Pas de Calais, and flows north-east through Belgium, to join the Scheldt at Ghent.

[106] Rises in French department of Haute Marne, flows mainly north-east, north, north-west, and west for 500 miles. In Holland it joins the left arm of the Rhine. The river is navigable from the sea to Verdun, some 135 miles from its source.

[107] Town on right bank of the Meuse, 17 miles by rail south by east of Namur. In the fifteenth century it was a busy manufacturing town, but prior to the war was a quiet tourist resort. The citadel stands on a cliff 300 feet above the river.

[108] *Na-mur´*, strongly fortified town, at the confluence of the Sambre and Meuse. The citadel stands on a height in the angle between the rivers, and the place was, before the war, encircled by nine forts on high ground, from 3 to 5 miles apart.

[109] *Sän'br´*, tributary of the Meuse. It rises in French department of Aisne, and becomes navigable 19 miles from its source.

[110] *Le-äzh´*, 50 miles east by south of Brussels.

[111] *Ar-den´*, wooded hill region between the Meuse and the Moselle; general elevation, 1,800 feet.

[112] State of taking no part on either of two sides. Belgium, by treaty, must never take sides in any war that is waged, and the Great Powers guarantee that she shall not be conquered. She can, of course, resist an invader.

[113] Independent Grand Duchy (area 997 sq. m.) between France, Belgium, and Germany. It forms a low plateau, and is drained by the Moselle and its tributary the Sauer. Mining and iron smelting are the chief occupations of the people.

[114] *Vōzh*. You will see their position on the map. The highest point (4,680 ft.) is at the south end. The western slopes of the mountains are thickly wooded, and the valleys give pasturage to many cattle.

[115] *Bāl*, largest and richest town of Switzerland, on the north bank of the Rhine, where it sweeps eastward.

[116] *Lor-rän´, äl-säs´*.

[117] *Say*.

[118] Born 1856; died 1879. After 1870 he lived with his mother at Chislehurst in Kent, and entered the Royal Military Academy at Woolwich.

[119] *Zar'brük-en*, on left bank of Saar, 38 miles east of Metz, in a coal-mining district.

[120] *Vīs'en-boorg*, 33 miles north-east of Strassburg.

[121] Born 1808; died 1893. He was made duke and field-marshal after saving the day at Magenta (see p. 88).

[122] *Vaert*, village, 12 miles south of Weissenburg.

[123] From Algeria (*Al-jē'ri-a*), African colony of France fronting the Mediterranean Sea, inhabited chiefly by Moors.

[124] *Fross-ar*, born 1807; died 1875. He had been a colonel in the Crimean War.

[125] *Stīn'mets*, born 1796; died 1877. Was in command of the Prussian army which gained victories over the Austrians in 1866.

[126] *Baz-ane'*, born 1811; died 1888. Marshal of France; previously saw service in Algeria, Spain, Italy, Morocco, the Crimea and Mexico. In 1873 he was denounced as a traitor and sentenced to death, but let off with twenty years' imprisonment. In August 1874 he escaped to Madrid, where he died.

[127] *Sha-lon*, on the Marne, 92 miles east of Paris. The camp (45 sq. m.) is 12 miles north of the town.

[128] Called by the French the battle of Borny; village 2½ miles from Metz.

[129] *Vār-dun'*, town and fortress of France on right bank of the Meuse; 35 miles by rail west of Metz.

[130] *Grav'lot*.

[131] *Reh-zon-veel'*.

[132] Nine miles north-west of Metz.

[133] One of the seven archangels, considered to be the guardian of Israel.

[134] *Seh-don'*.

[135] *Gee-von'*.

[136] *Vār-sa'y'*, French town, 11 miles south-west of Paris, containing a famous palace of Louis XIV., said to have cost £40,000,000.

[137] *Jofr*, born 1852.

[138] Born 1850.

[139] *Mah'di*, false prophet of the Mohammedans, who preached a holy war in the Sudan, that part of Africa south of Egypt and the Sahara. He was conquered by a British and Egyptian force at Omdurman in 1885.

[140] *Dō-dā'*, born 1840, died 1897, one of the greatest French novelists of the later nineteenth century. He has been compared, not unjustly, with Dickens.

[141] Children, Cooking, Church.

[142] See p. 81.

[143] *Lē'ber*, dear.

[144] See p. 80.

[145] For the story of how part of Poland was included in Prussia, see p. 48.

[146] *Boo'd'ha*, the founder of a religion largely professed in Tibet, parts of N. India, Ceylon, Burma, China, and Japan.

[147] The danger arising from the growing power of the Yellow peoples, chiefly the Chinese and Japanese.

[148] *Land'vair*.

[149] The Sultan of Turkey is the religious head of Mohammedans throughout the world.

[150] *Kō'ni-ā*, town, Asia Minor, about 300 m. east of Smyrna.

[151] Town of Mesopotamia, on the Tigris.

[152] Town on the Shat-el-Arab, 70 m. from the Persian Gulf.

[153] So called from the colour of its cover. It contains State documents explaining how the war arose.

[154] Country of N. Africa. In 1911 the Germans made a treaty with France, by which they agreed to let the French rule Morocco as a protectorate in return for territory in the French Congo.

[155] Born 1875, nephew of Leopold, King of the Belgians, whom he succeeded in 1909. He is a student, has travelled widely, and is greatly interested in improving the lot of his people. He is very popular with all classes of his subjects. The Socialists, of whom there are many in Belgium, say that when Belgium becomes a republic Albert will be their first president. His wife, Elizabeth, is a princess of Bavaria; she has qualified as an oculist.

[156] Since the war began its name has been changed to Petrograd.

[157] Born 1862. He was Under-Secretary for Foreign Affairs from 1892 to 1895, and became Foreign Secretary in Dec. 1905.

[158] See p. 13.

[159] Herr von Jagow (Ya-go), born 1863. He is a close personal friend of the Kaiser's, and has been the German Secretary of State for Foreign Affairs since 1913.

[160] See p. 30.

[161] Bethmann-Hollweg (*Betman-Holvech*), born 1856. He has been Chancellor—that is, chief minister of the German Empire—since 1909.

[162] Born 1847. In 1905 he became ambassador at Vienna, but was transferred to Berlin in 1908.

[163] France has colonies in Asia, Australasia, Africa, and certain islands of America, comprising in all an area of more than 4½ million square miles, with an estimated population of 41 millions.

[164] See p. 30.

[165] The rate which the Bank of England charges for giving ready money for a legal promise to pay money at a future date. The rise of the bank rate shows that money is scarce; its fall, that money is plentiful.

[166] Sailors who have left the Navy, but must return to it when required to do so.

[167] The Territorials are citizen soldiers from 17 to 35 years of age, who enlist for four years, and may be required to serve in any part of the United Kingdom, but not out of it without their own consent. They must put in a certain number of drills each year, and attend an annual camp. At the outbreak of war they numbered about 250,000.

[168] *Lon-wee´*, fortified town of France on the Belgian border, called by Louis the Fourteenth the "iron gate of France."

[169] *See-ra-lay-Forge*, manufacturing town in France, 33 miles east of Nancy.

[170] In the House of Commons the party or parties which support the Government sit on the Speaker's right; the party or parties which oppose the Government sit on the Speaker's left.

[171] Those Irishmen who desire Home Rule for Ireland.

[172] Residence of the German Ambassador in London. It was in Carlton House Terrace.

[173] Born 1859. He has been in the Navy since 1872, and has seen service in Egypt, and in China where he was wounded. When called to take chief command of the Fleet he was Second Sea Lord at the Admiralty, the headquarters of the Navy in Whitehall, London.

[174] See p. 181.

[175] Destroyers are fast warships, smaller than cruisers, and are meant to act against torpedo boats of the enemy. They also engage in scouting and patrol work. Some of them have a speed of more than 40 knots, and carry 105 men. All are armed with quick-firing guns and torpedoes.

[176] War vessels built mainly for speed. They were originally used for scouting, but nowadays they are little inferior in strength and gun power to

battleships. A battle cruiser is really a battleship with high speed. The *Lion*, for example, has a tonnage of 26,350 tons, and steams over 30 miles an hour. She carries eight 13.5-inch guns, and sixteen 4-inch guns. The *Lion*, the *Tiger*, the *Queen Mary*, and the *Princess Royal* are the most powerful battle cruisers in existence.

[177] *Am-fi′on.*

[178] For diagram see p. 192.

[179] Quoted from "First Lessons in War," by Spenser Wilkinson.

[180] Born 1761, died 1842. He invented shrapnel in 1787, and it was first employed by the British in 1804. Some of our victories in the Peninsular War were largely won by means of it, and it played an important part in the battle of Waterloo. The Prussians first used it in 1864.

[181] Millimetre. A millimetre is 1/1000 of a metre (3-1/3 ft.). Seventy-five millimetres is about three inches. This is the bore or *calibre* of the gun.

[182] Apparatus for signalling by flashing the sun's rays.

[183] See p. 109.

[184] The Austrian Switzerland, north of Italy and east of Switzerland. Its capital is Innsbrück, on the Inn.

[185] Belgian West Africa, mainly drained by the Congo and covering an area of some 800,000 square miles. It was explored by H. M. Stanley on behalf of Leopold, King of the Belgians, and became his property with the consent of the Great Powers. In 1889 Leopold bequeathed it to Belgium, and it was taken over by that country in 1908.

[186] *Brē-äl-mon′*, Henry Alexis, Belgian military engineer; born 1821, died 1903. The works which he planned along the Meuse were completed after his death.

[187] *Āks-la-shä-pel′*, or *Äch′en*, ancient city of Prussia, formerly the capital of Charlemagne, forty miles west-south-west of Cologne.

[188] *Mal-may-de.*

[189] *Stä′ve-lot.*

[190] *Vār-vi-ā′.*

[191] *Vee-zā′.*

[192] River of Belgium; after a north and west course of fifty miles joins the Nethe to form the Rupel, four miles north-west of Malines.

[193] Citizen soldiers for the defence of a town.

[194] *Lay-man*, born 1852; one of Belgium's most scientific soldiers.

[195] *Flair-on*.

[196] *Shōd-fon-taine*, means warm spring.

[197] French for *behold!*

[198] Born 1848; said to have been killed in a subsequent action.

[199] See p. 84.

[200] Under the will of Cecil Rhodes, a former Premier of Cape Colony, a sum of money was set aside to send colonial students to the University of Oxford. In addition, Oxford scholarships were founded for two students from each of the states of the United States and for fifteen students from Germany. The students were not to be merely bookworms, but clever youths, manly, truthful, upright, and successful in outdoor sports.

[201] On active service soldiers are supplied with compressed food which they may only eat when they cannot otherwise obtain supplies. In the British army the emergency ration is kept in a small sealed tin cylinder about five inches long. It consists of a cake of beef and a tablet of cocoa paste.

[202] *Ton'gr*. For this and other Belgian names, see map on page 226.

[203] German Lancers. The name comes from a Polish word derived from the Turkish.

[204] Seaport and first-class fortress, capital of province of West Prussia, 3 miles from the Baltic Sea and 285 miles by rail north-east of Berlin.

[205] So called from the cross which the Crusaders wore when they set out to free the Holy Land from the infidel. The First Crusade was preached in 1095, and lasted from 1096 to 1099.

[206] Ruled over Hungary, with his capital at Budapest. Became King of the Huns, 434 A.D.; died of intemperance, 453.

[207] An idyll is a story poem. The king is Arthur, who "in twelve great battles overcame the heathen hordes, and made a realm and reigned."

[208] Born 1478, died 1535; became Lord Chancellor of England. Was beheaded by Henry VIII.

[209] Means "Nowhere" (written 1516).

[210] Born 1466, died 1536; a native of Antwerp, and the greatest scholar and critic of his age.

[211] Born 1466, died 1530. His best pictures are in Antwerp.

[212] Fought in Germany between 1618 and 1648.

[213] The chief officer of a Dutch or Belgian town; the mayor.

[214] *Go-b'lan'*, so called from Gilles Gobelin, a famous tapestry maker of Paris in the fifteenth century.

[215] Sir Anthony Van Dyck, born 1599, died 1641. Many of his best portraits are to be found in private galleries in England.

[216] Peter Paul Rubens, born 1577, died 1640; the greatest painter of the Flemish school.

[217] The home of the Army Council and of the Headquarters Staff in Whitehall, London. The Army Council completely controls the army. At the head of it is the Secretary of State for War, who is a member of one of the Houses of Parliament and of the Cabinet.

[218] So called because raised by Lord Strathcona (1820-1914) who rose from a clerk in the Hudson Bay Company to be head of the company and High Commissioner for Canada. The construction of the Canadian Pacific Railway was almost entirely due to him.

[219] City of Saskatchewan, Canada; 400 miles west of Winnipeg, on the Canadian Pacific Railway.

[220] Chief city and commercial capital of Canada, on the St. Lawrence, Province of Quebec.

[221] Town, Canada, Province of Alberta; on the Canadian Pacific Railway, 2,262 miles west of Montreal.

[222] Capital of Ontario, Canada; second city of the Dominion; on north-west shore of Lake Ontario.

[223] Town, 60 miles south-west of Toronto.

[224] An over-great love of war.

[225] Winston Leonard Spencer Churchill, born 1874, First Lord of the Admiralty since 1911. He first became a minister in 1906.

[226] *Val-kar-tyā'*.

[227] Capital of Province of Quebec, on north bank of St. Lawrence, 145 miles north-east of Montreal.

[228] Parish priest.

[229] James Wolfe (1727-59) defeated the French on the Heights of Abraham, to the west of Quebec, and by this victory won Canada for the

British. He is referred to in the first verse of "The Maple Leaf," Canada's national song, which runs as follows:—

"In days of yore from Britain's shore
Wolfe, the dauntless hero, came,
And planted firm Britannia's flag
On Canada's fair domain!
Here may it wave, our boast, our pride;
And joined in love together,
The Thistle, Shamrock, Rose entwine
The Maple Leaf for ever!"

[230] Opposite to Quebec, on the other side of the river.

[231] To the east of Point Levis.

[232] Seaman of Devonshire, a relation of Sir Walter Raleigh, whom he assisted in founding Virginia. In 1591 he engaged a whole Spanish fleet with his single ship the *Revenge*, and was fatally wounded in the fight.

[233] Cousin of Sir Walter Raleigh. He took possession of Newfoundland (1583), but went down in the *Golden Hind* on the return voyage.

[234] Served under Drake, and fought against the Spanish Armada. Perished in the Arctic Ocean, 1594.

[235] Francis Drake (1540-1596), the greatest of English admirals, the first Englishman to sail round the world (1577-1580). He singed the King of Spain's beard in 1587, and fought against the Spanish Armada (1588).

[236] Group of twenty coral islands in the Indian Ocean, 700 miles south-west of Sumatra. They produce cocoanuts.

[237] German protectorate on the east coast of the Chinese province of Shantung. It was seized from China in 1897. The port is Tsing-tau. The Japanese first attacked this place on August 23, and declared that at the end of the war they would give it up to China.

[238] Largest city of New Zealand, in a fine harbour in the north of North Island.

[239] Tall, brown-skinned natives of New Zealand. They are a clever, cheerful race, very fond of games, riding, and feasting. Some of them visited this country in 1889, as members of a New Zealand football team.

[240] Louis Botha, born 1863, first Prime Minister of the Union of South Africa.

[241] Dutch farmers of what was formerly the South African Republic (Transvaal) and the Orange Free State.

[242] On August 7, 1914, the Prince of Wales founded a National Fund to relieve distress brought about by the war. He was its first treasurer, and he generously offered to pay the whole cost incurred in working the fund. Early in December 1914 it had reached £4,000,000.

[243] Close them up in ranks. The verses are adapted from W. E. Henley's "A New Song to an Old Tune."

[244] The Land of the Five Rivers, on the north-west frontier of India.

[245] Independent state of India, on the southern slopes of the Himalayas. It includes Mount Everest, the highest mountain of the world.

[246] Members of a secret society in China with the cry, "China for the Chinese." The German minister at Peking was murdered, and foreigners were besieged, and an expedition, in which British, French, Germans, Russians, Americans, and Japanese took part, relieved them (August 1900). China was forced to pay 64 millions of money.

[247] Native state of Madras, India; about as large as Scotland.

[248] Native state of Central India; nearly twice as large as Wales.

[249] Part of the Indian Empire, to the south of Afghanistan.

[250] The high priest and ruler of Tibet, and the head of the religion known as Lamaism. He lives at Lhassa, the capital of Tibet, a country of Central Asia north of the Himalayas.

[251] Aga Sultan Mohammed Shah, born 1875. He is a man of lofty character and great influence. He attended the coronation of Edward VII. as a guest of the nation.

[252] Ruler of Kashmir, the most northerly state of India.

[253] Both these generals were born in 1846.

[254] Surround them with troops, and thus form a screen behind which other troops can advance to engage the enemy.

[255] Province of Belgium, between the Meuse and the Scheldt, with Brussels as its chief town.

[256] Born 1713, died 1768. "Tristram Shandy" fills out nine volumes.

[257] Besieged in 1695.

[258] John Churchill, first Duke of Marlborough, born 1650, died 1722, was one of the most brilliant of British soldiers. He was sent to Flanders to

protect Holland against French invasion, and in 1702-3 seized the line of the Meuse. Afterwards he joined Prince Eugène on the Danube, and inflicted a crushing defeat on the Franco-Bavarian armies at Blenheim, 1705.

[259] Born 1811, died 1863. "Vanity Fair" and "Esmond" are his two greatest novels.

[260] Born 1816, died 1855. Her other great novel is "Jane Eyre."

[261] *Flam´-bō*, flaming torches.

[262] A disguise for the face worn during revels.

[263] "The Watch on the Rhine."

[264] It was written by Hoffmann von Fallenleben at Heligoland in 1841. There is a monument to the composer in Heligoland.

[265] German name for the Niemen.

[266] Tributary of the Po, North Italy. The sea is the Baltic.

[267] Sovereign duchy of the German Empire, chiefly surrounded by the provinces of Hanover, Saxony, and Westphalia.

[268] Named after the Prussian general Zieten (*tsĕt'en*), who gained great renown in the wars of Frederick the Great.

[269] Persons left with the enemy as pledges that certain conditions will be fulfilled.

[270] *Rex et Imperator*, Latin for "King and Emperor." Our King is also Emperor of India.

[271] The English come.

[272] Born 1852.

[273] Governor of the Sudan. He defended Khartum, at the junction of the Blue and White Niles, for several months against the followers of the Mahdi, and was killed by them two days before the relieving force came in sight of Khartum (1885).

[274] Town of Natal, on the Klip River; besieged by the Boers from November 2, 1899, to February 25, 1900.

[275] Diamond-mining centre of British South Africa, 646 miles by rail north-east of Cape Town. It was besieged by the Boers from October 15, 1899, to February 16, 1900.

[276] Thirty miles south-east of Kimberley, on the Modder River. The Boer leader Cronje was here forced to surrender with 4,000 men, February 27, 1900.

[277] Capital of the Transvaal. It surrendered to Lord Roberts on June 5, 1900.